English Words and Sentences: An Introduction

Hands-on, theory-neutral and non-technical, this textbook is a basic introduction to the structure of English words and sentences. Assuming no prior knowledge of linguistic analysis, it presents the facts in a straightforward manner, and offers a step-by-step guide from small to large building blocks of language. Every chapter contains numerous exercises and discussion questions, which provide essential self-study material, as well as in-chapter activities which lead students to a more comprehensive understanding of linguistic issues. The book also features concise chapter summaries, suggestions for further reading, an inclusive glossary and two consolidation chapters which encourage students to secure their understanding of the English language. The dedicated companion website includes further exercises, answers and solutions to the exercises, as well as useful links.

EVA DURAN EPPLER is Reader in English Language and Linguistics at Roehampton University, London.

GABRIEL OZÓN is a Teaching Fellow in English Language and Linguistics at the University of Sussex.

Cambridge Introductions to the English Language

Cambridge Introductions to the English Language is a series of accessible undergraduate textbooks on the key topics encountered in the study of the English Language. Tailored to suit the needs of individual taught course modules, each book is written by an author with extensive experience of teaching the topic to undergraduates. The books assume no prior subject knowledge, and present the basic facts in a clear and straightforward manner, making them ideal for beginners. They are designed to be maximally reader-friendly, with chapter summaries, glossaries, and suggestions for further reading. Extensive exercises and discussion questions are included, encouraging students to consolidate and develop their learning, and providing essential homework material. A website accompanies each book, featuring solutions to the exercises and useful additional resources. Set to become the leading introductions to the field, books in this series provide the essential knowledge and skills for those embarking on English Language studies.

Books in the series

The Sound Structure of English Chris McCully

Old English Jeremy J. Smith

English Around the World Edgar W. Schneider

English Words and Sentences Eva Duran Eppler and Gabriel Ozón

English Words and Sentences

An Introduction

Eva Duran Eppler

Gabriel Ozón

CAMBRIDGE UNIVERSITY PRESS
Cambridge, New York, Melbourne, Madrid, Cape Town,
Singapore, São Paulo, Delhi, Mexico City

Cambridge University Press
The Edinburgh Building, Cambridge CB2 8RU, UK

Published in the United States of America by Cambridge University Press,
New York

www.cambridge.org
Information on this title: www.cambridge.org/9780521171878

First published 2013

A catalogue record for this publication is available from the British Library

Library of Congress Cataloguing in Publication data
Eppler, Eva.
English words and sentences / Eva Duran Eppler and Gabriel Ozon.
   p.   cm.
Includes bibliographical references and index.
ISBN 978-0-521-17187-8 – ISBN 978-1-107-00132-9
1. English language – Grammar.   2. English language – Syntax.
3. English language – Morphology.   I. Ozon, Gabriel.   II. Title.
PE1112.E6   2012
425–dc23

                                                          2012016541

ISBN 978-1-107-00132-9 Hardback
ISBN 978-0-521-17187-8 Paperback

Additional resources for this publication at www.cambridge.org/eppler-ozon

Contents

Preface

This is a book of twelve chapters, divided into ten content chapters and two consolidation chapters. The organisation of each chapter is listed on its first page, in the content section. Throughout each chapter, *activities* encourage you to explore language yourself. Each activity appears in a box; and you should attempt to solve the activity before moving on with your reading. In many cases, we have answered the set questions in the chapter, but some are left for you to work out outside the covers of this book. Discussing these activities with colleagues in seminars or tutorials will give you an extra advantage in your learning. A fuller set of answers is provided on the webpages that accompany the book, available at the following URL: www. cambridge.org/eppler-ozon. Towards the end of each chapter, we give you a brief *summary* of the topics covered.

After the chapter summary, you'll find a set of *exercises*. These are labelled 'Exercise 1.1', etc. but, unlike in-chapter activities, they do not appear within a text box. Some exercises include a commentary, but most of the discussion has been placed on the relevant webpages. When working through the chapters, you will be acquiring basic knowledge about English words and sentences. You can build on this with the help of the texts suggested in *further reading* sections. Full *references* for these resources are given at the end of the book.

After Chapters 6 and 10, you will find two *consolidation chapters* with many more *tasks*, presented in the same way as end-of-chapter exercises. Like exercises, tasks only include commentaries when new ground is covered.

- **Activities** push the discussion forward; they are short and to the point.
- **Exercises** help you assess your understanding, and some of them develop the chapter content further.
- **Tasks** consolidate your knowledge, and often introduce different and more challenging perspectives on the topics.

You will also find a *glossary* towards the end of the book. The glossary contains all those key words which, on their first appearance in the text, are set in bold font. Altogether, key words, glossary and index help you navigate the book.

Acknowledgements

We are very grateful to our students at University of Roehampton, Edge Hill University and University College London for their ideas, suggestions and feedback. Thanks are also due to the many friends and colleagues who have read and commented on different parts of this book. We are grateful to Gerald Nelson, Georg Marko, Anthony Grant, Bas Aarts, as well as Trish and France Molyneux.

Our editors at CUP, Helen Barton, Raihanah Begum, Jo Breeze and Sarah Green, deserve special praise for their comments and tireless efforts in the production of this book. We are immensely grateful to all these people, whose input has improved this book in many respects. Any remaining errors are our own.

Finally, we would also like to thank our families for putting up with us during the writing of this book. Gabriel would like to thank Carolina, Victoria, Nicole and Santiago; Eva, as usual, is grateful for Mehmet's patience. We also thank our parents for putting us on the right track.

Many of the citations and extracts used in this book have been taken from the Cambridge International Corpus (CIC), and from the British component of the International Corpus of English (ICE-GB). The Word Grammar diagrams and analyses are used by kind permission of Dick Hudson and can be accessed on the WG home page http://www.phon.ucl.ac.uk/home/dick/wg.htm. The lovely and scary Little Red Riding Hood drawing in Chapter 10 is reproduced by permission of the artist Annie Rodrigue. Copyright for the cartoons in Chapter 9 has been obtained from Cartoonstock, and for the Pied Piper in Consolidation Chapter 2 from Shutterstock. Every effort has been made to secure necessary permissions to reproduce copyright material in this book, though in some cases it has proved impossible to trace or contact copyright holders. The Jabberwocky image in Consolidation Chapter 2, for example, is out of copyright, but can be accessed on http://www.fromoldbooks.org/LewisCarroll-AliceThroughTheLookingGlass/pages/023-the-Jabberwocky/. If any omissions are brought to our notice, we will be happy to include appropriate acknowledgements in reprinting and any subsequent edition.

CHAPTER 1

Language and this book

In this chapter ...

In this chapter we will introduce you to a system of thinking about, and then describing, English words and sentences. We will see that most words can have different forms. Combined according to rules of grammar (morpho-syntax), words can form larger units such as phrases, clauses and sentences. Many words can also be segmented into smaller meaningful units, which are called morphemes. We will discover that the most important shared characteristic of these units is that they all have internal structure. As we will see, in order to work systematically with English words and sentences, we need to analyse both: the structure that lies behind words (morphology), and the organising principles according to which native speakers assemble words into sentences (syntax). And we will see that, without this internal structure, we would not be able to communicate with language, and this is, after all, its purpose. We will not give you stylistic or prescriptive rules, but together we will discover the conventions underlying the use of standard English for communication.

Hi! How are you?
We do hope you are well.

Hi, how, are, you, we, do, hope and *well* are **words**. They are English words and they are written words. When you read them out loud, or simply say them to the next person you meet, they become spoken words. *How, are,* and *you* together, in this particular form and in this particular order, also make up a **sentence** (a specific type of sentence, a question). So do *we, do, hope, you, are* and *well*.

This book is called *English Words and Sentences*. On its very first page we are using English words and sentences. This is characteristic of the whole book: we will explore something which, if you are a native speaker of English, you already intuitively know. So why write a book about it? There are many reasons why it is better for you to also consciously know how English words and sentences work. We will look into this after two games with English words and sentences.

Activity 1.1

Use **all** six words from our reply, i.e. *we, do, hope, you, are* and *well* (without changing their form) to create at least three different sentences. If you manage to build more than five grammatical ones without changing any of the word forms, you beat us.

We presume you cursed at us for asking you not to change their form. The more or less sanctioned orders for the word-forms *we, do, hope, you, are* and *well* are

1. *You are well, we do hope.*
2. *Hope you are well, we do.*
3. *Well, you are, we do hope.*
4. *Well, we do hope you are.*

Without this restriction, the activity would have been easier and you would have been able to build more sentences. Try it now.

5. *We hope you are doing well.*
6. *You are hoping we do well.*
7. *We are hoping you do well.*
8. *?We did hope you are well.*
9. *We were hoping you did well, etc.*

What is the difference between our Activity 1.1 and the second version of this language game? In the original version, you were only allowed to change the order the words come in; now you could use different forms of the same word, which gave you more options.

So far we have looked at words and established that many of them come in slightly different forms. We have also established that combined according to rules of **grammar** and arranged in an order that is sanctioned by English grammar, words form sentences.

Now for the second creative activity with English words and sentences. This time we ask you to take the role of the teacher.

Activity 1.2

Imagine a non-native speaker of English is staying with you. She is a nice person and wants to help in the house. Before heading back to your home from town, she sends you a text message / SMS which reads 'I'm at the shop, should I bought anything for home?' How can you help your visitor improve her English?

If you are able to explain how English words and sentences work, you can not only help your friend with her English, you can also better comprehend your tutor's notes about your own language use in essays and assignments. Understanding the meaning of *tense*, *agreement*, *word order* will enable you to improve your own language use and get better grades. To help yourself and your non-native speaker friend with grammar in general, and not just with one specific utterance, you should be able to explain in a more general way why a sentence does not work and is ungrammatical (marked by an asterisk in linguistics). Sentences you could have made out of the six words from Activity 1.1 but which are ungrammatical because word forms are not right (examples 10 to 12) or they are not in the right order (examples 13 to 15) are listed below.

10. *We hopes you are doing well.*
11. *You is hoping we do well.*
12. *We are hoping you do weller.*
13. *Are did hope you are well we.*
14. *We well were hoping you did.*
15. *You we are hoping do well, etc.*

The same argument applies if you want to work as a classroom assistant, or go into teaching, or teach English to speakers of other languages (TESOL). If you intend to become a speech and language therapist, you will also need to be able to explain how words and sentences work. And knowledge about language not only facilitates all the creative uses of language in the media, journalism, drama, poetry, but also in more everyday tasks such as writing reports, reviews and presentations. It is highly **un**likely that you'll get through life without having to, or wanting to, perform any of these tasks. Knowing how language works is a transferable skill which will stand you in good stead in many life situations. After reflecting on a few reasons why it is good to know how English words and sentences work, we now return to the three notions we have already introduced: **words, sentences** and **grammar**.

1.1 Words

Recognising **words** is a task we tend to take for granted, because we have been using word-spaces to separate words since we first learned to read and write. OK, we can sometimes argue over whether *all right* is two words or one (*alright*), but generally the convention of using spaces to separate written words fits the realities of the language well, and by and large people agree as to what is or is not a word. Recognising word boundaries in spoken language is a much trickier task than in writing. Let's start with the most basic distinction, the one between **words** and **non-words**.

Activity 1.3

The following sentence has been modified from a scientific article on canine compulsive disorder:

A canine chromosome 7 locus that <u>wodoples</u> a high risk of compulsive disorder susceptibility has been identified.

How many non-words are there in the above sentence? Which ones are they? If you are not sure, where can you check?

You could look up all the unfamiliar words in a dictionary. Under which entry would you look for *wodoples*? We assume you would try the form *wodople*, safely assuming that *wodople-s* won't be listed. You won't find *wodople*, because it is a non-word in the English language. Non-words are neither listed in printed or online dictionaries, nor in the dictionary in our brain (also called our *mental lexicon*). If we successfully managed to introduce *wodople* into the English language, the words *wodopled* and *wodopling* would also be possible. All these words are different manifestations of the 'same' slightly more abstract vocabulary item and share a core meaning. The vocabulary items that are listed in the dictionary are generally referred to as **lexemes** (the 'lex-' component of 'lexeme' is taken from 'lexicon', which has more or less the same meaning as 'dictionary'). Lexemes are conventionally written in capital letters. The lexeme IDENTIFY, for example, has the different word forms *identifies, identified, identifying*.

The term 'word', however, is commonly used in a variety of different senses that are frequently not clearly distinguished. We'll distinguish them now to avoid confusion later on. In everyday language use, one meaning of 'word' is *lexeme*. But in everyday language use we also refer to spoken and written realisations of lexemes as **words**. For example, we call the last lexical unit in the example in Activity 1.3 'word', although strictly speaking *identified* is a word-form of the lexeme IDENTIFY.

Another sense of word we want to distinguish in some situations is best illustrated with an example. When we focus on the lexeme BID and the word-forms *bid* in the following two sentences, you will realise why we have to make this other distinction.

16.   *I never **bid** more than £50 on eBay.*
17.   *I **bid** £50 for an arm chair on eBay yesterday and it will get delivered in five days.*

The same word-form *bid*, belonging to the same lexeme BID, represents two different **grammatical words** in examples 16 and 17. In sentence 16, it is present tense; in sentence 17, on the other hand, it is past tense and refers to a time already past. This is why we should regard *bid* as representing two distinct grammatical words. Grammatical words are important in the discussion of the relationship between words and sentences.

For English we can assume that 'word' is the basic unit of language. Words stand out in contrast with other units of language, either smaller ones such as morphemes and phonemes, or larger ones such as phrases and sentences, because they typically combine a number of different characteristics. We'll use these characteristics to summarise our discussion of the first key term which also features in the title of this book.

The word is the largest unit relevant to spelling, and the unit marked by word spaces in conventional English spelling. *All right* and *mouse trap* are exceptions in that they behave more like a single word, but are sometimes written as two words. Words which combine two or more words (or roots) into a single word, i.e. compounds like *armchair*, *matchbox* but *chocolate-box* or *chocolate box*, are notoriously inconsistent in this respect and the hyphen is just a tentative word-space.

Words (in the sense of abstract vocabulary item or lexeme) tend to have one or more word-forms. The lexeme JUMP, for example, has the written word-forms

jump   jumped
jumps   jumping

The same word-form, on the other hand, can be two grammatical words. We looked at the example of *bid* earlier, another one would be *cut*. *Cut* can refer to an action in the present or past.

18.   *I normally **cut** white bread too thickly to fit into the toaster.*
19.   *Yesterday, however, I **cut** it so thinly that it burned in the toaster.*

However, when *cut* refers to the result of a cutting action, as in *The cut in Tom's middle finger does not heal*, it is a separate lexeme. It behaves differently in sentences and therefore belongs to a different word-class (as we will see in Chapter 2).

The word is also the basic unit of syntax. **Syntax** is concerned with the structural relationships among co-occurring words (we will discuss the term *syntax* in more detail in Section 1.5). Syntactic rules link words and phrases. And it is words, rather than phrases or morphemes, which are classified in terms of word-classes (see Chapter 2).

Some words are also the smallest unit of meaning, such as, for example, *apricot*. Phrases and sentences have meanings which are based in regular ways on the meanings of the words that make them up, but a word such as *apricot* has no smaller parts which contribute to its meaning. Exceptions to this characteristic of words are words that have no meaning as such (e.g. the first word in this chapter *hi!*, or *um*, or the *it* of *It rained)*, and idioms which have meanings which can't be worked out from the meanings of their parts (e.g. *cats and dogs* in *It rained cats and dogs*). The most frequent, regular and important exception to words being the smallest unit of meaning are the different (inflectional) forms of lexemes. The meaning of many inflected words (e.g. *dog-s*) can be worked out on the basis of the meanings of their constituent parts, but arguably it is the words themselves, rather than the morphemes, that have meaning.

1.2 Word structure: morphology

Based on the similarity between the different forms of the non-word WODOPLE, *wodople-s, wodopl-ing, wodopl-ed*, and the real-word lexeme JUMP, *jump-s, jump-ing, jump-ed*, we will now claim that words have structure. This may come as a surprise to you because normally speakers think of words as indivisible units of meaning. This is probably due to the fact that many English words are morphologically simple, as we saw in the *apricot* example. Other words that cannot be divided up into smaller parts that are themselves meaningful are, for example, *up, the, gentle, dog, coriander* and *shook*. When you compare these words with *jump-s, jump-ing, jump-ed*, you will notice that *up, the, gentle, dog, coriander* and *shook* cannot be segmented into smaller units that are themselves meaningful and are used in other words, too. Does this statement also hold true for *meander*? After all, there are many words that end in *-er*.

Activity 1.4

Collect at least ten words that end in *-er*. Then divide your ten words into two groups:

- group A in which the *-er* is a separable, recyclable (productive) unit of language, and
- group B in which *-er* just happen to be the last two letters of those words.

Which group does *meander* belong to?

In activity 1.4 on page 6, the group containing *meander* (group B) contains words like *number, remember, Mister* etc., the other group, on the other hand, contains words like *small-er, bright-er, call-er, runn-er*. Group A words can be broken down into smaller units that are meaningful; they are said to be morphologically complex. Other examples of morphologically complex English words are *jump-s, jump-ing, jump-ed*, or *comput-er-s, key-board-s, screen-s* or *tool-bar-s*. In the last four examples, *comput-er-s, key-board-s, screen-s* and *tool-bar-s*, the morphologically complex words denote more than one of the referred-to objects; if we take the *-s* off, they refer to one of them. The word-final *-s* therefore always has the same meaning 'more than one' and serves the same grammatical function, it indicates plurality.

The smallest indivisible meaningful units of language or grammatical function from which words are formed are called **morphemes**. Morphology is the linguistic discipline which devotes itself to the study of components of words which cannot be decomposed into smaller units that are either meaningful by themselves or mark a grammatical function (like plurality). Morphologists are linguists who study word structure. Morphemes can be compared to pieces of a building set or construction kit that can be used again and again to form different words. Recurrent parts of words that have the same meaning can be isolated and recognised as manifestations of the same morpheme. For example, *jump* in *jump-s, jump-ing, jump-ed* can be isolated and has the same meaning. In *sing-er, play-er, call-er*, the form *-er* is attached to verbs to derive nouns with the general meaning 'someone who does X' (where X indicates whatever action the verb involves, e.g. singing, playing, calling). We can therefore recognise the element *-er* as belonging to a given morpheme which contributes an identifiable meaning to the word which they are part of. In a similar way the *-s*, the *-ing* and the *-ed* can be isolated from *jump-s, jump-ing, jump-ed*. These morphemes have little semantic content, but each one of them has the same grammatical function when added to other words of the same word class (see Chapter 2 for a discussion of verbs).

Although there are no effective mechanical procedures for discovering the structure of words, or of a language in general, there exist reasonably reliable and widely accepted techniques that will help you. We have introduced the main procedure for discovering the structure of words, the *principle of contrast*. We have contrasted forms that differ in terms of their sound / letter sequences, and forms that differ in lexical meaning and / or grammatical function. Exercise 1.1 at the end of this chapter gives you practice in recognising when a single sound / letter or combination of sounds / letters represent a morpheme. We will also return to morphology in Chapters 3 and 4. For now it suffices if you can recognise when a word consists of one morpheme only, or when it is built up from two or more morphemes.

The morphological units words are composed of are not random; you can recognise them because they have the same shape and the same meaning or grammatical function in many other words. The way morphemes combine is also not random, but guided by rules (mainly morphological ones, but phonological ones are involved, too). You use these rules on a daily basis when you use the English language for communication, but we will make some of them more explicit in Chapters 3 and 4.

In this book on English words and sentences we have so far dealt with words and a little bit with their building blocks, morphemes. All morphemes have meaning and / or grammatical function, but some of them (called *bound morphemes*, see Chapter 3) need to combine with another morpheme to form a useful word. Words, on the other hand, can always stand alone as basic meaningful units of language. In a minimal way, words therefore already fulfil the main purpose or function of language: to communicate meaning – a message, an idea, a thought, a feeling. But we can only think of three groups of humans who tend to communicate in one-word utterances: grumpy people, adults with severe speech and language impairment and children who are under two years old. Remember this next time you are interacting with a toddler, and listen out for how much more children can communicate when they start combining first two, then three and eventually many words to form sentences.

1.3 Sentence structure: phrases, clauses and sentences

In contrast with words, which we have already identified as the smallest unit in grammar/syntax, **sentences** are the largest unit in grammar. Sentences are strings of words which are held together by syntactic relations. In writing, sentences tend to start with a capital letter and end with a full stop. Between the initial capital letter of a written sentence and the final full stop, or between the first and the last sounds of the first and the last words of an utterance, we encounter several different-sized units of language: **words**, **phrases** and **clauses**. We have already established a working notion of words. In everyday language use, a **phrase** is a group of words standing together as a conceptual unit. The linguistic definition of phrase includes these characteristics: a **phrase** is a group of semantically and grammatically related words which have an internal structure. Because phrases form conceptual and syntactic units, they can frequently be replaced by one word, or consist of a single word. A phrase therefore tends to be a grammatical unit intermediate between word and clause. We will look at phrases in more detail in Chapters 5 and 7.

Clause is the first term in this book which is not used much in everyday language; but it does have a very specific meaning in linguistics. A clause is a sentence that contains one lexical verb and whatever other sentence elements this verb requires. That is, it can consist of at least two phrases (phrases can consist of one word only). Here are three examples of simple or one-clause sentences.

20. *Alison laughed.*
21. *My cousins like chips.*
22. *It has been snowing in London recently.*

For linguistic units that contain only one lexical verb (represented by the lexemes LAUGH, LIKE and SNOW in the three example sentences above), the terms *clause* and *sentence* can be used interchangeably, because there is a one-to-one relationship between clauses and sentences. Not so in the following examples 23 to 25:

23. *Alison laughed about the fact that I had already forgotten our meeting.*
24. *My cousins, who live in Canada, like chips.*
25. *It has been snowing in London recently, because we had sub-zero temperatures and it was raining.*

Activity 1.5

How many clauses are there in examples 23 to 25?

Note that these sentences still contain representations of the lexemes LAUGH, LIKE and SNOW, but each of the complex sentences contains at least one other lexical verb.

We'll introduce criteria which will help you identify lexical verbs in the next chapter; for this activity it is sufficient to note that verbs tend to express a state, act, event or emotion. Once you have established the number of lexical verbs in examples 23 to 25, you will also know how many clauses these sentences contain.

In addition to LAUGH, example 23 contains the verb FORGET in the second clause, which starts with *that*. Example 24 contains LIKE and LIVE; LIKE being the verb of the main clause, LIVE being the verb of the embedded subordinate clause. Example 25 includes three lexical verbs: SNOW, RAIN and HAVE (in *we had sub-zero temperatures*). Example sentence 25 therefore contains three clauses. When talking about sentences like 23 to 25, we cannot use the linguistic terms *clause* and *sentence* interchangeably any longer, because in these examples there is no one-to-one relationship between number of clauses and number of sentences. Those sentences are more complex, and are composed of more than one clause: examples 23 and 24 are one sentence and two clauses respectively, and example 25 is one sentence containing three clauses. To be able to make this distinction, linguists added the term **clause** to their jargon. We use this term to refer to the linguistic unit that is intermediate between phrases and sentences.

We have now made a first parse through an English sentence, and established initial working definitions of its constituent parts. The smallest unit of an English sentence is a word, which in itself may be composed of one or more morphemes. If a word consists of one morpheme only, we call it *simple*; if it consists of two or more morphemes, we call it *complex*. Although a phrase can also consist of only one word, most of the time phrases consist of a group of related words with an internal structure. Phrases thus form a linguistic unit intermediate in size between words, and clauses and sentences. Sentences can also consist of one clause only. These sentences are called *simple sentences*. Sentences which are composed of two or more clauses are called *complex*. We can see that there are a lot of similarities between the linguistic units ranging from words, to phrases, to clauses, to sentences. The most important shared characteristic of all these units is that they all have internal structure.

Without this internal structure, we would not be able to communicate with language. We'll explore in the next section why parts of speech need to have internal structure, and why their combination needs to follow conventions / rules all its native speakers adhere to in order to be able to use language to communicate.

1.4 Structure and convention in language use

Activity 1.6
In this activity we let you play with the building blocks of language. We'll give you several language 'Lego' sets and ask you to build something with the blocks or units.

a. Make the word referring to the rebirth of a soul into a new body out of the morphemes
    carn, re, at, in and *ion*.
b. Make a phrase referring to a trendy or cool motor vehicle out of the following words
    bike, this, hot.

> c. Make a clause or simple sentence out of the phrase you created in (b) plus the verb *is* and the phrase *so fast*.
>
> d. Make a complex sentence out of the simple sentence constructed for (c), followed by the word *that* and the only word that can replace the whole phrase *this hot bike*; then add two verbs: first one that expresses a possibility, then *cause*; continue the sentence with the phrase *your soul*, and *to* plus the word you created in (a) without the morpheme *-ion*.

The rebirth of a soul into a new body is *re-in-carn-at-ion*; for step (d) we take the affix *-ion* off to get the verb *reincarnate*. Steps (b) and (c) are easy: [*this hot bike*] *is so fast*. The only words that can replace the whole phrase [*this hot bike*] are *it* (and *that*). Let's use *it*. This gives us the sentence fragment *this hot bike is so fast that it* ... Possibility is expressed by *may* (or *might* or *can* or *could*, but let's take *may*), which is then followed by *cause* according to the construction kit. When we then add *your soul* and *to reincarnate*, we get the complex sentence we were asked to build in step (d).

26. *This hot bike is so fast that it may cause your soul to reincarnate.*

This activity shows that all the linguistic building blocks we used have to be assembled according to a conventionalised structure; without this internal structure we would not communicate very successfully. We will illustrate this point with and for the English words, phrases and clauses of the sentence we have just created:

- Words have internal structure: if you assemble *carn -, re-,- at-,- in-* and- *ion* wrongly, you won't get the word *reincarnation*, but something completely incomprehensible like *carn-ation-in-re*.
- Phrases have internal structure: *hot bike this* also makes no sense, and *hot this bike* would only be said by either small children, or – with a very marked intonation – by an admirer of the motorbike using an unusual word order to emphasise their point.
- Clauses have internal structure: **Is so fast this hot bike* is not a simple sentence but an ungrammatical one.
- Sentences have internal structure: contrast the grammatical sentence in example 27 with example 28.

27. *This hot bike is so fast that it may cause your soul to reincarnate.*
28. **This carnationinre, that your soul, to hot fast may so is it.*

Example 28 is not only an ungrammatical sentence, it makes no sense what-soever. These examples show that violating only some of the morphological and syntactic conventions / rules of the English language has serious consequences for passing on a message. And if a message cannot be interpreted, there is little point in communicating it.

So when we speak, we follow the morphological and syntactic rules of our first language or mother tongue. If your first language is English, you know the rules for English. You acquired them by being exposed to spoken English from a young age. But only some of you – those who were taught grammar at school, and those who learned English as a foreign language – know some of these regularities and rules explicitly. In the remainder of this book we will explore the internal structure of English words and sentences, and the basic set of conventions / rules we adhere to when combining morphemes, words, phrases and clauses when using the English language to communicate.

1.5 Syntax, grammar and 'ungrammatical'

On the previous pages we used some terms which we haven't defined yet. These terms are **syntax**, **grammar** and **ungrammatical**. The first one, **syntax**, is mainly used in linguistics and means 'sentence construction', or how words group together to make phrases and sentences. So nothing new, really. Syntax can also mean 'the study of syntax', and in this use it outlines the scope of what we will study together in this book. At a basic level, we are going to be studying how English organises its morphology and syntax. Most of the organising principles that we flouted in (28) are word-order rules. The same holds true for all the ungrammatical sentences made from *we, do, hope, you, are, well* (examples 10 to 15) at the beginning of the chapter. But these are not the only rules of syntax. Syntax also includes those morphemes that provide the grammatical glue for sentences; the classification of words into classes or parts of speech; the structure of phrases, clauses and sentences; and the different constructions that English uses. The classification of words is the subject of Chapter 2; in Chapters 3 and 4 we will outline morphological rules of English; the structure of phrases is the main topic of Chapters 5 and 6, and the structure of clauses and sentences is the focus of Chapters 9 and 10. Chapter 7 will deal with grammatical functions, and Chapter 8 with coordination and subordination.

So if morphology is the study of word structure and syntax is the study of sentence construction, what is grammar? Unlike morphology and syntax, **grammar** is a term that is frequent in everyday language use and therefore used in many different ways. Some people use the term *grammar* in a quite narrow sense to mean the same as syntax; others follow the more recent practice of using it in a quite broad sense, whereby the grammar of a language includes all of its organising principles: information about the sound system (phonology), about the form of words (morphology and the lexicon), and some even include information about how we adjust language according to context (sociolinguistics, stylistics). In this book we will use the term *grammar* in its most traditional sense to include morphology and syntax. *Ungrammatical* according this definition then means 'violating morphological and syntactic conventions or rules of a language', English in our case.

1.6 Standard English, descriptive and prescriptive

But what kind of English? South African English? American English? Australian or New Zealand English? Scottish or Irish English? Hong Kong English? In this book we will consider 'standard' English examples. Standard English is the variety of English that is used for written communication, education (it is also the variety that is taught in English language courses), and in the media. In grammar, standard English is relatively uniform world-wide, this is why we get away with not having to specify which national standard we are talking about (for examples of non-standard English, see Exercises 1.2 and 1.3 at the end of this chapter).

We restrict our discussion to standard English for simplicity and space reasons. This book will be easier to understand, less complicated and shorter if we omit the morphological and syntactic conventions that are perfectly grammatical in, let's say, the English spoken on the Orkney Islands or on the southern Island of New Zealand. Somehow we don't think you want this book to be difficult, complicated and long, but should you worry about being caught short, we can assure you that the vast majority of morphological and syntactic rules are shared by all the Englishes listed above. All the documented varieties of UK English dialects, for example, only seem to differ in approximately fifteen morpho-syntactic constructions (there is, of course, more variation in World Englishes).

The reason why standard English is called 'standard' is because it has been codified, i.e. it has been recorded first in dictionaries, then in grammars and style books. We will turn to the distinction between grammars and style books next.

What we will be doing in this book is describing standard English. We will describe the language native speakers of English actually use, how they combine morphemes into words, and words into larger units like phrases, clauses and sentences. This book therefore is a descriptive grammar of English, not a prescriptive one. Prescriptive rules can be found in other books: handbooks, style books and manuals that tell people which usages to adopt or to avoid.

That is, prescriptive rules advise people what they should, or rather should *not*, do with language. An example of a prescriptive rule would be 'Don't use *like* as a conjunction.' This rule advises you to say *Speak as I do*, rather than what you may normally say, *Speak like I do*.

Activity 1.7

Which prescriptive rules of grammar were you taught at school? Write one of them down.

Make example sentences, two breaking this prescriptive rule, two following it.

Discuss why the sentence violating the prescriptive rule is not necessarily ungrammatical.

If nothing comes to mind, formulate the prescriptive rule that rates *Write down one of them* higher than *Write one of them down*.

One other thing we will not do in this book is discuss spelling variants produced by morphology. For example, why *royalty* is no longer spelt with a *y* when there is more than one of them, i.e. *royalties*; why *stop* gets another *p* when it refers to an event in the past, i.e. *stopped*; or why we put an *e* between *radish* and the plural morpheme *-s*, i.e. *radishes*. The last example has a good phonological reason (if you are interested, you can find out more about this in the phonological sister book in this series, *The Sound Structure of English*, see Further reading section), but many others don't. This is why we have decided not to deal with variations in spelling triggered by morphological changes to the words forms.

1.7 Chapter summary

In this chapter we took a first look at English words and sentences. We identified **words** as the smallest unit of **grammar** and **sentences** as the largest unit in grammar. Some words, e.g. *radish*, are one unit of language, other words are formed out of two or more units, e.g. *radish-es*. Units smaller than words are called **morphemes**, and the linguistics discipline concerned with the study of their structure is called **morphology**. Words are used to construct phrases, clauses and sentences. **Phrases** can consist of one or more words, **clauses** can consist of one or more phrases, and **sentences** can consist of one or more clauses. **Syntax** refers to how words group together to make phrases and sentences. **Grammar**, the way we use it in this book, is an umbrella term for morphology and syntax. That is, it describes how morphemes group together to make words, and how words group together to make phrases, clauses and sentences. In this light, while syntax describes the grammar of clauses and sentences, morphology is concerned with the grammar of words.

At this point, we want to make clear that we do not wish to tell you how to use the English language, we merely want to describe how it works. The variety of English we will describe is the one used worldwide in writing, i.e. standard English.

Key terms

Morpheme; lexeme; word; phrase; clause; sentence; grammar; syntax.

Exercises

Exercise 1.1   Which words from the list below belong to which lexeme?

starts	*brightest*	*understand*	*turkeys*	*be*	*geese*
turkey	*are*	*start*	*jumping*	*friendliest*	*starting*
brighter	*understands*	*friendly*	*bright*	*understood*	*friendlier*
goose	*was*	*jump*	*started*	*started*	*were*

Exercise 1.2   Here are two English sentences:

a. *Had you a good time last night?*
b. *Where's my book? – Ah, here it's.*

Now label them A–E:

A   I use this kind of grammatical construction myself.
B   I don't use this grammatical construction, but other English speakers do.
C   I've never heard anyone use a construction like this before, but I would guess that some native speakers do use it.
D   This is the sort of thing only a non-native speaker of English would say.
E   Nobody would say this.

Exercise 1.3   What does the following sentence mean?
     I don't <u>want</u> it but. (with heavy stress on *want*)

a.   I really don't want it.
b.   But I don't want it.
c.   I don't want it but I'll take it.
d.   _____

Discuss whether

- you can make grammaticality judgements about forms (of English) you do not use yourself.
- it is legitimate to include more than one variety of a language in a grammar.

Exercise 1.4 In Chapter 1 we introduced the main units of grammatical analysis. Try to identify all examples of morphemes, words, phrases, clauses and sentences in the following utterance. For units larger than words, put them in square brackets to indicate where they start and end.

Timmy loves aeroplanes and in March he will be very happy because he is going to be travelling round Europe by aeroplane.

Exercise 1.5 As a way of revising before you move on to the next chapter, define the key terms of this chapter in your own words. You get ten points per correct definition. Check your versions against the definitions given in Chapter 1 or the glossary of terms at the end of the book and award yourself points out of ten for each question. How many points did you get overall?

1) A **morpheme** is _____ ?/10
2) A **lexeme** is _____ ?/10
3) A **word** is _____ ?/10
4) We differentiate between **lexeme** and **word** because _____ ?/10
5) A **phrase** is _____ ?/10
6) A **clause** is _____ ?/10
7) A **sentence** is _____ ?/10
8) **Grammar** is _____ ?/10
9) **Syntax** is _____ ?/10
10) The difference between **syntax** and **grammar** is _____ ?/10

Further reading
For general reference, consult Quirk et al. (1985); Huddleston and Pullum et al. (2002); and Biber et al. (1999), among others. On prescriptivism, see Crystal (2006). You can find out more about phonological words and the 'segmentation problem' in a sister book in this series, McCully (2009).

CHAPTER 2

Word classes

In this chapter ...

In this chapter we will introduce the main word classes: nouns, determiners, pronouns, adjectives, verbs, adverbs, prepositions and conjunctions. We said that in order to work systematically with English words and sentences, we need to analyse both the structure that lies behind words (morphology) and the organising principles according to which sentences are assembled (syntax). In accordance with this principle, we will introduce you to morphological, syntactic and semantic criteria for word-class identification. We will see that word meaning is of course important for words to fit into a sentence; but their form characteristics are equally important. Each of the sections begins with a discussion of the shared properties of the word class under consideration. Once we have identified the typical characteristics of a word class, we will introduce you to different sub-types within it, if there are any. Activities on the fuzziness of different word classes, and on how distributional criteria allow us to shed some light on this fuzziness, will be relegated to the end of the chapter. In this chapter you will learn to work out which word class any word in any given sentence belongs to.

In this chapter we are going to do a training marathon. No, actually not a marathon, rather a sprint through the seven main word classes of the English language. There is more than one way of classifying the words of English: some grammatical theories work with marginally fewer word classes, others (those that wish to make more fine-grained distinctions) with a few more. This is not really important. Like athletes who have a speciality distance but also run other competitions, we aim to train you to recognise the most important distinctive features of seven English word classes. This will also enable you to recognise fewer (by subsuming some smaller categories into larger ones), or more (by making separate categories for words with enough different features to warrant a category of their own).

This chapter is a training session which will prepare us for what English words do in English sentences. This means that we will come back to the formal and distributional characteristics of English word classes in later chapters. Because words occupy such a central position in grammar, there are many links between this and other chapters. This makes the present chapter very important. But how do we know that individual words share characteristics and can therefore be grouped into categories or word classes (sometimes also called 'parts of speech')? We'll demonstrate this in the following two activities.

Activity 2.1

Which **single** words from the following list

played, in, insecticides, the, because, beautiful, lovingly, CDs, bright, ran, suddenly, a

can fill the empty slot in the sentence?

How useful did _____ seem to be?

Only two words from the list we gave you can fill the empty slot: *How useful did insecticides/CDs seem to be*. The other words don't fit for different reasons. In *How useful did because seem to be* the meaning of *because* does not work in the context of the sentence. Or their form does not fit, as illustrated by examples 1 to 5. In examples 6 to 10 we have only changed the form of the words from our list a bit, and all of a sudden they fit.

1. **How useful did **played** seem to be.*
2. **How useful did **beautiful** seem to be?*
3. **How useful did **lovingly** seem to be?*
4. **How useful did **bright** seem to be?*
5. **How useful did **run** seem to be?*
6. *How useful did **play** seem to be (in therapy)?*
7. *How useful did **beauty** seem to be?*
8. *How useful did **love** seem to be?*
9. *How useful did **brightness** seem to be?*
10. *How useful did **running** seem to be?*

What did we do? We changed the adjectives *beautiful* and *bright* into the nouns *beauty* and *brightness*. We changed the adverb *lovingly* into the noun it is derived from, i.e. *love*. And we changed the verbs *played* into the generic noun *play* (as in *children at play*) and the verb *run* into a form (gerund) that can be used as a noun, i.e. *running*. *In*, *because* and *that* are hopeless cases, because we cannot change their form. Activity 2.1 has thus shown us that word meaning is of course important for words to fit into a sentence; but their formal characteristics are equally important.

How restrictive grammar can be in terms of which words it allows in certain sentence positions is illustrated by Activity 2.2.

Activity 2.2

Fill the gap in the following sentence with ten single words.

The puppy was happy to _____.

What do all the ten words you found have in common?

The empty slot in Activity 2.2 can be filled with words like *play, run, lick, eat, drink, learn, sleep, bite, lie, slobber*. They share meaning (semantic), form (morphological) and functional characteristics, which we'll look at in more detail in Section 2.2. For now, we should note they are all verbs. Activity 2.2 demonstrates that only words which are members of the word class 'verbs' can fill the empty slot in the example sentence *The puppy was happy to* _____. Activity 2.1, on the other hand, showed that from the given list of words only the nouns *insecticides* and *CDs* can fill the gap in the example sentence *How useful did* _____ *seem to be?* The other words are a bit like Cinderella's sisters: their feet have to be chopped off, or cushioned out to fit the shoe. Together, Activities 2.1 and 2.2 have demonstrated that individual words share meaning, form and distributional characteristics and can therefore be grouped into categories or word classes.

We will start our training marathon with the largest, most important and most easily recognisable word classes which also featured in the first two activities: **nouns** and **verbs**. We subsume pronouns under nouns, and auxiliary and modal verbs under verbs. We will continue with one straightforward word class (**adjectives**), and one messy one (**adverbs**), before we move on to **determiners, prepositions** and **conjunctions**.

One group of words won't get its own section in this book. The deprived category are interjections, such as the first word in this book (*hi!*), or *Ouch!*, or *oh!* **Interjections** don't get their own section in this book because, from a grammatical point of view, they don't interact much with other words (note that in writing they are frequently separated by punctuation), and – more importantly – they do not allow us to make any generalisations beyond the fact that they tend to be uttered in exclamation. Other words that don't get their own section in this book are words that do not 'fit' anywhere (classless words) and should consequently be treated individually. One example of such a word is the infinitive marker *to*, as in *I want to swim*.

From Activities 2.1 and 2.2 we know that for individual words to work well in grammatical (standard English) sentences, they need to fulfil three criteria:

- their meaning must be suitable,
- their form must be right, and
- they must be able to fit into a specific position in the sentence.

We will follow a training programme in this chapter and look at these criteria in the same order: semantic (meaning) characteristics first, morphological (form) criteria second, and syntactic (distributional) characteristics of the individual word classes and their individual members last. Each of the sections will begin with a discussion of the shared properties of the word class under consideration. Once we have highlighted the typical character-istics of a word class, we will introduce you to different sub-types within it, if any. Activities on the fuzziness of different word classes, and on how dis-tributional criteria allow us to shed some light on this fuzziness, will be relegated to the end-of-chapter exercises. In working through the remainder of this chapter, you will acquire an initial ability to recognize and determine the word class of any given word within a given string.

2.1 Nouns

Nouns make up approximately a third of all the words you say or write. Several new members are added to this word class on a daily basis. For our grandmothers, *computer* was a new word and a new concept, for us *crunk* was a new noun. CRUNK is a type of hip-hop or rap music. The *Oxford English Dictionary* (OED) dates CRUNK back to the 1990s and suggests that it is either a *blend* (see Chapter 3) of CRAZY and DRUNK or an alternative past participle (see Section 2.3 and Chapter 4) of CRANK, as in *crank it up*. Because the noun class is open to the admission of new items, it is sometimes called an *open word class*. Other open word classes are verbs, adverbs and adjectives.

2.1.1 Meaning
A typical classroom definition of noun might be 'a noun is the name of a person, place or thing'. This informal definition correctly identifies many

members of this word class, e.g. *Tom*, *London* and *apple*, but runs into grave difficulty with others. Even the names of the days of the week, such as *Monday*, are difficult to determine as a 'thing' although they are clearly names. All abstract nouns, that is, nouns that do not denote physical objects such as *honesty* and *presence*, do not fit the semantic definition of nouns. In order to safely identify individual members of this word class as nouns, we need to supplement the semantic definition of nouns with morphological and distributional criteria.

2.1.2 Morphological features

Because nouns frequently denote physical objects, and physical objects tend to be countable, nouns generally have forms that contrast one occurrence of a physical object (singular) with two or more (plural) physical manifestations of this object: *chair / chairs*, *engine / engines*, etc. In other words, many languages distinguish nouns by number (singular vs. plural). The majority of English nouns, though certainly not all, express number in their morphology. The singular is unmarked, while the plural is most frequently expressed by a suffix *-s*. There are many irregularities in number-marking: some nouns add *-en* rather than *-s*, e.g. *child – children*, others change their central (or stem) vowel, e.g. *man – men*, others have identical singular and plural forms, e.g. *fish – fish*.

New members can be added to this word class by, for example, adding the morphemes / affixes *-er, -ee*, or *-ment* to verbs, or *-(i)ty* or *-ess* to adjectives.

Activity 2.3

Write down five words each ending in *-er, -ee, -ment; -ity* and *-ness*.
   For example, *sing-er, enjoy-ment, ment-ee, specific-ity* and *mad-ness*.
   The word *mentee* (but not the sometimes rather painful reality behind it) is a rather recent creation, and it means 'a person who is advised, trained or guided by a mentor'. Like in Activity 1.4, check that all the words you wrote down are nouns derived from verbs or adjectives by an added morpheme, rather than words that just end in these letters by coincidence. Which of the examples we gave you is not derived from a verb or adjective? (We will come back to this word twice in Section 3.6.2.)

2.1.3 Syntactic criteria

When nouns combine with other words to form phrases, they most frequently combine with determiners. If nouns are not names of things like persons, places and organisations (i.e. if they are not proper nouns), if the physical object denoted by the noun can be counted (i.e. if they are count nouns), and if the count does not yield more than one example (i.e. they are singular), the noun must combine with a determiner, as in *the sock*. The phrase *the sock* can then take the function of, for example subject or object (see Chapter 7) and combine with a verb to form a simple sentence, as in *The sock stinks* or *I changed the sock*. In Chapter 5 we will refer to phrases built up around nouns as noun phrases.

2.1.4 Sub-classes of nouns including pronouns

In Section 2.1.1 on the semantics of nouns, we distinguished between concrete nouns, which refer to people, places and other things made of atoms (*key, ball, tree*), and abstract nouns, which refer more to qualities, states or actions (*irony, pain, belief*).

In Section 2.1.2 on the morphology of nouns, we referred to the quality a lot of nouns have, i.e. that they are countable. Another group of nouns does not share this quality, they are uncountable or non-count / mass nouns: *milk, software, furniture* and *information*.

In Section 2.1.3 on the syntactic characteristics of nouns, we have already referred to the distinction between proper and common nouns. Proper nouns are the names of specific people, places or institutions; in English they tend to be the only nouns that begin with a capital letter (*Jenny, London, Bank of England*). Common nouns are nouns that are not names (*mouse, screen, battery*). Certain nouns can be both proper and common: *Hoover, Coke* and others started life in English as proper nouns (brand names) but have now been incorporated into everyday speech and are thus being used as common nouns (e.g. *I'd kill for a coke*, where any cola drink would do).

Why do we bother with these sub-classes of nouns in *English Words and Sentences*? For the same two reasons that we do NOT bother with interjections: concrete and abstract, count and mass, and proper and common nouns do interact with other words in phrases and sentences and we can make generalisations about these word classes. For example, count nouns can be accompanied by determiners that refer to distinctions in number: *a / one / every car*. Non-count nouns, on the other hand, can only be accompanied by determiners that do not refer to a distinction in number, e.g. *much / your software*. And any singular countable common noun must combine with a determiner.

For the same reason our noun category also covers **pronouns** such as *you* and *we* (for the full set of English personal, 'possessive' and reflexive pronouns, see Table 2.1 at the end of this section). The name *pronoun* already suggests that members of this word class are related to nouns. Pronouns also share several features with other members of the noun class. The most important syntactic similarity between pronouns and other nouns is that they occur essentially in the same range of positions in sentences as common and proper nouns, and they can largely serve the same functions as other nouns.

Activity 2.4

See if you can replace all the nouns in the following three sentences with pronouns.

a. *Helen likes cats and cats like Helen.*
b. *Cats easily get too much for Robert.*
c. *Software provides help.*

Activity 2.4 also illustrates some of the different pronoun types and some of the syntactic characteristics they retain in English (unlike common nouns and proper nouns, for example). Replacing all nouns in the first sentence with the appropriate personal pronouns, renders the following sentence.

11. *She likes them and they like her.*

This sentence illustrates similarities and differences between common and proper nouns, and pronouns. Like all other nouns, pronouns have number: that's why only the third-person singular pronouns *she* and *her* can replace *Helen*. *Cat-s*, on the other hand, has to be replaced with the third-person plural pronouns *them* and *they*. 'Third-person' means that reference is made to a third party and neither the speaker nor the addressees of the utterance are included in the pronominal reference. If we addressed the second sentence to Robert himself, we would use the second-person pronoun *you*, as in: *Cats easily get too much for you*. The sentence *I like cats, so they don't easily get too much for me* illustrates the first-person singular pronouns *I* and *me*; both of them indicate reference to the speaker.

But why do we have to replace *Helen* with *she* in the first clause, and with *her* in the second clause? We have to do this because *Helen* is in different sentence positions in the two clauses and serves different functions. In *Helen likes cats*, *Helen* is before the verb *likes* and serves as the subject of the sentence (see Chapter 7); in *Cats like Helen*, *Helen* is after the verb *like* and serves as the object of the sentence. In modern English, the position in the sentence largely marks the function of *Helen* and *cats* as subjects or objects respectively (English has subject–verb–object or SVO word order). The difference between *she* and *her* is one of **case**. *She* is nominative case which marks subject-hood, *her* is accusative case, which marks object-hood in English and other related languages (like German, Icelandic and the Scandinavian ones).

The other sub-classes of nouns which personal pronouns are most closely related to (in syntax and appearance) are the so-called possessive pronouns.

They come in two sets: *my, your, his, her, its, our, your, their* and *mine, yours, his, hers, its, ours, yours, theirs* (for an activity which draws an important syntactic distinction between these two sets on the basis of which we will reclassify the first set as determiners, go to Exercise 2.1 at the end of this chapter), and reflexive pronouns: *myself, yourself, himself, herself, itself, ourselves, yourselves* and *themselves*. Table 2.1 summarises all personal, possessive and reflexive pronouns in all persons (first, second and third) and all numbers (singular and plural).

Table 2.1. *Personal, 'possessive' and reflexive pronouns in all persons and all numbers*

	personal		possessive / genitive		reflexive
	nominative	accusative	determiner	independent	
first pers. sg.	I	me	my	mine	myself
second pers. sg.	you	you	your	yours	yourself
third pers. sg.	he / she / it	him / her / it	his / her / its	his / hers / its	him- / her- / itself
first pers. pl.	we	us	our	ours	ourselves
second pers. pl.	you	you	your	yours	yourselves
third pers. pl.	they	them	their	theirs	themselves

Because Helen likes cats and cats also like Helen, we can furthermore use a reciprocal pronoun and say Helen and cats like *each other* or *one another*.

Activity 2.5

The use of *each other* vs. *one another* has often been the subject of prescriptive rules of grammar. Do you remember them?

If one or more cats are in sight of the speaker who says *Helen likes cat(s)* and her audience, or if the speaker and addressee have already been talking about cats, we can replace *cat(s)* with demonstrative pronouns (*this, that, these* and *those*), as in *Helen likes these, but not those*. If, on the other hand, we don't know what Helen likes, we can replace *Helen* and *cats* with interrogative pronouns: *Who likes cats? Helen likes who(m)?* Apart from *who*, the more formal *whom* (which can only be used in object position) and *what*, there is only one other interrogative pronoun: *which*. These word-forms can also be used as relative pronouns when they introduce subordinate clauses, as in *I wonder what to do next*, but we will come back to this in Chapters 8, 9 and 10. Some grammarians recognise yet another sub-group of pronouns: indefinite pronouns which are said to include words such as *some, any, none, more, both, one*. For different classifications of these words see Exercise 2.1 at the end of this chapter.

To us, this seems like a sprint through nouns, but we are aware that it may seem more like a marathon to you. That's why we'll try to keep it brief on verbs (Chapter 6 is almost exclusively dedicated to verbs and the phrases they head) and other word classes.

2.2 Verbs

'a sentence without a verb is like a stage with actors and props but no script: they don't know what to do'   *(Tesnière 1959)*

Verbs are the most important words for syntax, because without verbs we don't even get simple English sentences. We can list as many nouns, adjectives, adverbs, determiners, prepositions and conjunctions as we want, but without a verb there won't be an English sentence. Such an unstructured list, including examples of the word classes just mentioned, is *light, green, brightly, the, on, her, and, him*. We can structure the list so that it starts resembling a sentence: *the green light brightly on her and him*, but without a verb, even this structured list will never become a grammatical English sentence like *The green light shines brightly on her and him*.

What's so special about verbs? Everything: their meaning, their morphology and their syntax. Unfortunately we can generalise less about the meaning, the morphological features and the syntactic behaviour of verbs than we could for nouns. That's why we will distinguish carefully between the subclasses of verbs: **main** or **lexical verbs**, on the one hand, **modal verbs** and **auxiliary verbs**, on the other.

2.2.1 Meaning

The meaning-based, primary-school definition of verb is 'a doing word'; a meaning-based secondary-school definition of verb would read something like 'a verb expresses an action, process or event'. Verbs, however, also include members which denote states and relationships (e.g. *seem, compare*), sensory perceptions (e.g. *smell, taste*) and cognitive processes (e.g. *contemplate, doubt*). The semantic reason why verbs are so important for syntax is that they tend to determine what kind of situation is expressed in a clause:

12.   *Dad swam one mile.*   [action]
13.   *The daughter stayed at home.*   [event]
14.   *The astronauts know the signal.*   [state]

As was the case with nouns, these semantic definitions are helpful for recognising individual words as verbs, but are by no means watertight. Morphological characteristics get us much further.

2.2.2 Morphological features

The most distinctive grammatical property of verbs is their inflectional morphology (see Chapter 4). Regular lexical verbs have five forms (e.g. *stop*, *stops*, *stopped* (past), *stopped* (participle), *stopping*). In all regular verbs (such as *stop* and *enjoy*, for example), and in many irregular verbs (such as *hear*), the forms of two grammatical words are identical (cf. *stopped* (past), *stopped* (participle); *heard* (past) and *heard* (participle)). The most basic form of lexical verbs, the one that corresponds to the lexeme and would therefore be entered in a dictionary, consists of just one morpheme (e.g. ENJOY / *enjoy*), as in

15.   *We enjoy the snow.*

(As we will see in Chapter 3, some lexical verbs can be a compound, as in *to fly-fish*.) When the enjoying takes place in the present time and is being done by a single person, the grammar of the English language requires us to add an -*s* to *enjoy*, as in

16.   *Our dog enjoy-s the snow.*

When the enjoying happened in past and is definitely over, we add an -*ed*, as in

17.   *Last week he enjoy-ed the snow.*

The snow in London has melted in the meantime, but our dog is still tired, because

18.   *He has enjoy-ed the snow.*

The forms of the lexeme *enjoy* in examples 17 and 18 are identical, but grammatically they are different words. That's one reason why we distinguished between lexemes, word forms and grammatical words in Chapter 1. The *enjoyed* in sentence (17) is the past (tense) form; the *enjoyed* in sentence (18), on the other hand, expresses perfective aspect: it is a so-called past participle form. We will return to this distinction in Chapters 4 and 6, but if you are a observant speaker of English, you will notice a subtle meaning difference between the situations expressed by the sentences *he enjoyed the snow* and *he has enjoyed the snow*. Anyway, today

19.   *Our dog is enjoy-ing the rest.*

The five forms of the verb *enjoy* with their corresponding names and syntactic functions are shown in Table 2.2.

Table 2.2. *Verb forms of ENJOY*

base form	s-form	ed-form (past)	ed-form (part)	ing-form (part)
enjoy present tense	*enjoy-s* present tense third pers. sg.	*enjoy-ed* past tense	*enjoy-ed* participle, perfective aspect	*enjoy-ing* participle, progressive aspect

These are the different morphological guises under which regular English verbs come. If you are not sure if an individual word in a sentence is a verb or not, you can always try to use it in another form or guise; if the sentence stays grammatical, you can be sure that the individual word in question is definitely a verb. Let's focus on the verb LAUGH in

20. *The girl is **laugh-ing** about the comedian.*

In different situational contexts, we could encounter this sentence and its lexical verb *laugh* in all of the following forms:

21. *The girl **laugh-s** about the comedian, but the boys don't **laugh**.*
22. *The girl **laugh-ed** about the comedian.*
23. *The girl has **laugh-ed** about the comedian.*

To the great annoyance of learners of English, there are also about fifty irregular English verbs. Like most irregular things in English, they originate in older forms of the language. Sometimes they disguise their lexeme family membership so well that you may not even associate them with the right lexeme. For example, if you don't know that *bought* is the past tense form of *buy*, you may not even connect it with *buy*, its infinitive form (that is the form under which it is listed in a dictionary). Fortunately not all English irregular verbs differ as much in their forms as *buy* and *bought*: the past and participle forms of *build, show, dig, lie* and *let*, for example are shown in Table 2.3.

Table 2.3. *Verb forms of BUILD, SHOW, DIG, LIE, and LET*

infinitive	past tense form	participle form
build	built	built
show	showed	shown
dig	dug	dug
lie	lay	lain
let	let	let

To help you solve the problem of associating irregular inflectional verb forms with the right lexeme, all good dictionaries list irregular verb forms as lexical entries and refer you back to the infinitive form for the main entry.

2.2.3 Syntactic criteria

The syntax of verbs is quite complex. Moreover, the syntax of lexical verbs differs so significantly from the syntax of auxiliary verbs that we will explore this in detail in Chapter 6. For now suffice to say that because verbs are the chief determinant of what kind of situation is expressed in a clause, they get to determine which other roles are required. The verb *rain*, for example, is happy with just *it*, as in *It rains*. The meaning of the verb *buy*, on the other hand, determines that somebody will have to do the buying and something will have to be bought, as in *Anna bought a present*. The verb *give* even requires three roles, somebody who does the giving, something that is given and a recipient, as in *Ali gave the toy to Max*. And it is the syntactic characteristics of the verbs *leave* and *arrive* that determine that we can simply add *the library* after *leave*, as in *I leave the library* now, but have to add the preposition *at* before *the library* after *arrive*, as in *I arrive at the library again on Monday morning*. In slightly more linguistic terminology, verbs license the occurrence of obligatory sentence elements (complements). Because verbs allow (or disallow) dependent sentence elements (as in the *It rains vs.* *It rains her*, *Anna bought a present* and *Ali gave the toy to Max* examples), and determine their kind (as in the *leave the library* vs. *arrive at the library* examples), verbs are the most important element in the group(s) of words they build around themselves, the verb phrase / predicate. We will develop this in Chapter 6, while Chapter 7 will build on the morpho-syntactic behaviour of verb phrases and explore how they function as predicates within clauses.

2.2.4 Sub-classes of verbs: auxiliary and modal verbs

English (and many other languages) have developed sub-classes of verbs whose semantic and morpho-syntactic behaviour is sufficiently similar to lexical verbs to still classify them as verbs, but also different enough to warrant sub-class(es). Auxiliary verbs (or auxiliaries, AUX) and a special kind of auxiliaries known as modal verbs (modals, MOD) developed out of lexical verbs during the last 600–700 years and have become more specialised in function(s), but have lost others. They, for example, can no longer be the only verb in a clause; they need a main verb to form a grammatical sentence. We will look at auxiliaries first.

Auxiliary verbs

The main or primary auxiliaries are *be*, *have* and *do*. In Chapter 1, we used the *cut* and *jump* example to illustrate why we have to distinguish between lexemes, word forms and grammatical words. One reason we have just explored in a bit more detail: *jumped* can be two different grammatical words (past and participle). Another reason is that some verbs can be used as both as lexical and as auxiliary verbs. They are then generally regarded as separate lexemes. Their contrasting use as lexical verbs and auxiliary verbs is illustrated by the following examples

24. *You have a fit.*   [lexical]
25. *We do our best.*   [lexical]
26. *I need you.*   [lexical]
27. *You have not calmed down yet.* [auxiliary]
28. *Do you enjoy it?*   [auxiliary]
29. *I need to tell you something.*   [auxiliary]

The contrast between examples 24 to 26 and examples 27 to 29 illustrates that, when used as the only verb in a sentence, these verbs have lexical meaning (e.g. *have* means 'possess, own, or hold', *do* means 'perform or carry out an action' and *need* means 'require'). As auxiliary verbs, on the other hand, they have more grammatical function than 'referential' meaning (meaning which tells you what the speaker is talking about). For example, in *Do you enjoy it?* the main distinctive load is carried by *enjoy*, not by *do*.

Activity 2.6

Find and label the auxiliary (AUX) and lexical verbs (V) in the following sentences first.

   a. *I am driving quite recklessly at times.*
   b. *On Saturday I was stopped by the police for a U-turn.*
   c. *I am riding my bicycle worse than ever.*
   d. *Unfortunately I'm not allowed on the roads for a month.*

Then try to identify the shared semantic and syntactic function of *be* in the above sentences.

The lexical verbs in (a) to (d) are *drive*, *stop*, *ride*, and *allow* respectively. All forms of BE in sentences (a) to (d) (*am*, *was* and *'m*) are auxiliary verbs. The semantic relation between them and the lexical verbs in the same clauses is one of co-reference, e.g. in *am driving* and *am not allowed*; the two verbs refer to the same event: the auxiliaries define the time, like the *-s* and *-ed* (past) morphemes on lexical verbs. The common function of the forms of BE in examples (a) to (d) therefore is to carry the tense (*am* is present tense and *was* is past tense). They also support various syntactic constructions (progressive, passive, predicative, negative). We will deal with them in Chapter 6.

Morphologically the auxiliaries *be* and *have* are the most irregular verbs in the English language. They have different forms in the present and past tenses, and for different number (singular vs. plural) and person subjects (first, second and third person).

Table 2.4. *BE and HAVE*

		first-, second, third-person singular	first-, second, third-person plural
BE	pres	I **am**, you **are**, he / she / it **is**	we **are**, you **are**, they **are**
BE	past	I **was**, you **were**, he / she / it **was**	we **were**, you **were**, they **were**
HAVE	pres	I **have**, you **have**, he / she/ it **has**	we **have**, you **have**, they **have**
HAVE	past	I **had**, you **had**, he / she/ it **had**	we **had**, you **had** they **had**

Morphologically the auxiliaries *be*, *have* and *do* behave more like lexical verbs than modal verbs (see next section), and we will carry out the full comparison once we have introduced the modals. For now suffice to note that Table 2.4 already contains the base, -*s*, and -*ed* (past) forms of BE and HAVE. Can you identify them? The base form of DO is *do*, its -*s* form is *does* and its past form is *did*. The only form we have not covered yet is the -*ing* (part / progressive aspect) form. Do the main auxiliaries have this form too? Yes, they do: *being*, *having* and *doing*.

Another characteristic of auxiliaries is that most of them have reduced forms (e.g. *am* ~ *'m*, *is* ~ *'s*, as in *I'm typing and he's cooking*), and only (tensed) auxiliary verbs accept -*n't* as in *They aren't tired* (the notable exception to this regularity is **amn't*). These reduced forms are called *clitics*. They straddle the boundaries between morphology, syntax and phonology. We won't go into them and move onto syntactic characteristics of auxiliaries.

When used as auxiliaries, *be* and *have* and *do* must combine with a main / lexical verb which they support (this is why they are called auxiliaries or 'helping' verbs).

30. *We are eating pizza again.*
31. **We are* _____ *pizza again.*
32. *We have eaten pizza again*
33. **We have* _____ *pizza again*
34. *Do you eat a lot of pizza, too?*
35. **Do you* _____ *a lot of pizza, too?*

The two most striking syntactic differences between auxiliary and lexical verbs are illustrated by questions and negative sentences.

Activity 2.7

Turn the following declarative sentences first into interrogative sentences (i.e. questions), and then into negative sentences.

   a.   *She has stopped the bus.*
   b.   *He paid the fine yesterday.*

Describe which words changed position.

---

36.   *Has she stopped the bus?*
37.   *She has not / hasn't stopped the bus.*
38.   *Did he pay the fine yesterday?*
39.   *He did not / didn't pay the fine yesterday.*

In the questions in examples 36 and 38, the subject pronouns (*she, he*) relinquished their sentence initial position to the auxiliary verbs *has* and *do* respectively. Because the subject and the (leftmost) auxiliary exchange place in questions, this is referred to as *subject-auxiliary inversion (SAI)*. Sentence (b) in Activity 2.7, *He paid the fine yesterday*, contains only a lexical verb PAY, but no auxiliary. In order to formulate a question, you had to add the appropriately tensed auxiliary *did*.

   In the negative sentences in examples 37 and 39, you inserted the negative marker *not* between the auxiliary and the main verbs. To make *He paid the fine yesterday* negative, we once again had to add the appropriate form of the 'dummy' word *do*, i.e. *did*. The two versions of the negative sentences furthermore show that most English auxiliaries (with the exception of *am* and the modals) have contracted negative forms in *-n't*. No lexical verb has forms of this kind: **writen't, *typen't, *screamn't*.

   Need and *dare* are good examples of non-typical auxiliaries/modals (which also point towards the fuzziness of word classes). We will discuss them in Exercise 2.5 at the end of this chapter.

Modal verbs

Modal verbs express either an expectation, evaluation, or judgement on whether an event was, is or will be likely to happen, as in:

40.   *We **may** go to the cinema tonight.*
41.   *The woman over there **could** be Andy's mother.*
42.   *I'm hungry, it **must** be lunchtime.*

or human control over events, as in:

43.   *You **must** also do the exercises at the end of the chapters.*
44.   *Ben **could** ride a bicycle when he was three years old.*
45.   *You **may** have your mobile / cell phone on as long as it is on silent mode.*

31

This is the specialisation in (semantic) function modal verbs have undergone, as mentioned in the introduction to Section 2.2.4.

Moving onto morpho-syntactic characteristics of modal verbs now, we observe that, like all lexical and auxiliary verbs, they have present and past tense forms (the exception is *must*).

Table 2.5. *Modal verbs and tense*

can	could
may	might
will	would
shall	should

The past forms of modal verbs are frequently used to refer to present or even future time, as in *I shall / will / may / can go for a swim now / tomorrow.* *Could*, *might*, *would*, *should* are also used when we want to be more polite. The past forms of modals are more polite, because they express a more remote possibility and are less imposing.

46. *I can help you with your shopping.*
47. *I could help you with your shopping.*
48. *I may finish the assignment tomorrow.*
49. *I might finish the assignment tomorrow.*
50. *I will pluck this hair for you.*
51. *I would pluck this hair for you, if you let me.*

We will look at other marginal members of the auxiliary / modal verb class (*need, dare, seem*) in Exercise 2.5 at the end of this chapter.

Another syntactic / distributional word order characteristic of modals is that they are the first to occur in a sequence of auxiliaries, as in *She must have been seeing him for several years.*

To summarise, the best way of recognising auxiliary and modal verbs is to formulate questions (interrogative) and negative sentences. If the verb swaps position with the subject (subject-auxiliary inversion) and shows up in sentence initial word-order position, it is likely to be an auxiliary or modal as in

52. *The winter sun is shining brightly today.*
53. *Is the winter sun shining brightly today?*

Equally, if in a negation the *not* squeezes in between two verbs, the one to its left will most probably be an auxiliary or modal verb, as in

54. *I can see the London Eye when I look out of the window.*
55. *I cannot/can't see the London Eye when I look out of the window.*

English auxiliaries and modals are small sub-classes of verbs whose members are characteristically used to mark syntactic categories. We have looked a bit at tense, interrogative mood and negation, but will deal more systematically with the syntactic categories marked by auxiliaries in English (aspect, mood, tense, voice) in Chapter 6.

2.3 Adjectives

Let's start again with the classroom definition of adjectives. They are 'describing words which modify a noun', that is, they express a quality or attribute of a noun. Note that even this basic semantic definition of adjectives already relies on you knowing what a noun is. The most prototypical adjectives denote properties of people or of concrete or abstract things. Because properties can be possessed in varying degrees, adjectives tend to be **gradable**. The degree of the coldness of a drink can, for example, be indicated in relation to the coldness of other drinks, e.g. *the Gin and Tonic is colder than the Black Russian and the Mojito is coldest*, or by words like *very*, *extremely*, *fairly*, etc., as in *the very cold cocktail*.

One special way of marking degree is by comparison. Short regular adjectives like *cold* or *fast* add the *-er*, *-est* morphemes to the end of their base to form the so called **comparative** (*fast-er*) and **superlative** (*fast-est*) forms. Longer gradable adjectives mark these three degree levels with *more* and *most*: *beautiful – more beautiful – most beautiful*. Adjectives belong to the group of open word classes and new adjectives are freely derived from many nouns (by adding e.g. *-able / -ible, -ful, -less, -ic, -ese, -ish*) or verbs (by adding *-able*, or *-ible*).

Unfortunately not all adjectives denote properties which are naturally gradable and therefore won't take degree modification either of the *-er / -est* or *more / most* form. For this type of adjectives, like for example *historical, married, editorial*, we have to rely on syntactic criteria to correctly identify them as adjectives.

As adjectives denote properties of nouns, most of the time they are placed immediately before the noun they modify, as in *the good breakfast*. In sentences which contain verbs such as *be, become, seem, feel*, adjectives can also be placed after the noun they modify and the verbs just listed, as in *the breakfast is good*. When the adjective precedes the noun it modifies, it is said to function **attributively**; when adjectives are placed to the right of the noun, they express a property of, they are said to function **predicatively** (we will return to the type of verbs which license this construction in Chapter 7). Most adjectives can be used both attributively and predicatively (for exceptions see Exercise 2.3 at the end of this chapter).

2.4 Adverbs

Adjectives and adverbs are linked by two contrasting characteristics, one morphological and one functional: the most prototypical adverbs are derived from adjectives by adding *-ly*; and adverbs modify words other than nouns. Otherwise, adverbs have few distinctive characteristics which unite them as a word class. We start again with the semantic ones before we elaborate a bit on the morphological and syntactic ones already mentioned.

The meaning of the most prototypical adverbs can be captured by the phrase 'adverbs express information about time, manner, place and frequency'. But this definition only works for the semantically most prototypical ones like *Tomorrow* I won't be *here*. For many other adverbs we better use morphological characteristics.

The easily recognisable adverbs are derived from adjectives by adding *-ly*, and fortunately there are quite a few of those (*quickly, fortunately, carefully*, etc.). The adverb *easily* in the previous sentence was derived from the adjective *easy* in the same manner. Be careful, however, because not all words ending in the morpheme *-ly* are adverbs: *deadly* in *the deadly virus*, for example, is an adjective. Can you say why? And by no means all adverbs are derived in this way; this includes some quite common ones like *almost, always, often, quite, rather, soon*. Another morphological criterion of a small number of adverbs is that they can be graded like adjectives: *hard – harder – hardest*.

By far the best distinctive characteristic of adverbs is their syntactic function. Adverbs mostly function as modifiers of verbs, as in *Anne laughs loudly*, but they can also modify adjectives, as in *the incredibly good cake*, or *the very expensive mobile phone*, or other adverbs (that follow them), as in *she laughs quite loudly*, or *the library will close quite soon*. In summary, the most prototypical adverbs are derived from adjectives by adding *-ly* and modify verbs, adjectives and other adverbs (but not nouns).

2.5 Determiners

In Section 2.3 we saw that the morpho-syntactic and semantic characteristics of auxiliary and modal verbs are sufficiently different from those of lexical verbs to warrant the formation of sub-classes. For determiners it is the other way round: this word class is composed of members that have traditionally been associated with other word classes. The most common determiners, A(N) and THE, for example, have been traditionally called

articles. Other typical examples of determiners you may have in the past associated with other word classes (like adjectives, quantifiers, numerals, pronouns) are SOME, ANY, FEW, ONE, MY, YOUR, HER, THEIR, THIS, THOSE. What unites determiners into a word class is that they all occur in phrases with nouns, and that they determine the (definite or indefinite) meaning of the noun phrase they belong to.

To work on the definite or indefinite meaning that determiners contribute to noun phrases, let's contrast two scenarios. At a library issue desk, a speaker (A) can say either 56 or 57:

56. *Give me **the** book, please*
57. *Give me **a** book, please.*

In the first scenario we can safely assume that everybody knows which book is being talked about. In the second scenario, on the other hand, neither the speaker of the sentence nor the addressee(s) knows exactly which book is being talked about. In this case, it is left to the addressee to either choose a book (and risk it may be the wrong one), or to ask the speaker to select one, which could trigger an exchange like

58. B: *Which one?*
    A: *The one [book] on the table.*

If the speaker and the addressee(s) are both familiar with the referent of the noun, a definite determiner is used, as in *the book*; if the referent is not known, an indefinite determiner is used, as in *a book*. Naturally, SOME, ANY, FEW, MY (and all possessive determiners), THIS (and all demonstrative determiners) can have such a variety of different meanings and referents that we cannot generalize about their semantics.

Recall that in Activity 2.1 we grouped the two determiners *the* and *a* with the 'hopeless' word classes that couldn't be made to fit the noun slot in our example sentence *How useful did ____ seem to be?* This was done on the basis that their form couldn't be changed. In other words, determiners are free morphemes and do not take any inflectional (for example *the-ed, *the-ing, *the-s) or derivational endings (for example, *the-able, *un-the). This is why they belong to the so called *closed word classes*. Syntactically, on the other hand, determiners stand much more of a chance of filling a noun slot, as we shall see in the next paragraph.

Determiners are controlled by one very general rule, which we have already encountered in connection with nouns: any singular countable common noun must combine with a determiner, as in *I found *(a) book* (i.e. *a* cannot be omitted). This rule applies to all determiners when the nouns they combine with are explicitly spelled out. Sometimes, however, the referent of the noun combining with the determiner is understood by all participants in the conversation, and can therefore be left out (this is called **ellipsis**). When we have already been talking about books, I can safely omit the noun *book(s)*, as in

59. *I found some (books).*
60. *Which (books) did you read?*
61. *I like this (book).*
62. *I have read two (books).*
63. *I read a few (books).*
64. *I haven't read any (books).*

If the meaning can be reconstructed on the basis of the preceding context, we can also omit *insecticides* and *CDs* from our example sentence from Activity 2.1 (e.g. *How useful did those (insecticides / CDs) seem to be?*) and leave just *those* in the noun (phrase) slot. How would you classify *those* now? As a determiner or a (pro)noun? To summarise, syntactically determiners do not pair with any other word class but nouns; they only occur in syntactic relations with nouns.

2.6 Prepositions

Prepositions were also branded as 'hopeless' in Activity 2.1 because they can never ever fill a noun slot in an English sentence. Prepositions cannot do this because of their meaning, their unchangeable form, and their distribution in relation to other English words in English sentences. Typical prepositions are ABOUT, ABOVE, ACROSS, AFTER, AROUND, AT, BEFORE, BEHIND, BELOW, BESIDE, BETWEEN, BY, DURING, FOR, FROM, IN, OF, OVER, PAST, SINCE, TO (as in *I go to school* and not the classless infinitive maker *to* that can precede verbs, as in *I want to give him a book*), etc. There are more (some even consist of two words, like *in between*) but nonetheless prepositions are definitely a closed class.

Semantically, the role of prepositions is to define relationships between the words they link. For example, in *picture of Pat* the preposition *of* defines the relationship between the picture and Pat, and contrasts with other prepositions, for example *for: picture for Pat*. Most prepositions denote relations in space or time.

Prepositions cannot be further analysed into smaller morphs. Syntactically they have three main distinguishing characteristics:

- They usually come before a noun (phrase): they are called 'pre-positions' because of their position before (*pre-*) a noun;

- Prepositional phrases can further modify almost any class of words, including nouns (*picture of Pat*), verbs *(think of Pat)*, adjectives *(proud of Pat)*, and adverbs *(unfortunately for Pat)*
- In questions, they can be 'stranded' at the end of the clause, as in *Who are you thinking of?* This is sometimes considered to be 'bad' grammar by prescriptive grammarians. In formal language, prepositions can be 'pied-piped' to the front of the clause, along with the question words starting in *wh-*, as in *Of whom are you thinking?*

2.7 Conjunctions

Conjunctions were also hopeless in Activity 2.1, at least when it comes to filling noun slots in English sentences. Conjunctions are similar to prepositions (some linguists even treat them as the same word class) in that they link together, or con-join, linguistics units. Conjunctions furthermore form a closed class, or rather two: *coordinators* and *subordinators*.

2.7.1 Coordinators
Coordinators form a very small class whose most obvious members are AND, OR and BUT. Their primary function is to signal coordination. Coordination is the joining of two elements, which have equal syntactic status and are usually also of the same kind, to make a larger constituent of the same kind and level (see Chapter 8). The coordinated elements are in square brackets in the following examples.

65. *[Cats] and [dogs] tend to fight.*
66. *It's up to [the young woman] and [the not quite so young man] to have a good life.*
67. *[It is raining heavily] but [the sun is shining].*

Equal syntactic status does not mean same number of words, or the same meaning. Equal syntactic status means neither of the units depends on the other. Both clauses in the last sentence, for example, can stand on their own. This contrasts sharply with the unequal relationships subordinators establish between two clauses.

2.7.2 Subordinators
Subordinating conjunctions only come at the beginning of a subordinate clause. The most central members of the subordinator category are *that*, *whether* and the *if* that means *whether*, as in *I'm not sure if the sun is*

shining. The subordinator *if* has turned the second clause from example 67 above into a subordinate clause. *If the sun is shining* can no longer stand on its own, the conjunction *if* has made *the sun is shining* a subordinate clause. Don't worry if this goes over your head at the moment; we will return to conjunctions in Chapter 8 when we look at the phrase or clause types they introduce or conjoin. For now suffice that when you find two main lexical verbs in a sentence, it may be worth checking if you can divide the sentence in two clauses which are linked either by co- or by subordination.

2.8 Chapter summary

In this chapter we demonstrated that individual words share meaning, form and distributional characteristics and can therefore be grouped into word classes. In Activities 2.1 and 2.2 we established that meaning is of course important in determining if a word fits into a specific slot in a sentence or not, but formal characteristics are even more important. For some word classes (nouns, verbs, adjectives and adverbs) we can change the word forms quite easily (by means we will explore further in the next chapter) without drastically changing their meaning. They belong to the *open word classes*. Members of other word classes (determiners, prepositions and conjunctions) are unable to change their form, and because these classes do not accept new members they are called *closed*. We then followed an effective but rather strenuous training routine by going through the semantic (meaning), morphological (form) and syntactic (distributional) characteristics of the seven main word classes of the English language: nouns, verbs, adjectives, adverbs, determiners, prepositions and conjunctions. For nouns, verbs and conjunctions we had to establish sub-classes because pronouns, auxiliary and modal verbs and coordinating and subordinating conjunctions differ enough in morpho-syntactic behaviour to form sub-groups within the larger word classes they belong to. So far we have mainly looked at typical nouns, verbs, prepositions, etc., but, like anywhere else in nature, there are also atypical examples that do not fit the main characteristics we have just established and / or show exceptional behaviour. We will look at some of the dolphins, whales, ostriches of language in the following exercises.

Key terms
(Pro)noun; lexical; auxiliary; modal verb; adjective; adverb; determiner; preposition; conjunction; gradable; comparative; superlative; attributive; predicative.

Exercises

Exercise 2.1　Make one sentence each with the two different sets of possessive / genitive (case) pronouns

my, your, his / her / its, our, your, their　mine, yours, his / hers / its, ours, yours, theirs
*I am going to drink **my** coffee.*　　　*Don't you dare drink it, it's **mine**.*

What is their difference in usage? Are you clear about why we called *mine,* *yours, his / hers / its, ours, yours, theirs* independent? Equally, can you see that the 'dependent' ones (*my, your, his / her / its, our, your, their*) syntactically behave just like the articles / determiners *a* and *the,* as in *I am going to drink a / the / my / your / his / her / its / our / your / their coffee*?

Exercise 2.2　Using the semantic, formal and especially syntactic criteria we established in Sections 2.6 and 2.7, determine which word class *after* belongs to in the following two sentences:

a.　*I visited Maureen after I had had dinner with Annabelle.*
b.　*I visited Maureen after dinner.*

In sentence (a), you most probably (or hopefully) classified *after* as a member of the word class discussed in Section 2.7. In sentence (b), on the other hand, you put it in with the parts of speech introduced in Section 2.6. Think whether it makes sense to say that *after* is a _____ when it introduces a clause, as in sentence ___, and to call it a _____ when it introduces a phrase, as in sentence ___ .

Exercise 2.3　Make pairs of sentences in which you use the following adjectives attributively and predicatively respectively: *tasty, affirmative, calm, main, sheer, afraid* and *glad,* as in:

Attributive	Predicative
Mariana enjoyed the tasty stir fry.	*The stir fry is tasty.*

Can you use all the adjectives from the list we gave you both attributively and predicatively?

Exercise 2.4   Our Table 2.3 includes examples with *show* and *lie*. Insert the form of these words you would normally use into the gap in the following sentences.

a. *The caretaker has _____ (show) me where the new recycling containers are.*
b. *Our neighbour is very ill. She has _____ (lie) in bed for the last weeks.*

Now go back to Table 2.3 and compare the form you used to the one listed in the table. If the words forms are different, explain in morphological terms how you arrived at the participle forms you used. When introducing auxiliary and modal verbs, we mentioned that the English language has been and is changing. Can we attribute the discrepancy between the *shown* and *show-ed* and *lain* and *lie-ed* to a similar reason, i.e. language change?

Exercise 2.5   In Section 2.2.4, we mentioned *need* and *dare* when discussing auxiliary verbs, and *ought to*, *had to* when discussing modals, but relegated them to the end-of-chapter exercises because they do not share some of the core characteristics of these sub-classes of verbs. Let's check this out now. What are the core syntactic criteria of members of the auxiliary and modal class? They are illustrated in the following examples

a. *Are you going to work today?*
b. *You are not going to work today.*
c. *Must you go to work today?*
d. *You must not go to work today.*

Subject *dare, need* and *ought (to)* to these two tests now by forming negative sentences and questions with them. What do you think, are they grammatical, marginally grammatical (indicated by '?' instead of '*' in linguistics) or good? Ask the first person you meet in the kitchen when you make your next cup of coffee or tea what they make of your *dare* and *need* and *ought (to)* questions and negative sentences. Put * / ? / nothing against the sentences. You have successfully collected your first grammaticality judgement, a legitimate scientific (linguistic) data collection technique. In the past, frequently this was the only method used; today most linguists also check their and their informants' intuition against examples of the same construction type in big language corpora.

Further reading

On word classes see Aarts and Haegeman (2006), Greenbaum and Nelson (2009) and Huddleston and Pullum (2005). On verbs, consult Palmer (1987) and Leech (2004). Auxiliaries are discussed in depth in Warner (1993). Wales (1996) is very useful for personal pronouns. On adjectives, see Thompson (1988). An excellent study of noun phrases in English is Keizer (2007); see also Mahlberg (2005).

CHAPTER 3

Derivational morphology

In this chapter . . .

We are going to introduce you to morphology proper. We will start by revisiting the concepts of morpheme and morph and briefly introduce the notion of allomorph. Analogous to what we did with words in Chapter 2, we are then going to develop our understanding of morphemes by looking at different ways of classifying them into free and bound morphemes; affixes which either attach to the left or the right of a base and are then called prefixes and suffixes respectively; and last but not least the important but not always clear-cut distinction between inflection and derivation. We will then focus on derivational morphology. In the activities we will explore how derivational morphological operations can change the class of a word and how this affects their distribution and behaviour in sentences. Towards the end of the chapter we will look at other word-formation processes which are productive in English: compounding, conversion, backformation, clipping, blending, acronyms and abbreviations.

During our sprint through the main seven word classes of the English language in the last chapter, did you manage to make it to the end? If you collapsed, first catch your breath and then go back to where you broke down and finish the chapter. You will feel better, and because of your knowledge about the morphological characteristics of the different word classes you will find the next two chapters easy; the syntactic characteristics will stand you in excellent stead in Chapters 5 and 6 and the remainder of this book. From our perspective, we are glad we managed to fit the most important shared characteristics of English word classes into approximately twenty-six pages (the marathon distance in miles) and not forty-one pages (the marathon distance in kilometres). The other good news is that

- derivational morphology, the main topic of this chapter, is fun, and
- you already know a few things about *morphology* and *syntax*, so we don't start from scratch.

3.1 Morphemes, morphs and allomorphs

In Chapter 1, for example, we discussed the principle of contrast as the main procedure for discovering the structure of words and the grammatical structure of language in general. In Chapters 1 and 2 we contrasted word forms that differ in shape, in meaning (both lexical meaning and grammatical function) and in their distribution. From the principle of contrast we arrived at the definition of **morpheme** as the smallest grammatical unit of meaning. This is the smallest grammatical (not phonological) unit that matches up with the smallest difference in word or sentence meaning, or in grammatical structure. This difference also manifests itself in word shape. By contrasting examples 1 and 2 below

1. *Jasper unlocked the bike.*
2. *Jasper locked the bike.*

we, for example, discover that *un-* is a **morph**, i.e. a physical shape associated with a **morpheme**. In this case it's very obvious why and how: *un-locking* something is the reverse process of locking. The difference between *lock* and *unlock* thus correlates with the smallest difference in word and sentence meaning. By contrasting 3 and 4 below

3. *Jasper cycles through the park.*
4. *Jasper cycled through the park.*

we discover that both *-s* and *-d* are morphs associated with the morphemes *-s* and *-ed* respectively. In this case it is maybe a bit less obvious why and how, but again it is the difference between *-s* and *-d* at the end of the verb *cycle* that correlates with the smallest difference in word and sentence meaning (*cycles* refers to the present, whereas *cycled* refers to the past) and grammatical structure (*cycles* is present tense and *cycled* is past tense). The words *lock* and *unlock* and *cycles* and *cycled* differ in exactly one morpheme. This is why in the second paragraph of this chapter we defined **morpheme**, slightly more technically than in Chapter 1, as the smallest difference in word shape that correlates with the smallest difference in (word or sentence) meaning or in grammatical structure.

In this and the next chapter we will hopefully discover enough about the structure of words (i.e. morphology) and how word-internal units (i.e. morphemes) work so that you can move on to more specialised courses in syntax as well as in morphology. Concepts we first introduced in the opening chapter will be dealt with at a slightly more technical level in this one. Only one distinction, the one between morphs and **allomorphs**, will merely be touched upon here at the beginning of the chapter, because allomorphs are not really relevant to morphology and syntax.

Both morphs and allomorphs are physical shapes associated with a morpheme. A **morph** is the realization of a morpheme; an *allomorph* is one of two or more complementary morphs which manifest a morpheme in its different phonological or morphological environments. For example, sentences 1, 2 and 4 all contain the abstract past tense morpheme *-ed*, realised as the morphs *-(e)d* in *(un)locked* and *cycled*. Read these two words out loud and you will notice that in *locked* this past tense morpheme is pronounced /t/; whereas in *cycled* it is pronounced /d/. Verbs like *want* and *need* already end in /t/ and /d/ respectively. Because it is difficult to pronounce sounds that are produced in the same place (like /t/ and /d/) in succession, we insert a vowel before the past tense morpheme, as in /niːdɪd/ (the colon represents a long /i/ sound). These examples illustrate that the past tense morpheme can take three different physical shapes: /t/, /d/ and /ɪd/. Which of these three allomorphs actually represents the past tense morpheme in spoken language depends on the sound environment it occurs in. In this case, we therefore say that an *allomorph* is a phonologically conditioned realisation of a morpheme. For a different example of allomorphs, pronounce the three words *hats*, *dogs* and *boxes*. You will notice that the plural morpheme also manifests itself in three different allomorphs. For our purposes, however, it is important that these allomorphs represent the abstract morphemes *-ed* (past) and *-s* (plural). Just as we do not concern ourselves with the different spelling variants of words when morphemes are attached (for example, the doubling of *t* in *potted*), we do not concern ourselves with pronunciation variations (allomorphs) of morphemes.

In comparison with Chapter 1, we have now stepped our discussion of morphology up a bit by saying that a **morpheme** is an element of language, smaller than the word, which represents a correlation between form and meaning. A **morph** is the realisation of a morpheme, and an *allomorph* is one of two or more complementary morphs which manifest a morpheme in its different phonological and morphological environments. We are now ready to take a closer look at the morphological structure of words.

3.2 **Free and bound morphemes**

In the previous chapter, we noticed that some words have more in common than others. We therefore grouped them into classes. Utilising the principle of contrast again, we will now discover that some morphemes also have more in common than others. We can therefore usefully classify morphemes into **free** and **bound morphs**, or **roots** and **affixes**. We will see that, like nouns, verbs and conjunctions, affixes are usefully further sub-divided into **prefixes** and **suffixes**. The most crucial morphological distinction, however, is the one between **derivation** and **inflection**. In this chapter we will play with derivational morphological processes once we have indentified and named the different types of morphemes. Inflectional morphology gets its own chapter, Chapter 4.

The same techniques that allow us to segment sentences into word-forms also allow us to segment word-forms. We have already looked at all of the following words in one or another context in Chapters 1 and 2. They all have two things in common.

Activity 3.1

Which morphological characteristics do the following words share? Can you segment them into morphemes? Can all the morphemes you identified stand on their own?

brightness, unlock, jumps, painted, jumping, dogs, faster

The two things the words in Activity 3.1 have in common are:

(a) all these word forms can be divided into two parts, or morphs: *bright-ness, un-lock, jump-s, paint-ed, jump-ing, dog-s, fast-er*;

(b) only one of the morphs that make up the word-forms given in Activity 3.1 is a word-form on its own. They are *bright, lock, jump, paint, dog, insect* and *fast*.

Those units or morphs that can stand on their own are called **free morphs**. They are not further analysable into smaller grammatical units. All free morphs in Activity 3.1 (listed under (b)) also realise lexemes. In English, most free morphs are lexemes. The basic irreducible core of a word, the part of a word-form that remains when we have taken all recurrent units off, is called the **root**. This is easy to remember if you think about the root of a plant or a tree. Roots can be extended by adding other morphs. In *planters*, for example, PLANT constitutes the **root** of the word form. This root is then extended to form first *PLANT-er* and then *PLANT-er-s*. In the word-form *PLANTer-s*, *planter* forms the **base** (underlined) to which another morph (*-s*) is attached. Base, therefore, is a broader term than root. Any part of a word to which an affix is added is called a **base**. This means that a root can be a base (when we attach another morpheme to it), but a base does not have to be a root (which, by definition, is the irreducible core of a word). In the following examples the root is again in capitals, and the base is underlined: RECOGNISE, RECOGNIS-able, un-RECOGNIS-able. Every English word must contain at least one free morpheme.

Morphological units which cannot be word-forms by themselves and which need to be attached to other morphs are said to be **bound**. The bound morphemes in our example words from Activity 3.1 are highlighted in bold now: *bright-**ness**, **un**-lock, jump-**s**, paint-**ed**, jump-**ing**, dog-**s**, fast-**er**.* Bound morphs are also called **affixes**. Affixes can be added directly to a root, as in all the examples in Activity 3.1, or they can be added to a **base**, as in *PLANT-er-s*, *un-RECOGNIS-able*, and *FOOL-ish-ness*.

So far we have only looked at what the words from Activity 3.1 have in common. Before we look at the differences, we will briefly revise the new terminology we introduced on the previous page: all word-forms in Activity 3.1 are composed of two morphs. Morphs / word-forms which can't be dissected into smaller units are called **roots**. Because roots can stand on their own, they are also called **free morphs**. The type of morph that must be attached to some other morpheme is called **bound morph**. Bound morphs which do *not* realise lexemes are called **affixes**. You only have to look at the first two examples of affixes in Activity 3.1 (*bright-**ness**, **un**-lock*) to notice that affixes also differ in their distribution. Affixes which attach before the root / base, like *un-*, are called **prefixes**; affixes which attach to the right of a root / base, like *-ness*, are called **suffixes**. The word *un-lock-ed* from example sentence 1 consists of a root LOCK, a prefix *un-* and a suffix *-ed*.

In English we don't really have any other affixes. Bauer (2003) and Katamba and Stonham (2006) both list *kanga-bloody-roo* as an example of an *infix*, an affix which is attached inside its base.

3.3 Derivational and inflectional morphemes

The difference between affixes is easy: if they attach to the left of a root, they are called **prefixes**, if the attach to the right of the root, they are called **suffixes**. There is, however, a far more important distinction in morphology which is illustrated by the contrasting function of the bound morphemes of the first two and the last five word-forms from Activity 3.1.

Activity 3.2

Describe and contrast the function of the bound morphemes of the following words.

*bright-**ness**, **un**-lock, jump-s, paint-ed, jump-**ing**, insecticide-s, fast-er.*

For example,

a. *bright-**ness**: -ness* turns the adjective *bright* into a noun
b. ***un**-lock*_____
versus
c. *jump-s: -s* has to be added if the action takes place in the present, is not continuous, and who or whatever is doing the jumping can be replaced by a third-person-singular pronoun, as in *He /She / It jumps.*
d. *paint-ed* _____
e. *jump-**ing*** _____
f. *insecticide-s* _____
g. *fast-er* _____

Examples (a) and (b) are derivational morphemes; derivational morphemes either change the meaning (like the *un-* in *unlock*) or the word class (like the *-ness* in *brightness*) of a word. We assume that you referred more to grammatical concepts in your description of the remaining five suffixes in (c) to (g). This is because they are inflectional morphemes (see Chapter 4). For now suffice that inflectional morphemes modify a word / lexeme so that it reflects grammatical (i.e. relational) information, such as tense (as the *-ed* in *painted)*, person (the *-s* in *jumps* actually relates to both present tense and third person), number (the *-s* in *insecticides)*, etc.

The ratio of two derivational morphemes to five inflectional morphemes in Activity 3.2 is actually a very unfair representation of how many derivational and how many inflectional morphemes there are in modern English: numerically there are many more derivational morphemes than there are inflectional ones. The few inflectional morphemes there are in the English language, however, are very frequent, because they are obligatory. We have already introduced both categories of morphemes, we just have not named them yet, nor have we described their function. This is what we will do next.

3.3.1 Derivational morphology: class-changing

In Chapter 2 we have already encountered some of the most common morphemes that can help us obtain / derive nouns, adjectives and adverbs from words belonging to other word classes. The sentence 'new members can be added to this world class [nouns] by . . . adding the affixes *-er, -ee,* or *-ment* to verbs, or *-(i)ty* or *-ess* to adjectives', for example, is lifted straight out of the section on morphological characteristics of nouns (Section 2.1.2). And you have just formed words with these derivational suffixes (in Activity 3.2). Since we seem to have a greater need for naming people, places or things than for naming actions or qualities, English and most other languages generally have more means for deriving nouns than for deriving verbs and adjectives, but there are also many **derivational** affixes that **derive** adjectives from other words.

The sentence 'adjectives are an open word class and new adjectives are freely derived from many nouns (by e.g. *-able / -ible, -ful, -less, -ic, -al, -ese, -ish*) or verbs (by *-able*, or *-ible*)' is again repeated from the section on morphological characteristics of adjectives (Section 2.3). The next Activity (3.3) is the flip side of the coin of Activity 3.2: in Activity 3.2 we derived nouns from verbs and adjectives; now we are going to derive adjectives from nouns and verbs.

Activity 3.3

Write down at least five adjectives that are derived from nouns by adding the affixes *-able / -ible, -ful, -less, -ic, -al, -ese, -ish*. For example, *help-ful, metal(l)-ic, styl(e)-ish*. Think of at least five adjective derived from verbs by affixation of *-able, -ible, -y, -ive*.

The sentence 'the most easily recognisable adverbs are those derived from adjectives by adding *-ly*' should also ring a bell; you first came across it in the section on the morphological characteristics of adverbs (Section 2.4). As a rule, it is possible to derive an adverb by adding the suffix *-ly* to an adjectival base; therefore examples are almost innumerable: *kindly, simply* and *lovingly* we have already encountered; *attentively, superficially, quietly, hotly* are just a few new examples. The *-ly* affix is therefore said to be very productive. Morphological productivity is the property of a morphological process to give rise to new formations on a systematic basis.

Have you noticed that verbs very often form the input to word-formation processes, but are less frequently the output of derivational morphological processes? Generally verb-deriving patterns are less numerous and diverse than noun-deriving patterns, and derived adjectives are even less common than derived verbs.

Word formation is one of the two functions of derivational morphology. Derivational operations change the word class of the base lexeme by affixing derivational morphemes that produce new lexemes from a base. We can therefore describe all word-formation processes by giving the word class of the input base, naming the derivational suffix involved in the process and its meaning and stating the word class of the output word.

Table 3.1. *Describing affixation (-ness)*

Input	Suffix	Meaning	Output	Example
Adjective, e.g. *kind*	*-ness*	'quality, state, condition'	Noun (abstract)	*kind-ness*

If you want to make sure that you describe derivational morphological processes systematically, you can used Table 3.1 as a template.

The grammatical change caused by the presence of derivational affixes, however, does not always have to be as drastic as moving a base from one word class to another. Derivational suffixes may also merely shift a base to a different sub-class within the same broader word class. Nice examples of these types of derivational affixes are the diminutives (meaning 'small something') *-ling* and *-let*: Winnie the Pooh's friend, for example, is a really small pig. A. A. Milne therefore used the common noun *pig* and turned it into a diminutive (still a noun) by adding *-let*. Note that by using the diminutive to name the character in his book, A. A. Milne furthermore shifted *Pig-let* into yet another sub-class of nouns, i.e. proper nouns or names. The derivational suffix *-ling* has the same function / meaning: a *duckling* is a small duck. We can do a similar table for *-ling* and *-let* as we did for *kind-ness*, the only difference being that the broader word class of the input and output words is the same, only the sub-class changes, as in Table 3.2.

Table 3.2. *Describing affixation (-let, -ling)*

Input	Suffix	Meaning	Output	Example
Noun (common) e.g. *duck*	*-ling*	'small something'	Noun (diminutive)	*duckling*

Derivational suffixes are notoriously inconsistent. It took the morphologist Hans Marchand a lifetime to get some order into the English system. Consider the examples below. The first example is adult language use. The second example shows that children who are in the process of acquiring language struggle with these inconsistencies before they work out the adult forms.

5. *The engine-er is relying on the machin-ist to carry out the job.*
6. *The flutist is sitting in the first row, the *drummist in the last.*

3.3.2 Derivational morphology: meaning-changing

The other function of derivational morphemes is illustrated by the word *un-lock*. *Un-* here changes the meaning of the root *lock* to which it is attached. The derivational prefix *un-* reverses the action / process / state denoted by the verb *lock*. *Un-* can also be prefixed to adjectives, as in *friendly* vs. *un-friendly*. When prefixed to adjectives, *un-* basically means 'not' and *unfriendly* therefore has the opposite meaning of *friendly*, but both words are adjectives. In the same way both *obey* and *dis-obey* are verbs, but they have opposite meanings. The derivational prefix *dis-* can not only attach to verbs, but also to nouns, and adjectives. Laying this information out in table format again illustrates clearly what is going on – see Table 3.3.

Table 3.3. *Describing affixation* (un-, dis-)

Input	Prefix	Meaning	Output	Example
verb, e.g. *lock*	*un-*	'reverse'	verb	*un-lock*
adjective, e.g. *friendly*	*un-*	'not'	adjective	*un-friendly*
verb, e.g. *engage*	*dis-*	'not' / 'reverse'	verb	*dis-engage*
noun, e.g. *favour*	*dis-*	'not'	noun (abstract)	*dis-favour*

Before we do ourselves a disfavour, you disengage and get very disconsolate (unhappy and unable to be comforted), we're going to summarise what we have found out about derivational morphology so far and move on. Derivational affixes / processes:

- create new lexemes.
- can change the word class of the base to which they are added; this may entail a possible change in meaning, as in to *court* (V), and *court-ship* (N abstract); if they do not move a word into a different word class altogether, they may cause a shift in the grammatical sub-class of that word, as in the *duckling* and *piglet* examples.
- can modify the meaning of the base to which they are attached; the change in meaning can be significant, as in *kind* vs. *un-kind*, or not so drastic, as in *create* vs. *recreate*. These derivational affixes do not necessarily change the word class to which they attach, and they may not have a regular meaning.
- do not necessarily attach to any word of a certain word class, the English prefix *be-*, for example, can change nouns into verbs, as in *witch* (N) *bewitch* (V). But *be-* cannot attach to all English nouns, e.g. **be-wizard* (thanks to Laurie Bauer for this lovely example).

Useful rules for derivational suffixes are that, in English, prefixes are always derivational; and derivational affixes are always nearer the root than inflectional ones, as in *plant-er*$_{Der}$*-s*$_{Inf}$. The latter rule is one of the few universal rules that apply to all languages.

Now that we have introduced morphology properly, we can move on the creative and enjoyable word formation processes we promised you at the outset of this chapter.

Activity 3.4

You may not have come across the following words yet, but they are not non-words. They are neologisms, i.e. newly coined words. Analyse them into their constituent morphs, and describe their meaning and function as well as you can.

  googleability
  doomers

Google is the name of a company that originally developed an internet search engine, so *Google* is a proper noun. *Googleable*, on the other hand, is an adjective. It describes the quality of something that can be searched for by an internet search engine. *Googleability*, on the other hand, is a noun again. The word-form can be found in combinations like *googleability test*, or sentences like *What's your googleability quotient?*

Just to give you an idea how 'young' these words are and how productive these derivational processes are: *Google* is already listed in the **Oxford English Dictionary**, which dates its first recorded use to 1999. *Googleable* has not made it into the OED yet, but was accepted into the Macmillan dictionary in 2008. At the beginning of 2010 we got 16,600 hits when searching for *googleability* on Google, by the beginning of 2011 this number has gone down to 16,300. It may be interesting to check how many hits you get when you are working on this example. You will then get a better idea if this word is catching on or not.

Doom is a noun meaning 'death, destruction, or other terrible fate'. The *-er* suffix therefore does not change the general world class of *doom*, but just moves it into a sub-class. A *doomer* is 'a person who is concerned that petroleum depletion will lead to a severe economic recession or a great economic depression'. This neologism further combines with inflectional affixes, as in *doom-er-s*, derivational affixes, as in *ex-doom-er*, and other free morphemes, as in *doomer news*.

The neologisms *googleability* and *doomers* illustrate that multiple affixation is possible. *Doomers* furthermore illustrates the linguistic universal 'derivational affixes are always nearer the root than inflectional ones'. First the derivational morpheme *-er* attaches to the root *doom*, which then forms the base to which the inflectional plural suffix *-s* gets attached to arrive at the word-form *doomers*. These multiple affixed forms can form the input to other word-formation processes, for example compounding.

3.4 Compounding

Googleability test and *doomer news* are compounds, i.e. words formed by adjoining two (or more) lexemes. In the most typical cases, it is bare roots that are combined in compounds, as in *teapot, motor insurance* or *weekend*, and these compounds are therefore called root compounds. But *googleability test* and *doomer news* illustrate that complex morphemes can also contribute to this very productive word-formation process.

Activity 3.5

What is main meaning of the following compounds? For example, is a *sea-bird* a kind of *sea* or a kind of *bird*, or neither?

   teapot, egg-head, motor insurance, highbrow, weekend, redskin (N)

For some of the six words in the list, the answer is obvious: a *teapot* is a kind of pot, a *motor insurance* is a kind of insurance, and the *weekend* is the end of a week. In each of these cases, the main meaning of the whole compound lies 'within' one of its two lexemes, and the compound as a whole refers to a sub-class of the main (or head) element the compound is composed of. These compounds are called *endocentric*. This term becomes self-explanatory if you recall that *endo-* means 'within'; i.e. the meaning of these compounds lies within their most important element. For the other examples, the answer is less straightforward, but they clearly do not refer to a sub-class of the head lexeme, the most important of the two free morphemes: a *redskin* (N) does not denote a type of skin; an *egg-head* is not a head, and a *highbrow* person does not have to have arched eyebrows. *Redskin* is a word used to refer to native Americans and, like all *exocentric* compounds (*exo-* means 'without'), it denotes one, usually quite outstanding, feature of the entity which is denoted by the compound, in this case skin colour; but their meaning does not reside 'within' one of the compound's constituent lexemes.

To summarise, compounding is a very important way of adding new words to the word stock of English and many other languages. Compounds, e.g. *tourist bus*, are lexemes in which we can identify other lexemes, in this case *tourist* and *bus*. For syntax, however, the internal composition of compounds is not important. When we start analysing phrases, whole clauses and sentences, compounds will therefore be treated as a single lexeme (noun).

3.5 **Conversion**

In this chapter we have been looking at complex words, i.e. words that consist of more than one morpheme. We saw that complex words may either be formed by:

- *affixation*, i.e. attaching a free morpheme to a bound morpheme, as in *doom-er*;
- *compounding*, i.e. a combination of two free morphemes or lexemes, as in *seabird*;

or by a combination of the two, as in *doomer news*.

There is an even easier and more 'economical' way of forming new words. *Conversion* follows the following recipe: don't change the form of the input word, just shift it into a different word class and use it like a member of that class. For example, convert the noun *sign* into a verb and use it like one. The verb *sign* occurs twice in the following example sentence, once as a verb and once as a noun. Which one is which?

7.   *I can sign the word 'table' in British Sign Language.*

The first *sign* is a lexical verb; the second *sign* is a lexical noun (which forms part of the endocentric compound noun *British Sign Language)*. The distributional and syntactic behaviour of *sign* (V) vs. *sign* (N) shows that the word has changed class membership and undergone a word-formation process, but one that does not change the form of the input word, i.e. conversion. Because conversion changes the word class of a word without any overt modification of the word-form, it is sometimes called zero derivation. Other examples of conversion include *convert* (N/V), *combine* (N/V), *fish* (N/V), *comment* (N/V), *contest* (N/V).

Activity 3.6

In written language we have to rely entirely on distributional / syntactic criteria to work out whether *sign, convert, combine, fish, comment* and *contest* are nouns or verbs. Make one sentence each with *fish, comment, contest*; then list the syntactic features that help you identify the word class as a noun or as a verb for each usage.

Now read your example sentences out loud. Is it easier to distinguish the noun and the verb usages for some of these words in speech? If yes, why?

3.6 **Shortening bases**

3.6.1 Blending

As a derivational process, blending is comparable to compounding. In compounding a new complex base is formed from a combination of two (or more) unmodified lexemes. A blend is also a new lexeme formed from two (or more) lexemes, but only parts of them. In blending, part of one word is 'stitched' onto another word without any regard for morpheme or lexeme boundaries. One or both of the source bases are chopped, and then merged at a point where the spelling or the sound structures facilitate it. *Smog*, for example, was blended from *smoke* and *fog* at the point where the words overlap in spelling, i.e. at the *o*. Other examples of blends are

stagflation	(from stagnation and inflation)
motel	(from motor and hotel)
infotainment	(from information and entertainment)
breathalyzer	(from breath and analyzer)
splog	(from spam and blog)

These examples show that blends should be made up of morphs or meaningful parts of the original lexemes. In the process of blending the original lexemes may, however, become totally unrecognizable.

3.6.2 Backformation

Is a derivational process which can best be described as the opposite of affixation. Instead of adding an affix, in backformation an element which either is (or looks like) a morph is subtracted from the word-form. This means that the output word is actually shorter than the input word. The noun *editor*, for example, underwent this process to yield the verb *edit*, as in *Tonight I will edit the chapter*. We have already looked at a word that illustrates both backformation and affixation: to arrive at *mentee*, the affix *-or*, which forms agent nouns, was first taken off the word-form *mentor* to give *ment*; then the affix *-ee*, which forms 'patient' nouns, was added to give *mentee*. Maybe this explains why this is such an awful word. How do we know which word came first? Is it a chicken-and-egg question, or can we actually answer it? For spoken English it is a chicken-and-egg question; for written English, on the other hand, we can answer it. The first documented use of *editor* in its present-day usage is in Addison's *Spectator* in 1712 according to the *Oxford English Dictionary*; *to edit* is eighty-one years younger. The age gap between *mentor* (1735) and *mentee* (1965) is even bigger.

In order not to end our discussion of backformation on this downbeat note, here is a nice example in which P. G. Wodehouse is playing with backformation.

I could see that, if not actually disgruntled, he was far from being gruntled.
(P. G. Wodehouse, *The Man Upstairs*)

These examples also illustrate that all output forms of the word-formation processes discussed in this chapter are originally neologisms. Some of them get accepted into everyday language use, e.g. *to edit*; others don't. Although *gruntled* would be a valid backformation from *disgruntled*, it never caught on.

3.6.3 Clipping

When we clip a word, we shorten it without changing its meaning or part of speech. A clipping tripped one of us up big time when first arriving in England. The landlady was constantly talking about a *fridge*, but one of the authors had no idea that *fridge* was the clipped form of *refrigerator*, a word learned at school. Other frequent examples of clippings are given in Activity 3.7.

Activity 3.7

Based on the following examples of full forms and clippings, try to work out:

a. which end of the word-form tends to get clipped?
b. how much of a word tends to get clipped?
c. what part of a word-form tends to be retained?

full form	clipping
telephone	*phone*
delicatessen	*deli*
microphone	*mike*
science fiction	*sci-fi*

Did you find a consistent pattern? Not likely, and we apologize for sending you on a wild goose chase. These examples illustrate that there is no way of predicting how much of a word will be chopped off, nor which end of the word will get affected, nor what will be left over after this word-formation process has been applied. Because of this lack of systematicity, clipping and abbreviations are not really word-formation, but rather word-creation processes.

3.6.4 Abbreviations and acronyms

Abbreviations and acronyms are similar in that both of them are based on the initial letters of a sequence of words, and both of them tend to be written in upper-case letters. They differ only in the way they are pronounced.

When the initial letters of the words in a name, title, or phrase are spelled out as a pronounceable word, we get an *acronym*.

- *AIDS* – Acquired Immune Deficiency Syndrome – for example, is an acronym because it can easily be pronounced; therefore it also rhymes with words such as *raids* (n. pl.), *maids* (n. pl.), and *fades* (v., third pers. sg.)
- *TESOL* – Teaching of English as a Second or Other Language – is pronounced /tesol/, and
- *LIPPS* – Language Interaction in Plurilingual and Plurilectal Speakers – is an acronym that was created on the basis of a pronounceable existing word of the English language.

Abbreviations, on the other hand, just string together the names of the initial letters of the words in the names, titles or phrases they stand for. DNA, for example, is spelled out by simply pronouncing the names of the letters DNA: /di/ /en/ /ei/. Other well-known abbreviations are TV for *television*, and UN for *United Nations*.

Because of this small difference between acronyms and abbreviations, you may not always know whether you are dealing with one or the other when you first come across them in print. The other way round, sometimes we have heard an acronym or abbreviation so often that we treat them like words, because we are unaware of their origin as acronyms. Two examples of this are *scuba* as in *scuba diving* which has been derived from *Self-Contained Underwater Breathing Apparatus*, and *radar*, which comes from *Radio Detecting And Ranging*. From a linguistic point of view the distinction does not matter either; both abbreviations and acronyms are nouns and behave accordingly in syntax.

3.7 Chapter summary

We saw in this chapter that morphemes can be free or bound: in English **free morphemes** tend to be lexemes and can stand on their own. **Bound morphemes** are affixes which have to be attached to a root, a base, or, as we will see in the next chapter, a stem. **Affixes** which attach to the left of a root or base are called **prefixes**. Prefixes are always derivational. Derivational morphemes either change the meaning of a word or its word-class membership. **Suffixes** attach to the right of a root, base (or stem) and can either be derivational or inflectional. Inflectional morphemes act as syntactic glue in the construction of sentences. The following table provides you with brief definitions and examples of the most important concepts relating to morphology, the study of word forms.

Name	Definition	Example
Morpheme	An abstract entity that expresses a single concept within a word	*function*, *dys-* and *-ed* are morphemes
Morph	the concrete physical shape of a morpheme	spoken or written *function*, *dys-* and *-al*
Root	the irreducible core of a word	*function* is the root of *dys-function-al*
Base	any unit to which affixes can be attached	*dysfunction* is a base
Stem	a root or base without inflectional affixes	*function* without *-s* or *-ing* is a stem
Free morpheme	a root which can stand on its own	*function* is a free morpheme
Bound morpheme	a morpheme which cannot stand on its own	*dys-* and *-al* are bound morphemes
Affix	a bound morpheme which only occurs when attached to a root / free morpheme	*dys-* and *-al* are affixes
Prefix	an affix attached to the left of a word	*dys-* is a prefix
Suffix	an affix attached to the right of a word	*-al* is a suffix
Compounds	words formed by adjoining two (or more) lexemes	*trouser press*, *mountain bike*

Key terms
Morpheme; morph; root; base; stem; affix; prefix; suffix.

Exercises

Exercise 3.1   Activity 2.1 in the previous chapter was quite restrictive. We made the words *played*, *beautiful*, *lovingly*, *bright*, *ran* fit into the noun (NP) slot in the sentence

How useful did _____ seem to be?

We are now in a position to be more creative. Rather than making the words fit the sentence, let's build short grammatical English sentences around the words *played, beautiful, lovingly, bright, ran*. For example, *I played the guitar*.

a. Write your sentences next to the words

played	How useful did **play** seem to be?
beautiful	How useful did **beauty** seem to be?
lovingly	How useful did **love** seem to be?
bright	How useful did **brightness** seem to be?
ran	How useful did **running** seem to be?

b. Now determine the word class of the words *played, beautiful, lovingly, bright, ran*. Write them or the abbreviations we are using for them above the words.

c. Try to describe and name the morphological operations / processes that turned the lexemes *played, beautiful, lovingly, bright, ran* into the nouns *play, beauty, love, brightness* and *running*. Make sure that you first determine the underlying lexemes, before you start looking into the word-formation processes.

d. State how the change in word-class membership affects the syntactic behaviour of our example words. Do this by contrasting the distribution / word order position of *played* with *play*, *beautiful* with *beauty*, etc. We left the sentences with the nouns in the right-hand column, so that you can compare the syntactic behavior of *play, beauty, love, brightness* and *running* in the right-hand column with that of *played, beautiful, lovingly, bright, ran* in your newly created sentences in the left-hand column. Note that the core meaning of the word remains unaffected by many derivational processes, but the lexemes, the word-forms, the word classes and the distribution of the words in the sentence have changed.

Exercise 3.2   Complete the sentences in section (a) of this activity, fill the gap in (b), and delete the inappropriate terms in (c).

a. For example *We dry our hair with a hairdryer.*
   Builders mix cement with a _____.
   Japanese people cook rice with a _____.
   I open the bottle with a _____.

b. A *hairdryer* is a kind of dryer, therefore *hairdryer* is an _____ compound.

c. The head element of the compound *hairdryer*, ie. *dry-er*, is a noun / verb derived from the noun / verb *dry* by affixation of the inflectional / derivational prefix / infix / suffix -*er*.

From our example sentence *We dry our hair* we also know that *our hair* is an obligatory sentence element (an object) required by the meaning of the verb *dry* (we need to dry something!). Compounds whose right-hand or head element contains a verbal base and other (left-hand / modifying) element, which can occur as an argument of that verb in a sentence, as in *We dry our hair*, are called *synthetic compounds*.

Exercise 3.3   Which word class do the lexemes *round* belong to in the following sentences?

The baby is playing with a round ball.
The shepherd is rounding the sheep up in the pen.
My ex-husband insists on playing another round of poker.

Which derivational process has created these lexemes?

Exercise 3.4   Can you work out which original lexemes were involved in the following blends?

Mockumentary	from
Carjacking	from
Spork	from
Galumph	from
Mocktail	from

Exercise 3.5   NFL is an acronym that means very different things for different people:

For American football fans it means *National Football League*.
For Canadians it means *Newfoundland*.
For catering personnel it means *No Free Lunch*.
For some people it means *New Found Love*.
For others *Not For Long*.

Find out what else NFL can stand for.

Further reading

For more on morphology in general, see Bauer (2003); Bauer (2004) (especially Chapter 3); Haspelmath (2002) (especially Chapter 2); Katamba and Stonham (2006); Matthews (1991); Spencer (1991); Carstairs-McCarthy (2002); Aronoff and Fudeman (2005); Katamba (2004); Lieber (1992); Spencer and Zwicky (1998); and Williams (1981). On word formation, see Bauer (1983); Adams (2001); and Plag (2003).

CHAPTER 4

Inflectional morphology

This chapter . . .

This chapter starts with a comparison of derivational and inflectional morphology. We will then deal with principles of inflectional morphology, morphology that reflects grammatical (i.e. relational) information. We will focus on the grammatical categories number, tense and agreement, concepts that are important in the English language. We will see that today's English has little inflectional morphology in comparison with earlier versions of English and other languages. We are going to illustrate this with examples from Shakespeare's English, Russian, German and Nez Perce. We will introduce some of the ways in which morphology is related to syntax and demonstrate this in the activities and the exercises at the end of the chapter. This provides a natural transition to the topic of syntax which we are going to examine in the rest of the book.

In the last chapter we revisited the concept of morpheme (first introduced in Chapter 1) and refined it by looking at different ways of classifying morphemes: free and bound; root; base; affix; prefix; and suffix. This chapter will concentrate on inflectional morphology, and as a way of checking that you are familiar with the morphological concepts we also need in this chapter, do Activity 4.1.

Activity 4.1
First write brief definitions of the following morphological key terminology, and give at least one example for each. Then state the difference between two contrasting terms.

A **free morpheme** is _____

A **bound morpheme** is_____

The difference between a **free** and a **bound morpheme** is _____

A **root** is _____

A **base** is _____

If a **base** is not a **root**, the difference between them is _____

An **affix** is _____

Affix is an umbrella term for **prefixes** and **suffixes** because _____

A **prefix** attaches to the left / right (cross out the incorrect answer) of a root or base, a **suffix**, on the other hand, attaches to the left / right of a root or base.

Now run a quick check over your answers by consulting the Glossary at the end of this book. If the content of your definitions matches those in the glossary, we can move on. If not, reread Sections 3.1 and 3.2. In Section 3.3 we discussed derivational morphology; as a way of revising it, we are now going to compare derivational patterns with inflectional categories, which we will concentrate on in this chapter. For our discussion of inflectional morphology we need to introduce just one other term: **stem**. A stem is the base for any inflectional affixes. This is why we introduce it in this and not the last chapter.

4.1 Differences between derivation and inflection

We have already said that

- derivational morphemes are more diverse than inflectional categories (which means that this chapter will be shorter but perhaps more difficult than the last one), and that
- derivational processes commonly change
  - the word class of the base lexeme (we have, for example, derived adjectives from nouns and verbs in Activity 3.3, nouns from verbs and adjectives in Activity 3.2), or
  - the meaning of the base to which they are attached, as in *lock* vs. *un-lock*.

Other properties of derivational and inflectional morphology that can be used to distinguish between the two are contrasted in Table 4.1 (adapted from Haspelmath 2002).

Table 4.1. *Properties of derivation and inflection*

	Derivational morphology	Inflectional morphology
1	is not relevant to syntax	is relevant to syntax
2	the output is replaceable by a simple word	the output is not replaceable by a simple word
3	is optional	is obligatory
4	more likely to be semantically irregular	semantically regular
5	is very relevant to base meaning	is less relevant to base meaning
6	the output is a new concept	the output is the same concept as the base
7	has relatively concrete meaning	has relatively abstract meaning
8	limited / sporadic applicability	unlimited / automatic applicability
9	is expressed close to the base	is expressed at word periphery
10	the process can be repeated	the process cannot be repeated

Some of the ten criteria listed in Table 4.1 are all-or-nothing properties, while others are relative. The relative properties are of course not so useful if we want to classify morphemes into two neat, distinct and non-overlapping categories (derivational and inflectional). Some morphologists want to do this; others see the different patterns as lying on a continuum ranging from the most strongly derivational patterns to the most clearly inflectional ones. As we shall see, we find the latter view more convincing. And of course it's great when we have young morphologists in the 'Introduction to Morphology and Syntax' classes we teach. They identify themselves by asking critical questions like: 'Last week we identified -*ly* as a derivational morpheme. This week you tell us that derivational morphology is not relevant to syntax. But in weeks two and three we learnt that the -*ly* morph changes the word class of a base, and thus its syntactic behaviour. Is this not supposed to be relevant to syntax?' Or they challenge us on the content of the first teaching week / chapter: 'Is *nicely* really a separate lexeme from *nice*? Or is it just another word-form of the lexeme of *nice*?' These are really good and valid questions, so pertinent actually that theoretical morphologists have been discussing them since the 1980s and still have not reached a consensus.

Apart from the last three, all properties listed in Table 4.1 have already been illustrated in relation to derivational morphology. In the following discussion we will therefore focus on inflection, and only contrast it with derivation when particularly useful. We will also show that most of the ten criteria are relative.

4.1.1 Relevance to syntax

The first and the second criteria sound very different, but amount to pretty much the same thing. That inflection is relevant to syntax (criterion 1) is best illustrated with a sentence like

1. *She stopped buying clothes.*

The verb *stop* needs to be followed by a verb with the suffix *-ing*. The only reason we get the *-ing* on *buy* is the specific syntactic relationship between *stop* and *buy*. Most of the other inflectional categories, however, are less obviously relevant to syntax.

As far as derivational morphology is concerned, we have already observed (in the context of our discussion of *nice* vs. *nice-ly*) that the statement 'derivational morphology is not relevant to syntax' is too strong. The two lexemes *develop* (verb) and *develop-ment* (noun) illustrate the same point: they have very similar meanings, but their syntactic behaviour differs considerably. Consider:

2. *The architect developed a prototype.*
3. *The developments are in the planning stage.*

The verb, for example, is marked for past tense (*-ed*); the noun for plural (*-s*). The verb follows the subject (*the architect*) and selects one object (*a proto-type* in this case); *the developments* is the subject and cannot select any other sentence elements. We will discuss the syntactic behaviour of different word classes further in the next two chapters.

4.1.2 Replaceability
Some inflected word forms really can't be replaced by forms that consist of only one morpheme. Try to replace the *high-er* in the following sentence with a mono-morphemic form. You are bound to fail.

4. *The Alps are higher than the Tatra.*

But this criterion does not work for the inflectional categories of verbal tense (and aspect) or nominal plural, which are replaceable by simple words.

5. *The dog loses / lost the stick.*
6. *The dogs / dog lost the stick.*

Criterion 2, however, works quite well for derivational morphology. Contrast sentence 3 (repeated below as sentence 7) with sentence 8:

7. *The developments are in the planning stage.*
8. *The estates are in the planning stage.*

Syntactically a derived noun like *development*, for example, does not behave differently from a simple noun like *estate*.

4.1.3 Obligatoriness
Another popular criterion that can be used to distinguish derivation and inflection (number 3 in Table 4.1) is that inflection is obligatory to the sentence, whereas derivation is optional.

9. *She buys clothes.*
10. **She buy clothes.*

The inflectional suffix *-s* on *buy* in example 9 is obligatory: the sentence becomes ungrammatical if we do not use the third-person-singular present-tense suffix *-s* when the subject of the sentence is third-person singular (i.e. can be replaced with *he*, *she* or *it*).

On the other hand, whether we use a simple form, like *kind*, or a complex derived lexeme, like *kind-ness*, to express the concept of 'having or being of a good or benevolent nature or disposition' is optional. Contrast 11 and 12 below:

11. *Andy is a very kind man.*
12. *Andy's kindness is legendary.*

The contrast between *kind* and *kindness* is not one of meaning: *kind-ness* does not mean 'not having the quality of being kind'.

Criteria 1–3 are supposed to be all-or-nothing criteria for delimiting derivation and inflection, but we have seen that all of them have their problems. According to the remaining criteria, derivation and inflection form a continuum, with one end marked by clearly inflectional categories and the other one marked by clearly derivational forms. Properties 4–7 are semantic or meaning-based criteria.

4.1.4 Semantic regularity

According to criterion 4, inflectional categories always make the same predictable semantic contribution to their base. The plural suffix *-s*, for example, always 'means' more than one, as in

13. *The dog is really muddy.*
14. *The dogs are really muddy.*
15. *This abstraction works.*
16. *Those abstractions don't work.*

Derived lexemes, on the other hand, are often semantically more irregular and idiosyncratic. We have already seen that the *un-* in *unlock* denotes a reversal of action; in *un-fussed*, on the other hand, it expresses negation, i.e. not fussed. A good example for the idiosyncratic meaning of derivational morphology is *ignorance* (noun), which is derived from *ignore*, but the meaning of *ignorance* can only be guessed from the two constituent morphemes *ignore* and *-ance*.

4.1.5 Semantic effect

Criterion 5 states that inflectional morphology is less relevant to the base meaning than derivational morphology. This works for well for agreement morphology like the *-s* on the verb *shops* in

17.   *He shops for his life.*

The *-s* is clearly not relevant to the base meaning of the verb – it just expresses agreement, that is, it marks the syntactic relation between the word *shop* and the word *he* in the sentence.

Those derivational morphemes that change the meaning of the base to which they are attached are by definition meaning-changing, frequently in a rather drastic way, e.g. *stable* vs. *un-stable*; and a *build-er* is also something quite different from the act / process of *building*.

Criteria 6 and 7 are also semantic, meaning-based criteria tend to be quite vague.

4.1.6 New concepts

According to criterion 6, inflected word-forms express the same concept as the base. This works well for *to buy* vs. *she buys*, as it did for *shop* vs. *he shops* in the previous section, but arguably less well for *shoe* vs. *shoes* (one shoe is not the same as a pair of shoes).

Derived lexemes, on the other hand, often express a new concept. Children use this principle to fill gaps in their lexicon.

Activity 4.2

When children do not yet know the words for concepts they want to refer to / name / talk about, they sometimes use derivational and other word formation processes to 'make' the words they need. Describe the word formation processes used in the following examples using the terminology you learned in the last chapter. The children's ages are given in brackets.

1.a *lesson-er* (4;0) = 'teacher'
1.b *driv-er* (3;0) = 'ignition key'
2.a *plant-man* (3;0) = 'gardener'
2.b *fix-man* (3;0) = 'mechanic'
3.a *You have to scale it.* (2;4) = 'to weigh'
3.b *String me up mummy.* (3;2) = 'do the string up' (of a hat)
4.a *unsad* = 'happy'
4.b *unbig* = 'small'

(all examples are taken from Eve Clark's work)

Activity 4.2 illustrates that children are wonderfully creative language users. Some of their innovative forms, however, express meanings for which there is already a conventional, established term in the language.

Children give these innovations up once they have acquired the conventional established form.

Words which have been created by derivational morphological processes thus frequently express new concepts – or at least they are supposed to. *Kindness*, however, is not a drastically different concept from *kind*, as we have already noted.

4.1.7 Abstract vs. concrete meaning

The abstract (inflection) vs. concrete (derivation) meaning criterion (no. 7) works well for inflection: we struggle to find meanings for many inflectional suffixes, because they are quite abstract. (The most notable exception to this regularity is plural *-s*, which, for the same reason, featured strongly in the previous two sections.) The segmented *-ed* and *-ing* in example sentence 18 are reasonably good examples of this characteristic of inflectional morphology (careful, the *-ed* is not the past-tense morpheme here).

18. *She has phon-ed the boy she is interested in and now she is wonder-ing whether this was the right thing to do.*

Derivational morphemes that change the meaning of words (those discussed in Section 3.3.2, e.g. *dis-*, *un-*) must have concrete meanings, but there are also derivational meanings that are just as abstract as inflectional ones. This mainly applies to derivational morphs that either change the word class of the base (as in *kind-ness*), or move the lexeme into a different sub-class, as for example *-hood* in *sisterhood* (which moved the concrete noun *sister* into the abstract noun sub-class; see Section 3.3 for more examples of the latter category).

4.1.8 Applicability

Inflectional morphemes can generally be applied to a base without arbitrary limitations (no. 8). It is because inflections are regular that we could use them in Chapter 2 to help us identify word-class memberships. For example, all verbs tend to have past-tense forms (as in *jumped*), and all adjectives have comparative forms (as in *bright, bright-er, bright-est*). There are not many exceptions to this rule in English, and the ones there are are logically straightforward: if *the rat is dead*, it cannot be *dead-er* (adjective), and now that you *know* something about morphology, this is hopefully a permanent state, and we need not stress that it is continuous, as in

19. *You are know-ing something about morphology now.

In derivational morphology, on the other hand, we find many 'gaps' without obvious semantic explanations: if *actress* and *heiress* are useful ways of distinguishing the gender of actors and heirs, why does nobody want to distinguish Gabriel and Eva as *lecturer* and *lecturess*?

4.1.9 Proximity to the base

Criterion number 9 is a beauty because it is universal, but paradoxically it is a relative and not an absolute property.

Activity 4.3

Recycle some of the nouns you derived from verbs and adjectives by adding the suffixes *-er*, *-ee*, *-ment*, *-ity* and *-ness* in Activity 3.2 and now put them in the plural, e.g. *sprint-er-s*. Where in relation to the different bases and the inflectional plural suffix are the derivational morphemes placed?

The words you created all have one derivational and one inflectional suffix, and the derivational affix almost always occurs between the root and the inflectional affix. Did you find any exceptions to this rule? If not, make sure you don't skip Consolidation Section 1.4.

4.1.10 Recursion

The final criterion states that inflection is more restricted than derivation in that derivational processes can be performed repeatedly, whereas inflectional affixes cannot be iterated. Iteration is not terribly widespread with derivation either, but we tend to joke that our literature colleagues have moved into the *post-post-post-modern* phase now, and both our grandmothers were *great-great-grand-mothers*. It's not obvious why we can't say **wrote-ed* to refer to writing in a more remote past, or *book-s-es* to refer to the pile of books, but reiterated (or double) inflections are virtually unattested in English and other languages.

We've stepped the level of difficulty up a bit now, haven't we? Can you tell what's different between, for example, Chapter 2 and this chapter? In Chapter 2 we kept it nice and simple by relegating the words that are difficult to classify to the end of chapter activities. We did this because a marathon is always a 'flat race'. In this chapter we have discussed properties of inflectional and derivational morphology, but we have also started looking into how well the individual criteria work for individual examples or groups of examples. We had to find that some of them work better than others, but none of them are absolute properties.

4.1.11 Gerunds

Even the criterion we used in Chapter 3 to define derivational morphology is not absolute: derivational processes can change the word class of a base. It is often claimed that inflectional categories never change the word class of the base, but there is one exception to this 'rule': nouns derived from verbs, such as *washing* in

20.   *I enjoy not washing clothes.*

These inflectional deverbal nouns are so frequent in the English language that they've even got a name; they are called **gerunds**. Gerunds combine the characteristics of both nouns and verbs in a particularly interesting way. The meaning of ENJOY implies that something has to be enjoyed. In this case it is (not) *washing*, so *washing* is the object (see Glossary and Chapter 7) of the verb *enjoy*. But the object of ENJOY is normally a noun, as in

21.   *I enjoy the sun / it.*

Therefore *washing* must be a noun in *I enjoy not washing clothes*. On the other hand, there are equally good syntactic reasons why *washing* must be a verb: *washing* itself has an object (namely clothes), and it is preceded by NOT, something that is typical of verbs and not nouns. In this brief deliberation of gerunds we've talked a lot about how the deverbal noun *washing* interacts with other words in the sentence. This means that we've already been talking about syntax. From our discussion of gerunds we have therefore learned two important things. First, there are word-class-changing inflections (because gerunds combine the characteristics of both nouns and verbs), and second, there is a close relationship between morphology and syntax – but it is inflectional categories that are more closely related to syntax than derivational ones (our criterion 1).

We've really come across a few hurdles and ditches in this chapter, but hurdles, fences and ditches are only used in races over short distances – we haven't forgotten that we promised you a short chapter! And we can keep our promise, because the English language has lost a lot of its original inflectional morphology over the last 800 years. All languages change, but why English has decided to shed this type of morphology while a lot of its close relatives (the Scandinavian languages, Icelandic and German, to name just a few) retained it, nobody is really sure. The closest linguists come to answers to this question can be found in books on historical linguistics and language change.

Before we look at the inflectional categories English retained, let's summarise what we have learned out about inflectional categories in general so far. Often inflectional categories do not have a clearly identifiable meaning, but only a syntactic function. Inflectional categories are often naturally grouped together: English present and past tense, for example, have to do with the relation between the time an utterance is made and the time the related event takes / took place. Present and past are both categories of the dimension **tense** and they can never occur together on the same verb, e.g. **jump-s-ed* (see criterion 10). Most inflectional categories fall into one of three groups. Table 4.2 (again adapted from Haspelmath 2002) presents these groups in three columns headed by the word classes on which the inflectional categories are expressed: on verbs, or nouns, or agreement shown on nouns, verbs (and adjectives and pre- (or post-) positions in languages other than English).

Table 4.2. *Inflectional categories*

On verbs	On nouns	On nouns, verbs, adjectives
Tense (present, past, etc.)	Number (singular, plural, etc.)	Agreement in number, case, person, etc.
Aspect (perfective, progressive, etc.)	Case (nominative, accusative, genitive, etc.)	
Mood (indicative, subjunctive, imperative, etc.)		

We have already seen examples of most of these categories, and when we go through them more systematically in the next sections, we won't have to deal with all possible combinations of the above inflectional categories, because some of them hardly ever occur together. Some combinations of aspect, tense and mood, for example, don't make sense. Let's look at one example.

Activity 4.4

I'm quite sure you have never heard anybody say *Sat on the chair!* but you have overheard *Sit on the chair!* thousands of times.
Why is *Sat on the chair!* so distinctly odd?

Sat on the chair! is a command (or imperative mood). The verb SIT, however, is in its past-tense grammatical form *sat*. It is this combination of imperative mood and past tense that does not work: what's the point in telling somebody to sit down in the past (probably that's why most parents occasionally revert to *I told you so!*).

Our discussion of the inflectional categories will start with the middle group, i.e. inflectional categories expressed on nouns, because one inflectional category that is expressed on nouns is easy (number), and the other one (case) has almost disappeared in English.

4.2 Inflectional morphology on nouns: number

Every noun has a number: *dog* is singular and *dog-s* is plural. We don't explicitly have to spell out the exact number, as in *one dog* vs. *two / three / hundred dogs* to know that *dog* and *dogs* contrast in number. And we know this even though it is only the plural that is overtly marked by an inflectional morpheme (*-s*) in English. If we consider the plural *-s* in word-forms like *dogs*, *bicycles*, *cards*, *bottles* and so on, the difference in meaning between the base and the affixed form is always the same: 'more than one'. So the inflectional category of number fulfils criterion no. 4, i.e. it is semantically regular.

But what about criterion no. 8 (unlimited applicability), which states that that if you can add an inflectional affix to one member of a class, you can generally add it to all members of that class? Some learners of English over-generalise this rule and apply the *-s* morph to irregular plural forms like, for example, **children-s*, **men-s* and **sheep-s*. There are a few other exceptions to the prototypical syntactic, morphological and semantic characteristics of number we have just discussed:

- Some plural nouns refer to an individual thing or substance – e.g. TROUSERS, SCALES and GLASSES.
- 'Collective' nouns, like FAMILY and STAFF automatically mean 'more than one'; but note that we say both *Susan's family is / are going on a day-trip*. We will return to subject–verb agreement in Section 4.4 below.
- There are some cases where number does not match the morphology: both *linguistic-s* and *new-s* have the plural suffix *-s*, but are singular as clearly indicated again by agreement: *The news is sad*, and *Linguistics is interesting*.

Table 4.2 also lists **case** as an inflectional category marked on nouns. We have already come across this grammatical category in Section 2.1.4 on pronouns. In Activity 2.4 we found that we can replace *Helen* with *she* and *cats* with *them* in the first clause of example 22:

22. *Helen likes cats and cats like Helen.*

In the second clause of this sentence (the one following the coordinating conjunction *and)*, on the other hand, we have to replace *cats* with *they* and *Helen* with *her*. From the order these words appear in the two clauses we know that *Helen* and *cats* have swapped syntactic function (from subject to object and the other way round – more on this in Chapter 7). Subjects are associated with nominative case and objects with accusative case. This difference is preserved only in the pronominal system in English, but not on other nouns. This is, case is not inflectionally marked in English any more. English case inflections had disappeared well before Shakespeare's time (late Middle English).

4.3 Inflectional morphology on verbs

4.3.1 Tense

Tense is a morpho-syntactic way of referring to the time when some action, event or state takes place (e.g. in the past, present or future) in relation to the moment of speaking. Tense is marked inflectionally on verbs.

The English present tense inflectional morph is -s, as in *She laugh-s now*. The physical form / shape of the past-tense morpheme, however, only shows when the subject of the sentence can be replaced with one of the three third-person-singular pronouns *he / she / it*, as in: *The man / he laughs*; *The woman / she laughs*; *The child / it laughs*. The sentences *I / we laugh* are also present tense, but the present tense is inflectionally unmarked (like the singular on nouns), if the subject is *I* or can be replaced with *you*, *we* or *they*.

The past tense, on the other hand, is always marked in English, and with the exception of irregular verbs, it is always marked with the inflectional suffix -ed, as in: *I / you / he / she / it / we / you / they /also laugh-ed yesterday*. And if you look closely, you will also notice some regularity in the irregular past-tense forms.

Activity 4.5

Group the following 'irregular' past-tense forms of English verbs into three categories depending on how they are formed

> *Awake – awoke, bend – bent, become – became, bet – bet, come – came, hurt – hurt, lend – lent, let – let, mean – meant, put – put, run – ran, send – sent, spend – spent, stink – stank, wake – woke, wed – wed.*

Which of the listed past-tense forms do you no longer use? Which form do you use instead?

In one group of irregular past-tense forms there is no change of form whatsoever: *bet – bet, hurt – hurt, let – let, put – put*. I doubt you use the word *wed* much at all, let alone its irregular past-tense form *wed*. Can you remember the name of the morphological process that produces new lexemes of a different word class and new grammatical words without changing the form of the input word? We encountered conversion in Chapter 3 on derivational morphology, but the same term is also used for inflectional relationships of this type. In another group of irregular verbs, the base is modified: in *awake – awoke, become – became*, etc. It is the vowel of the stem that contrasts the present- and past-tense form of the verb. Note that stem vowel change is also used in the formation of irregular plural nouns such as *foot – feet, tooth – teeth*, etc. In the last group of irregular verbs from Activity 4.4 the word final *d* becomes *t*, as in *bend – bent, lend – lent*, etc. It does not matter which morphological process is used, the difference between present and past tense is always coded by the morphology of the verb. But what about the future?

There is no shortage of ways of referring to the future with the English language:

23. *Tomorrow I will go to Isabella Plantation to see the witch hazel flower.*
24. *The party starts at 5 p.m. tonight.* (it is 2 p.m. at the moment of writing / speaking)
25. *I should / ought to get ready.*
26. *Cats like milk.* (So much so that we can safely assume they will still like it tomorrow and the day after)

But note that, unlike the past tense suffix *-ed*, or other 'irregular' regular morphological processes, there is no single inflectional category that marks verbs as future. This is, future is not inflectionally marked in English.

4.3.2 Aspect

Aspect is more difficult than tense, but it is another important inflectional dimension of verbs, not just English ones. Aspect has to do with the temporal unfolding of an event.

If we change a present-tense verb (example 27) to the past tense (example 28), we change the reference of the sentence from present to past time.

27. *The boy **runs** to the playground.*
28. *The boy **ran** to the playground.*

But if we change the verb form from *runs* (29) to *(is) running* (30), the time (and tense) remains the same, i.e. present.

29. *The boy **runs** to the playground.*
30. *The boy **is running** to the playground.*

For the difference between sentences 29 and 30, the speaker is firmly placed in the present, so tense is no longer the issue, and the difference becomes one of point of view: in 29 the speaker is making a general statement, as in *The boy runs to the playground every day*. In *The boy is running to the play-ground* the speaker is focusing on the internal unfolding of the event. What is important about the action / event now is that it is in progress or ongoing. This perspective remains the same in sentence 31, which is in the past tense:

31. *The boy **was running** to the playground.*

The boy is still running, i.e. the action is ongoing or in progress, but the speaker has, as it were, been beamed into the past in a time-travel machine. When we take an internal view at a situation and it is ongoing, we use progressive aspect.

   So far so good. Contrasting progressive aspect (32) with non-progressive (33) is fine.

32. *I am / was closing the laptop.*
33. *I close / closed the laptop.*

But what about the difference in meaning and morphosyntactic structure between sentence 32, on the one hand, and sentences 34 and 35, on the other?

34. *I have clos-ed the laptop.*
35. *The boy has run to the playground.*

Native speakers of English know intuitively that in both sentences 34 and 35 the action is completed: my laptop is closed and the boy is already at the playground. In sentence 32, on the other hand, the action is not over.

   But what is the *-ed* suffix on lexical verb *clos-ed* in sentence 34? Is it the past-tense suffix? If it were, we ought to have the past-tense form *ran* (see Activity 4.5) in sentence 35.

36. **The boy has ran to the playground.*

Sentence 36 is clearly ungrammatical. The *-ed* on *close* only has the same form as the past-tense suffix, but it represents a different morpheme: the (past) participle. For *run* the participle form is the same as the present-tense form, but look at *begin – began* (past) – *begun* (participle):

37. *I am beginning to understand* is progressive aspect (and present tense).
38. *I have begun my homework* is perfective aspect (and present tense).

Note that at the time of uttering sentence 38, the homework may not be completed. Once we have begun our homework, the action of beginning is completed. This is why we use perfective aspect.

   We know that this can be confusing. We have been explaining the difference between tense and aspect for more than ten years and therefore know that the combination of present tense and perfective aspect as in 38 is counter-intuitive. Martin Haspelmath and Andrea Sims (2010: 65) state that 'perfective aspect (which implies that an event is viewed in its totality) does not go together well with present tense (which implies that the speaker is still in the middle of the event)' and they call this combination of aspect and tense 'unusual' (and only marginally better that the 'downright exotic' combination of past tense and imperative mood we looked at in Activity 4.4).

The sentence

39.   *We think we have never explained the difference between tense and aspect better.*

ought to get your hopes up for two reasons: First, you know we tried our best, and second, although this sentence is in the present tense (*have . . .*), it is also perfective in aspect (*. . . explain-ed*), which means that our discussion of aspect is completed, over, finito, finished!

4.3.3 Mood

Mood is also an inherent verbal category. The unmarked mood, *indicative*, tends to be associated with factual assertions as in

40.   *I sit on the chair.*

The function of other 'moods' is to describe events in terms of whether they are necessary, possible, permissible, desirable and the like. We have already had one example of the *imperative* mood:

41.   *Sit on the chair!*

is a command. Note that no inflectional morphology is involved in the imperative mood in English. The same holds true for all the example sentences in Activity 4.6.

Activity 4.6
The following sentences describe an event in terms of whether it is necessary, possible, permissible, desirable and the like. Which sub-class of verbs is used to express mood?

You can stop soon   which expresses possibility/permission
You may stop soon   which expresses permission
You ought to stop soon   which expresses desirability
You must stop soon   which expresses necessity

In English, modal verbs (see Section 2.2.4) are used to denote other modalities.

Many languages also mark *subjunctive* mood morphologically. Semantically / pragmatically the subjunctive tends to mark desire (42), unreality (43) or subordination. Because English does not mark the subjunctive morphologically, two (very dramatic) examples will suffice.

42.   *I wish he were here.*
43.   *It is as though she had never died.*

4.4 Agreement

Agreement is a kind of syntactic relation in which the inflectional form of a word or phrase is determined by the properties of another word or phrase, which is almost always a noun. Agreement relations are quite restricted, especially in English: two or more words in a sentence may agree in person, number and case, as well as in grammatical gender (in those strange languages in which tables can be feminine, as in French *la table*, or masculine, as in German *der Tisch*). In English, only agreement in person and number is expressed by inflectional morphology.

In *this rose* and *those flowers* the determiners / demonstrative pronouns *this* (singular) and *those* (plural) agree in number with the nouns they form a phrase with, i.e. *rose* (singular) and *flowers* (plural). In this example, the agreement is marked among the words that group around the noun, i.e. the noun phrase.

Agreement, however, can also mark syntactic relations within a sentence. In example 44 below, the verb *sleeps* agrees with *the dog* (singular) in number and person.

44.   *The dog sleeps.*

How do we know this? To test agreement in number, we can contrast *the dog sleep-s* (singular) with

45.   *We / you / they / the dogs sleep_. (plural)*

The verb *sleeps* also agrees with *the dog* in person: the dog can either be a he, a she, or – if a stray dog – an it (the third-person-singular personal pronouns which can stand for all third-person-singular noun phrases), but verbs do not overtly 'agree' with first- (*I*) and second-person (*you*) singular agents, as in

46.   *I / you sleep_.*

The principle of contrast therefore shows us that we get the inflectional ending *-s* on the present-tense verb only when the subject noun (phrase) of the clause is third-person singular. And we only get the agreement marker when the verb refers to present time, as the contrast between *he sleeps* (present tense) and *he slept* (past tense) reveals.

These examples illustrate that **agreement** is a morphological change to a word which reflects the characteristics of some other word it is in a syntactic relation with. We left inflectional morphology and especially agreement to the end of our discussion of morphology because these topics provide a natural transition to the topic of syntax examined in the rest of the volume.

4.5 **Morphology in other languages**

Present-day English has very little inflectional morphology left. To illustrate our point, we are first going to look at a line from Shakespeare's sonnet no. 128. The version of English Shakespeare used in his writing is called Early Modern English (1500–1700) by historical linguists. It is the direct ancestor of the English we are using today and is marked by more forms and more inflectional morphology, as in

47. *With thy sweet fingers when thou gently sway'st.* (Sonnet no. 128.3 from the Shakespeare Database Project http://www.shkspr.uni-muenster.de)

This one line illustrates that you got away lightly in two respects: first, the summary of the current English pronominal system, including personal, possessive and reflexive pronouns, in Chapter 2 does not include *thy* and *thou*. Can you work out which person and which number of which type of pronoun these two forms are? *Thy* is second person singular possessive in its dependent / determiner usage; and *thou* is again second person singular, but this time a personal pronoun. The third and last form that may require an explanation is *sway'st*. We have no problem understanding the verb *sway*, but what about the *-est*? It's the same type of morpheme as the present-day third person singular *-s*, i.e. an agreement morpheme, but not for the third-but for the second person singular.

We are going to step it up a bit now. Consider the Russian verb *byt* 'be', presented here in its word- and morphological form, with a morphological gloss and a free translation. The word-form does not give us any indication as to how many morphemes this example contains. The morphological form, in which segmentable morphemes are separated by hyphens, reveals that. But the free translation does not tell us which morpheme has which 'meaning' or grammatical function. This is why linguists use morphological glosses. The gloss identifies the *by* as the root, the *-l* as a past-tense morpheme and the *-a* as a feminine-singular agreement marker.

word form	*Tanja byla doma.*
morphological form	Tanja by-l-a doma.
morphological gloss	Tanya be-PST-F.SG at.home
free translation	'Tanya was at home.'

(Corbett 2007: 24)

If you think that's bad, we promise you it can get much, much worse, as in Nez Perce, for example. Nez Perce is spoken by a tribe of Native Americans who live in the Pacific Northwest region (Columbia River Plateau) of the United States. It is a polysynthetic language, which means that it has a rich morphological system which allows complex propositions to be expressed at the word level. The simple English clause *He / she / it ran* can be conveyed in only one word. The example is again given in its word- and morphological forms with a gloss and a translation.

word form	*hiwlé·ke•yke*
morphological form	hi-wilé·-ke•éyVC-k-e
morphological gloss	3NOM-run-move/change.location.or.position-K. ELEMENT-PST
free translation	'He / she / it ran.'

(Cash Cash 2004: 1)

Without looking it up, we could work out that 3NOM in the morphological gloss line means third-person nominative (the 'subject' case as opposed to accusative ACC, the 'object' case, as in English *him / her / it*) and that PST means 'past', like in the Russian example. But we've got no idea what K.ELEMENT means. Fortunately there is a standard set of conventions that linguists can consult to find out, the so called Leipzig Glossing rules. They consist of ten recommendations for how to gloss and a proposed 'lexicon' of abbreviated category labels. The recommendations and abbreviations are freely available on the web (www.eva.mpg.de/lingua/resources/glossing-rules.php). It's good to know about them; maybe you'll need them one day.

4.6 Chapter summary

In Chapter 1, we had a first basic look at the units of morpho-syntactic analysis: morphemes, words, clauses and sentences. In Chapter 2 we established that, fortunately, all the words of all the world's languages share some characteristics, and this is why we can group them into word classes. We focused on the shared characteristics of English nouns, verbs, adjectives, adverbs, determiners, prepositions and conjunctions before we started looking inside the words, i.e. at morphology (Chapters 3 and 4). In the previous chapter we established an inventory of morphological categories (free and bound morphemes, root, base, affix, prefix and suffix) we could then use to investigate derivational morphology with. We looked at the most important word-formation processes in English before turning our attention to the type of morphology that is most relevant to syntax: inflectional morphology.

In this chapter, we contrasted the properties of derivational morphology with those of inflectional morphology before examining the meagre remains of English inflectional categories. We found that all English inflectional morphemes are always suffixes. Nouns have the feature / attribute **number** (singular and plural), and some pronouns still have **case** (illustrated by the contrast between *I* and *me*, *we* and *us*, etc.). Inflectional categories such as **number** can be reflected on other words. We can discover them with the principle of contrast: *this plant* (singular) vs. *these plants* (plural). Words that indicate through their morphological form that they form a syntactic relationship / unit are said to **agree** with each other. Our list of properties of inflectional morphology (see Table 4.1) states that inflectional morphemes are obligatory. Violations of inflectional category or agreement marking therefore result in ungrammaticality.

**Five plant_* violates obligatory number marking on nouns
*Them are very fond of they has the wrong case in both subject and object
*this plants *these plant the determiners and nouns 'disagree' in number

In English, verbs have the inflectional dimensions of **tense** (present, past), **aspect** (progressive vs. perfective) and **mood** (indicative, imperative, subjunctive). When verbs refer to an action, event or state in the present, and their subject is a third-person-singular form, they also have to **agree** with that subject in person and number, as in

He watch-es TV (3SG) vs. *They watch TV* (3PL)
*He watch_ TV vs. **They watches TV*

Therefore inflectional morphology in general, and agreement in particular, already help establish relations between words. This is what we will move on to now: groups of words or phrases.

Key terms
Inflection; tense; aspect; mood; number; case; agreement; gerund.

Exercises

Exercise 4.1   If this chapter was difficult, imagine how difficult it must be for children to learn morphology. Morphological acquisition requires a child to correctly segment words into morphemes and to correctly categorize words into classes. Children, however, do not seem to be fazed by this task, even though they initially make a few mistakes. The following examples under 1–3 illustrate three distinct error mechanisms involving morpheme segmentation and word-class allocation. What are they?

1a.   *Jei, Kei, Elemeno, Pi* . . . (a child reciting the alphabet)
1b.   *He throw-uped at the party.*
1c.   *I like jump-roping.*

After a child was told her behaviour was inappropriate, she replied

2a.   *No, I'm out of propirate.*
2b.   *Daddy, you are interring-upt me.*
2c.   Kids referring to grown-ups as *dults*

In the examples under 1, the children segmented the words or phrases into too many / too few (delete as appropriate) morphemes; they under-segmented. In the examples under 2, on the other hand, the children broke the words up into too many / too few (delete as appropriate) morphemes; they over-segmented. What's going on in 3 and 4?

3a.   *I am jellying my bread.*
3b.   *I got manys.*
3c.   *He runs fastly.*
4a.   *I saw to many polices.*
4b.   *I am hating her.*

In the examples under 3 the children put the words into the wrong _____ . In the examples under 4, on the other hand, they 'only' put them into the wrong sub-_____ .   *(Examples from Owens 2008)*

Exercise 4.2   In Activity 4.3 we asked you to derive nouns from verbs by adding the suffix *-er*. Every time we use this activity in class, answers include words such as *runner, manager, harder, reader, faster, player, newer* and *diver*. Exactly half of these answers are correct, the other half are not. Sort the words into two piles. Then identify which other morpheme *-er* can be. What is its function? Is it derivational or inflectional? Use the criteria listed in Table 4.1 to answer the last question.

Exercise 4.3 Between age the ages of two and a half and five children are frequently heard to produce the following over-generalised forms

 a. *foots, mens*
 b. *goed, bringed, buyed, breaked, broked*

Do you have an idea why children may be using these forms?

Exercise 4.4 Consider the German noun phrase *unsern Vätern* 'to our fathers'. Can you identify the roots / stems of both words? What does the identical gloss for the morph -*n* mean? In which inflectional categories do the determiner and the noun agree?

word-form	*unsern Vätern*
morphological form	*unser-n Väter-n*
morphological gloss	our-DAT.PL father.PL-DAT.pl
free translation	*'to our fathers'*

The morphological gloss for the German example singles *unser* and *Vätern* out as the roots / stems and identifies the -*n* as dative (case) and plural. This suffix is present on both the determiner and the noun to show that they belong together, or 'agree'.

Further reading

On differences between inflection and derivation, see Haspelmath (2002) (especially Chapter 4); Blevins (2006); and Bauer (2003) (especially Chapter 6). On language change, see Trask (1994). More on our Russian and Nez Perce examples can be found in Corbett (2007) and Cash Cash (2004).

CHAPTER 5

Phrase structure 1

In this chapter ...

We are going to move onto the next larger units in language. We are going to turn our attention to the relationships between words and the ways in which these relationships can be captured. We start by linking every word in a sentence to at least one other word in the same sentence, and by describing the grammatical and meaning relations between the words we joined up. From there on, we will introduce different phrase categories, and show that phrasal categories have an internal structure for which the concept of head is crucial. We will explore this first on the pre-modification of nouns (NP), and are then going to demonstrate that the same template can be applied to other types of phrases (e.g. AdjP, AdvP). We continue with a discussion of NP post-modifiers, which lead us into other phrase types (e.g. PP).

In the first four chapters of this book we looked at how morphemes are put together in order to build words, and how these form natural – but fuzzy – classes depending on their morphological, syntactic and semantic similarities. In the next chapters we will explore how words are combined in order to build phrases and sentences and how these again form natural classes because of their morpho-syntactic, semantic and pragmatic similarities. The fact that morphemes, words, phrases and sentences form natural classes is great for us as language users, because it saves us a lot of time. Any idea why?

Consider how the many uses of the suffix -*s* economise language learning and use.

Having worked through Chapter 2, you should already be able to determine the word class of every word in a given string of words. Try it out on Activity 5.1. If you have problems with any word token, go back to Chapter 2 and remind yourself of the morphological, syntactic and semantic clues for identifying word classes.

Activity 5.1

Label every word in the following sentence for the word class it belongs to. Use the notation system we introduced in Chapter 2, i.e. N for nouns, V for verbs, Adj for adjectives, Adv for adverbs, P for prepositions, C for conjunctions.

Henry, the white cat with a stripy tail, pounced clumsily on those sparrows.

You should have found four nouns (one name and three common nouns), three determiners, two adjectives, two prepositions, one verb and an adverb. There is no conjunction in the above sentence. *Henry* is the name of the cat; the common nouns are *cat*, *tail* and *sparrows*; the determiners are *the*, *a* and *those*; *with* and *on* are prepositions; *white* and *stripy* are adjectives; *pounced* is the verb; and *clumsily* is the adverb.

5.1 Relations between words

The sentence in Activity 5.1 communicates a message. It does so because its words are related to one another; both in terms of meaning (semantically) and in terms of grammatical structure (morphologically and syntactically). This is a book about morphology and syntax, and we will focus on structural relations, but these do not exist without meaning relations. The next activity guides you towards identifying some of these relations.

Activity 5.2

Relate every word in the example sentence from Activity 5.1. (repeated below) to at least one other word in the same sentence and try to describe the grammatical and meaning relations between the words.

Henry, the white cat with a stripy tail, pounced clumsily on those sparrows.

Example: *those* and *sparrows*

A grammatical indicator that the determiner *those* and the noun *sparrows* are related is that both are plural (*that sparrow* would be singular), which means that the two words **agree** in number. There is also a meaning relation between *those* and *sparrows*: when you come across this combination of words, you know that the sparrows are in the speaker's field of vision, but somewhere in the distance, and that there is another group of sparrows closer by. If there was only one group of sparrows, the narrator would have said *the sparrows*; and if he / she was talking about the sparrows closer by, he / she would have said *these sparrows*.

Some of the relations you may have identified are discussed below:

- *Henry* and *the white cat with a stripy tail* refer to the same animal; the name can replace the whole group of words, and *the white cat with a stripy tail* simply expands on *Henry*. This type of relation is called **apposition.**
- *the* and *cat* are related; *the* refers to a specific cat (otherwise the speaker would have said *a cat*). The sentence is about one cat only (otherwise the speaker would have said *cat-s* or *the cat-s*). The determiner and the noun agree in number like *those* and *sparrows*, but *the* and *cat* are both singular. Without a determiner, the phrase / sentence would not be grammatical in Standard British English. Remember, the symbol for *ungrammatical* is *, as in **Cat with a stripy tail*.
- *Henry* furthermore has two features the speaker finds worth mentioning: (i) he is white, and (ii) he has a stripy tail. The adjective *white* squeezes in between the determiner and the noun, and this word order leaves no doubt that it is the cat who is white and not, for example, the sparrows. The preposition *with* establishes the second relation: *with* immediately follows *cat* (and not *sparrows*) and precedes *stripy tail*, which again indicates that it is the cat who possesses a stripy tail (and not the sparrows).
- The verb *pounced* establishes the most important relation in this sentence: it links Henry, the agent of the action with the target, the sparrows. Note that if the narrator had told the story in the present tense, the verb *pounce* would carry the suffix *-s* to mark that it **agrees** with the third-person-singular subject.
- The way *Henry* pounces is *clumsily*, so you know that *clumsily* relates to the verb *pounce*. To show that it modifies a verb and not a noun, the stem *clumsy* carries the adverbial ending *-ly*.
- Finally, *Henry* pounced in the direction of the poor sparrows; the preposition *on* establishes this spatial relation.

In this sketchy description of how some of the words in Activity 5.2 relate to one another to create a message, we considered structural and meaning relations. The word meanings establish the semantic relations; the morphology and the syntax (including word order) form the morpho-syntactic relations between words. The meaning relations are primary and most obvious, but no language we know of operates purely on semantic relations. In other words, every documented language also uses morpho-syntactic relations and word order to build sentences and convey meaning. Languages, however, vary in the extent to which they use morpho-syntax and / or word order to indicate which words are related. In the past, English made heavy use of morpho-syntactic relations (like **agreement**) to indicate that two or more words belonged together. Over the last 800 years, however, English lost much of its morphology and now relies heavily on syntax, especially word order, to express syntactic relations. Nowadays, related words tend to be next to each other in all varieties of English.

After this summary of the key points on structural and meaning relations, we will show you (i) that related words form groups or **phrases** which have an internal structure, and (ii) that in these groups of words one element tends to give the phrase its basic meaning and grammatical character.

5.2 What are 'heads' in syntax?

In a group of related words, one of them largely determines the group's meaning and grammatical character. This word is called the **head**; the other words are called **dependents**. The head of a phrase bears the most important semantic information and incorporates the most essential grammatical characteristics of the whole group of words. Heads thus tend to:

- be obligatory; they cannot normally be omitted. *The white _ with a stripy tail* is ungrammatical;
- be able to stand for the phrase as a whole, wherever the phrase occurs. Because *cat* is the head of the whole phrase *the white cat with a stripy tail* and *cat* is co-referential with *Henry*, *Henry* (or just *he*) can replace the whole phrase (e.g. *Henry pounced*; *the white cat with a stripy tail pounced*; *he pounced*). In linguistic analysis, a phrase can therefore consist of just one word;
- determine the word class of the entire phrase. The word class of the head in *The white _ with a stripy tail* determines and gives the name to the whole group of words.

Heads dominate the word(s) they are head of: they determine many of the grammatical properties of the phrase. For example, heads provide slots for the words they enter into morpho-syntactic relations with (*with* in Activity 5.1

provides the possibility for *a stripy tail* to occur); and they frequently specify the grammatical properties required of the elements they select, i.e. their dependents. For example, because *sparrows* is plural, *those* is plural, too. Heads thus often require their dependents to agree with some or all of their grammatical features, overtly or covertly. Whether the agreement is explicitly morphologically marked or not largely depends on how much agreement morphology a given language has. English has little, so we only get the two types of overt agreement discussed in the previous chapter: the agreement in number between the determiner and the noun already illustrated with *those sparrows*, and agreement in person and number between the subject and present-tense verbs, as in *Henry pounces*.

Heads also largely determine the relation between the phrase they are head of, and the 'world' beyond the phrase, i.e. the sentence they are embedded in. In other words, heads determine the external relations a phrase can enter into: for example, *with* determines that *a stripy tail* can occur with *cat*, as in ... *cat with a stripy tail*. Heads do for phrases what periscopes do for submarines: they keep contact with the outside world.

Despite their importance, the concept of head is quite controversial in syntax. We know that heads exist, but there is still debate on whether all phrases have heads, whether all heads behave in the same way, and whether heads are always necessary. Let's look at some examples of head-dependent relationships.

5.3 Nouns and the words they combine with

5.3.1 Determiners

We will now focus on the three nouns in Activity 5.2. We are going to start with *cat* and *tail*, and will then use *sparrows* to illustrate that any word(s) we relate to *sparrows* will behave (morpho-syntactically) quite similarly to any word(s) we relate to *cats* (and this is not because cats and sparrows are both animals ;-).

> Activity 5.3
>
> Recycle your answers to Activity 5.2 for this one. You will find that every single common noun in the example sentence is syntactically related to a token of another word class. Which word class are we talking about?
>
> *Henry, the white cat with a stripy tail, pounced clumsily on those sparrows.*

Cat is related to *the*; *tail* is related to *the*; and *sparrows* is related to *these*. The answer to Activity 5.3 therefore is that all three nouns are morpho-syntactically related to determiners (two definite articles, and a demonstrative pronoun acting as a determiner). To establish whether all English nouns have to combine with a determiner, go to Exercise 5.1 at the end of this chapter.

Activity 5.3 shows you that in English:

- singular countable common nouns, like *cat* or *tail*, need one determiner;
- plural nouns like *houses*, *sparrows* and *cars* don't need (but can take) a determiner;
- names (or proper nouns) either resist (**the Henry*) or demand a definite article; if they require one, it has to be *the*, as in *the White House*, *the Titanic*, *the Bronx*, *the Atlantic*.
- singular mass nouns, like *water* and *furniture*, don't need a determiner, but (just like plural nouns) can combine with one. For example, if you want to pick out a specific *water*, you can say *the water I drank in Ararat tasted great*.

The example of the syntactic relation between determiners and various types of noun shows us that some syntactic relations are obligatory and some are optional. In obligatory syntactic relations, the whole construction becomes ungrammatical if the head or the dependent are missing. (For a useful activity on identifying obligatory versus optional syntactic relations, check the consolidation chapter following Chapter 6.) In a determiner–noun relation, the whole group of words (and consequently the whole sentence) becomes ungrammatical if either the determiner or the noun is missing.

But which is the head in the determiner–noun relation? The noun is clearly the semantic head; the noun also specifies many of the properties (number, gender, etc.) of the elements it is syntactically related to. In all contexts, the presence of determiners presupposes the existence of a noun, but there are no nouns which always presuppose the presence of a determiner (we looked into this in Chapter 2). So there are good arguments for both the noun and the determiner being the syntactic head in determiner–noun relations (if you want to know more about this, consult the literature suggested in the Further reading section at the end of this chapter). We are going to assume that the noun is the head in determiner–noun relations.

At present we are looking at how nouns combine with other words in phrases and sentences in order to communicate a message that goes beyond an aggregate of word meanings. Without any modification, nouns can refer to too many things. For example, if you say *cats are lovely*, you think that all cats are lovely, whereas if you say *these cats are lovely* you're only talking about a particular bunch of cats; you may even hate cats, but love these specific ones, for all we know! To narrow a noun's reference down to what we consider to be relevant, we can use determiners (as well as other elements introduced in the coming sections).

5.3.2 Other ways of limiting noun reference

> **Activity 5.4**
>
> Determiners got their name because they determine (i.e. limit, restrict) the potential reference of nouns. Which other words can do this? See if you can limit the reference / meaning of the examples below by using words other than determiners (and adjectives, which express a quality or attribute of a noun, see Section 2.3 as well as the next section).
> a. countable nouns like *car*, *rat* and *screen* (e.g. *Sheila likes _ cars*)
> b. uncountable nouns like *water*, *dough* and *cyberspace* (*My neighbour wastes _ water*)

Depending on their kind, noun reference can also be limited with numerals and words like *both*, *every*, *each*, *all*, *some*, *many*, *more*, *most*, among many others.

Yet another way of limiting the reference of nouns is by specifying possession (this only works for nouns denoting objects or people, because only these can be 'owned'). This can either be done with possessive determiners (*my*, *your*, *his*, *her*, *its*, *our*, *your*, *their*) preceding the noun, as in *her cat has a stripy tail*; or with prepositions; or with the so-called possessive -'s. In writing, this possessive -'s is added to singular nouns after an apostrophe ('), as in *Val's cat has a stripy tail*; plural nouns only take an apostrophe, as in *The girls' cat has a stripy tail*. Readers (and listeners) will interpret *Val*, *her* and the possessive -'s as referring to one *specific* instance of the noun they combine with (*the cat of Val*, not *a cat of Val*). Both *her* and *Val's* therefore help determine the reference of the noun *cat*. Competent adult users of English can extend the possessive -'s construction further to, for example, *this squirrel's nuts* or *Val's cat's tail*. Children, non-native speakers and even many native speakers find this quite difficult, and rightly so. To find out why this is a rather complex grammatical construction, go to Exercise 5.2 at the end of this chapter.

An easier, but possibly less beautiful, way of specifying possession is by linking the referents of owner and object with a preposition, as we have seen in the examples *the cat of Val* and *a cat of Val*. We will discuss this construction type further when we have moved on to the syntactic relations between nouns and the words that follow them.

To recapitulate, we can use articles, demonstrative and possessive deter-miners, possessive -'s, numerals, words like *both*, *every*, *each*, *all*, *some*, *many*, *more*, *most*, as well as prepositions, to restrict the reference of nouns. We are not necessarily aware of this when we produce speech.

All we are doing in this book is to make you aware of the underlying regularities at work every time you use language. On the perception side, your audience (most of the time) understands what you are doing with language and interprets it correctly, despite some of the constructions being far from straightforward.

5.3.3 Nouns and adjectives

You can also single out a cat from a group of cats by, for example, describing its colour (as in *the white cat*); or you can single a *tail* out from of group of tails by, for example, describing its pattern (as in *a stripy tail*). Both groups of words *the white cat* and *a stripy tail* are grammatical and *white* and s*tripy* clearly describe or **modify** *cat* and *tail* respectively. Because *white* and *stripy* are placed before the nouns they modify, we say that they **pre-modify** them. (You will have a chance of working with other pre-modifiers in our first consolidation chapter, which elaborates on this term, using linguistic knowledge you have acquired by working through this book.) These examples therefore show us that it is possible for nouns to relate syntactically to adjectives. Once this has been established, there are two more questions every respectable scientist / linguist needs to ask him/herself: (i) 'Is this generally true?', and (ii) 'Is this obligatory or optional?'

We can find the answer to question (i) by trying to add one or more adjectives before nouns, for example in our sentence: *Henry, the beautiful young white cat with a long stripy tail, pounces on these poor sparrows.* It therefore seems that the meaning of nouns can generally be limited by one or more adjectives which precede them. You will find that almost indefinitely long strings of adjectives can occur before nouns. The placing of adjectives before nouns is recursive, i.e. it can be repeated again and again. *Recursive* implies that there is no limit to this process, but in fact there is. This restriction, however, is not grammatical, but our (short-term) memory. We will have problems processing the whole sentence if the string of adjectives gets too long. A discipline of linguistics / psychology which is called psycholinguistics deals with these kind of processes and restrictions.

To answer question (ii), consider the results of deleting the adjectives pre-modifying the nouns in our example sentence. We find that it does not become ungrammatical when we delete *white* or *stripy*. Unlike determiners, adjectives are *not* in an obligatory syntactic relation with nouns, but in an optional one. Strangely enough, the fact that we can stack adjectives up in front of nouns is evidence for them being optional elements; recursiveness tends to be a characteristic of optional syntactic relations.

Because heads play a more prominent role in most syntactic relations than other elements, it is always useful to know which element is the head in a grammatical relation or phrase. So which is the head in a pre-modifying adjective–noun relation? We said that heads are words that play a primary role in giving the phrase its basic meaning and grammatical character. Given that adjectives simply modify the meaning of the noun they combine with, it is fairly obvious that the noun is the semantic head. The fact that pre-modifying adjectives are optional also suggests that the noun is the grammatical head in a noun–adjective syntactic relation.

The flip side of the coin (i.e. that we can have any number of adjectives occurring before the noun) also supports the argument that the head of a syntactic relation containing a noun and an adjective is the noun, not the adjective. We can therefore conclude that adjectives before nouns depend on the nouns they modify. But what about adjectives in other word-order / sentence positions? Do they also depend on the head noun, or do they depend on one another? Exercise 5.3 at the end of this chapter will guide you to the answer to this question (and we will come back to it when we look at pre-modifiers of adjectives and adjective phrases).

So far we have looked at two syntactic relations nouns enter: determiner–noun and adjective–noun relations. We found that the syntactic relation *cat* enters with *the* is identical to the syntactic relation *tail* enters with *a* (Section 5.3.1). We have just established that the morpho-syntactic relation *cat* enters with *white* is identical to the one *tail* enters with *stripy* (and you are welcome to run the same analysis over any other adjective pre-modifying a noun). This relates to something useful we mentioned earlier: any word we relate to *sparrows* will behave quite similarly to any word we relate to *cats*. This is not because both cats and sparrows are animals, but because the words referring to cats and sparrows are both nouns.

To native speakers of English it seems obvious and natural that adjectives slot in before the noun, but not so for native speakers of Spanish. The majority of Spanish adjectives follow nouns. In Spanish therefore most adjectives **post-modify** the noun. *Post-* means after, and *post-modify* therefore means 'modify by being placed after'. One of the three nouns in our main example sentence is also post-modified, but not by an adjective.

Activity 5.5

Which noun in our example sentence is post-modified? *Cat, tail,* or *sparrows*?

Henry, the white cat with a stripy tail, pounced on those sparrows.

What is the first word in the post-modifying phrase and which word class does it belong to?

5.3.4 Nouns and prepositions

Cat is described further by *with a stripy tail*. This group of words occurs after the noun it modifies; it therefore post-modifies the noun *cat*. From Activity 5.1 we know that the first word in this post-modifying group of words is a preposition, i.e. *with*. But what's the function of *with a stripy tail*? *The white cat* isn't specific enough, and the post-modifying prepositional phrase restricts or specifies the meaning and singles Henry out from among all other white cats. There is a semantic or pragmatic reason for adding *with a stripy tail* to that sentence, but from a grammatical point of view this post-modifying phrase is not strictly necessary. When we delete *with a stripy tail*, the sentence does not become ungrammatical.

Henry, the white cat _ , pounced clumsily on those sparrows.

We can therefore conclude that this group of words is in an optional syntactic relation with *cat*.

How do we know that *with a stripy tail* forms a group of words that belong together as a phrase? Well, as soon as you have said the preposition *with*, you can't just stop there; you have to add a noun or a group of words headed by a noun, i.e. a noun phrase: **The white cat [with _] pounces clumsily on those sparrows.* So the preposition *with* is in an obligatory relation with the (extended) noun phrase *a stripy tail*. (The noun phrase is extended because here *tail* is optionally pre-modified by *stripy*.)

But do prepositions obligatorily combine with noun phrases?

Activity 5.6

Some other English prepositions are: *on*, *under*, *at*, *of*, *by*, *to*, *about* and *without*. Construct phrases containing these prepositions and observe what follows them,

e.g. *I stand by Mehmet / him / water / lakes / the beautiful lakeside.*

We assume you placed either a name, or a mass noun, or a pronoun, or a plural noun, or a count-noun with a determiner, i.e. a simple (or extended) noun phrase after the prepositions above. When you delete the noun phrases, your sentences become ungrammatical. This suggests that prepositions combine obligatorily with nouns / noun phrases.

The only exceptions to this rule are 'prepositions' that form a very close idiomatic relation with verbs. The combination *speed up*, for example, means 'accelerate' in *Come on, let's speed up. Up* in this so called phrasal verb construction is not really an independent preposition and is therefore called a particle. A particle must be a preposition, but it must not combine with a noun phrase complement. If you find this difficult, make sure you do the task on phrasal verbs in the first consolidation chapter. Here we are going to continue our exploration of prepositions and nouns.

We said that it is always helpful to know which word plays the most prominent role in a syntactic relation or phrase. Let's look at the phrases you constructed for Activity 5.6. They all express relationships established by the preposition. The element that plays a primary role in giving the phrase its basic meaning and grammatical character therefore appears to be the preposition. Internally, the preposition 'dominates' the phrase in that it determines the grammatical properties of the phrase: it provides the syntactic slot for the noun (phrase) inside it, $_{PP}[with_{NP}[a\ stripy\ tail]]$, and it determines what this slot has to be filled with, i.e. a noun (phrase). This means that the primary player in the prepositional phrase *with a stripy tail* is the preposition *with*. This is why syntactic relations / groups of words that are headed by a preposition are called prepositional phrases or PPs.

As with other heads, the preposition functions as the periscope of the whole phrase in that it establishes the external relation(s) the phrase enters into. By external we mean outside the square brackets of the phrase they head. What is the external syntactic relation *with* establishes in our example sentence?

Activity 5.7

Recycle the sentences you constructed for Activity 5.6. This time don't focus on what goes on after the preposition, but rather on the preceding noun. In our example sentence, this word is the noun *cat*; *with* links the (extended) noun phrase *a stripy tail* with *cat*.

The preposition *with* therefore establishes an external syntactic relation with the head (*cat*) of the preceding / 'higher' noun phrase *the white cat*, as in

$_{NP}[the\ white\ cat\ _{PP}[with\ _{NP}[a\ stripy\ tail]]]$

The preposition therefore lives up to its definition (given in Section 2.6): it sets up and spells out the relationship between the words / phrases it links.

We have taken a reasonably close look at language in this book so far. Let's step back a bit for a moment and take in the bigger picture. Language is one of the things we use daily in our lives; this can only mean that communication is hugely beneficial to us. We communicate competently in our first language, and more or less competently in other languages. But unless we learn a foreign language, or study languages or linguistics, we don't have to be aware of how it works, any more than you need to know about mechanics in order to drive a car. The first four chapters of this book tried to show you how linguistic units up to the size of words are put together. In this chapter we have turned our attention to the assembly of words into larger structures such as phrases and sentences. Up to now we have looked at two major word classes and the syntactic relations they enter into, nouns and prepositions. Tokens of these two word classes are also among the first words children utter, but at the age of two they still tend to utter words in isolation. Ask any carer of a two-year-old how much guesswork is involved in trying to work out what the child wants to communicate when he / she says *cat*, or *tail*, or *up* or *tail up*. This is why they learn really quickly to combine words into larger structures. What we are doing here is to try to deduce some of the regularities children and adults follow in building word and sentence structure. You may have noticed that we are asking the same questions again and again. What are these questions?

In order to work out how larger structures like phrases and sentences are put together from individual words, we first and foremost need to establish which word in an utterance is related to which other word(s). Establishing grammatical relations is primary for communicating meanings. Second, it is also very helpful to be able to identify the essential bits of a message. The important words tend to be tied together by obligatory syntactic relations; optional add-ons must be important enough to the speaker to get mentioned, but they are not essential for communicating the basic message. For example, should you phone the RSPCA (Royal Society for the Prevention of Cruelty to Animals) with a complaint about Henry, your main message would most probably not be *Henry, the white cat with a stripy tail, pounces clumsily on those sparrows*, but *A cat is slaughtering sparrows in my garden*, and only then would you provide more specific information about Henry's colour and tail. Third, you need to be able to answer the question what modifies what. English has shed most of its inflectional morphology in the last 800 years, so the order in which words occur is very important. We have all experienced communication break-downs caused by non-native speakers who know the words for the key concepts they want to communicate, but assemble them in a way that does not make sense. The order in which syntactically related words occur in a sentence is therefore also important.

The main questions we have been asking and will be asking when analysing the structure of phrases and sentences are:

1. Which word(s) is the word we are looking at related to?
2. Is the other word obligatory or optional?
3. Does the word stand before or after it?
4. Which of the two words is dominant?
5. Do the answers to questions 1–4 hold true for most / all cases of this syntactic relation?

In more precise technical terminology, these questions are

1. Which word(s) does the word enter into semantic and morpho-syntactic relations with?
2. Are these relations obligatory or optional?
3. Are they pre- or post-modifying relations?
4. Which of the two words is the head?
5. Is this syntactic relation productive / generative?

In the remainder of this chapter we will be asking these questions regarding two other word classes: adjectives and adverbs.

5.4 **Adjectives and words they combine with**

Adjectives featured prominently in Chapter 2; in this chapter we have looked at *white* and *stripy* in relation to the nouns they combine with. We said that they are optional sentence elements which can be removed without rendering our example sentence ungrammatical. They are in an optional syntactic relation with the nouns they modify, i.e. *cat* and *tail*. Because they precede *cat* and *tail*, we call them pre-modifiers. The traditional name for an adjective used as a pre-modifier to a common noun is **attributive** adjective (because the adjective ascribes certain attributes or characteristics to the noun it modifies). We have furthermore established that every noun can be pre-modified by more than one adjective (e.g. *a long stripy tail*), all of which depend on the noun and not on each other. But what about *amazingly* in *the amazingly long tail*?

> **Activity 5.8**
> Which word class does the word *amazingly* belong to?
> In the phrase *the amazingly long tail*, which word does *amazingly* modify?
> Is *amazingly* in an obligatory or optional syntactic relation with that word?
> Does *amazingly* pre- or post-modify that word?

The adverb *amazingly* pre-modifies the adjective *long*. *Amazingly* is not compulsory. *Amazingly* is therefore an adverb functioning as an optional pre-modifier to the head of the syntactic relation, i.e. the adjective *long*. The head of this pair of words is the adjective *long*, which along with *amazingly* forms an adjective phrase which is embedded in the noun phrase *the amazingly long tail*, as in $_{NP}[the_{AdjP}[amazingly\ long]\ tail]]$. Note that the process at work here is similar to the process we observed for nouns: like nouns, adjectives can be pre-modified and expanded to phrases. And like a noun

93

phrase (in fact, like all other phrases), an adjective phrase can consist of one or more words. The syntactic generalisation we have established, i.e. that adjectives can optionally be pre-modified by adverbs, is productive in the sense that it tells us in a formal and explicit way that this string of basic elements of the English language is grammatical in all cases. Let's try it out on a few more examples.

Activity 5.9

Test the syntactic statement 'adjectives can optionally be pre-modified by adverbs' on the adjectives in the following noun phrases:

the pretty cat, the poor sparrows, the powerful engine, the great galaxy

using the following list of adverbs:

incredibly, very, stupidly, hesitantly, quite, unfortunately

Can all adjectives be pre-modified by adverbs?

All English adjectives can be pre-modified by adverbs, but not by all adverbs (degree adverbs like *very* and *quite* always work, but some of the other adverbs from the list above don't, as you've noticed).

Adjective phrases furthermore fit directly into a noun phrase, between the determiner and the noun, to be more precise. When an adjective phrase appears as part of the noun (phrase) it modifies, it is said to be in **attributive** position.

Adjective phrases, however, can also describe a characteristic of a noun phrase that occurs before it.

Activity 5.10

Try to construct a grammatical English sentence similar in meaning to *a stripy tail*, in which the adjective is placed after the noun *tail*. Use the words *the*, *tail* and *stripy* and a verb of your choice (hint: the most frequent and easiest verb that allows nouns to be post-modified by adjective phrases is the verb *to be*).

In *the tail is stripy*, the adjective follows the noun and is therefore used **predicatively**. Many adjectives can appear in either position, attributively or predicatively; for example *the sweet cherry* vs. *the cherry is sweet*, or *the very greedy squirrel* vs. *the squirrel is very greedy*, others can't. Exercise 5.4 at the end of this chapter introduces you to some adjectives that are not as flexible, i.e. they can occur only in one position.

5.5 Adverbs and words they combine with

There remain two other word classes to be discussed, illustrated by *pounced* and *clumsily* in our example sentence. We will leave *pounce* until later, and focus on *clumsily* now. Establishing the word class of *clumsily* is as easy as it was to establish the word class of *amazingly* in the previous section. Both words are derived from adjectives (*clumsy* and *amazing*) by adding the *-ly* suffix. The name of the word class *ad-verbs* then provides us with the answer to our first question: *ad* means 'to' in Latin

1. Which word(s) are adverbs related to?

Clumsily is related to the verb *pounce*, but adverbs can also modify adjectives (as we worked out in Section 5.4, *amazingly long tail*), and other adverbs (e.g. *very clumsily*).

2. Is the word obligatory or optional?

It is optional, cf. *The cat with a stripy tail pounces ~~clumsily~~ on those sparrows*. Unlike prepositions, adverbs never require the occurrence of another sentence element.

3. Does the word it is related to stand before or after it?

In our original example (e.g. *Henry pounced clumsily*), the adverb post-modifies the verb, but adverbs can also pre-modify verbs (e.g. *I slowly cycle to Covent Garden*). Adverbs can modify verbs, adjectives and even whole sentences. This versatility naturally influences their positioning in the sentence. Generally speaking though, adverbs tend to appear near the word they modify (see Exercise 5.5 at the end of this chapter).

4. Which of the two words is dominant?

Clumsily is optional; verbs are generally the most important part of every sentence. The verb *pounced* is thus the head of the syntactic relation, not the adverb *clumsily*.

5. Are the answers to questions 1 to 4 true for most / all instances of this syntactic relation?

Yes, adverbs can generally pre- or post-modify verbs. If they modify adjectives or other adverbs, they generally pre-modify them.

 OK, so *clumsily* is an optional post-dependent of *pounce* in our example sentence. But can adverbs also be heads? Let's try to modify the adverb *slowly* in the sentence *I cycle slowly to Covent Garden*. You can cycle more or less slowly and express this verbally by modifying *slowly* with another adverb describing this variation in speed. Degree adverbs include words like *quite*, *too*, *extremely*, *really* and the most frequent one: *very*. Not all of them fit into our sentence but *quite*, *extremely*, *rather*, and *very* do. Let's take *very*: *I cycle very slowly to Covent Garden* and apply our set of questions to the syntactic relation between *very* and *slowly*.

Activity 5.11

In the sentence *I cycle very slowly to Covent Garden*

1. Which word is *slowly* related to?
2. Is the other word obligatory or optional?
3. Does the word stand before or after it?
4. Which of the two words is dominant?
5. Do the answers to questions 1 to 4 hold true for most / all cases of this syntactic relation?

The degree adverb *very* limits the sense of the adverb *slowly* and therefore modifies it (this answers questions 1 and 4). A degree adverb cannot normally appear on its own in the adverb phrase slot (e.g. **I snore very*). *Slowly* creates the syntactic slot for *very* (but note that *slowly* does not need the occurrence of *very*; *very* is optional), so from a distributional (grammatical) perspective it is *very* which is the less dominant word in this syntactic relation, and *slowly* appears to be the head. An adverb phrase, then, consists of an adverb *optionally* (answer to question 2) *preceded* (answer to question 3) by a degree adverb. Post-modified adverb phrases exist but are quite rare.

You can use all the degree adverbs we listed above to pre-modify adverbs of your choice to obtain a partial answer to question 5 above. You may run out of patience before you arrive at a full answer, because combining all English degree adverbs with all English adverbs is a very tedious task. And by the time you think you are done, somebody may have created / invented a new adverb by adding *-ly* to another word. The good news is that this new adverb will behave (morpho-syntactically) just like all other adverbs. So while language is creative, it tends to be creative within the boundaries of its own parameters, i.e. its grammar.

5.6 Chapter summary

In this chapter we looked at the morpho-syntactic relations words enter with other words to – eventually – create sentence and text meaning. In spoken and written language use, words form groups or phrases; one word in a group (the head) plays the most important role in terms of meaning and grammatical properties. Phrases are named after this head word. We then looked at how nouns, adjectives, adverbs and prepositions combine with other words and came to the conclusion that words from the same word class behave similarly with respect to their dependents. Finally we arrived at a set of five questions which gets us quite a long way in any morpho-syntactic analysis. These questions are

1. Which word(s) does the word we are looking at enter into semantic and morpho-syntactic relations with?
2. Are these relations obligatory or optional?
3. Are they pre- or post-modifying relations?
4. Which of the two words is the head?
5. Is this syntactic relation productive / generative?

Key terms
Phrase; head; dependent; pre-modifier; post-modifier; apposition.

Exercises

Exercise 5.1   In this chapter we raised the question whether all English nouns have to combine with a determiner. Try it out by deleting the determiners in the example sentence below:

Henry, the white cat with a stripy tail, pounces clumsily on these sparrows.

We are asking you to make grammaticality judgements; i.e. we are asking you to tell us whether this sentence or construction is grammatical or well formed according to your knowledge of English. Note that answers to questions about grammaticality may vary between speakers of different social, regional and ethnic backgrounds. But they should not vary in this case.

We can immediately tell that the name *Henry*, for example, is perfectly happy without a determiner; in fact, most English names don't require a determiner, but some do. Which category do the following examples fall into?

I am cycling along ___ Thames in ___ London, UK.
___ United States of America are bailing out the banks.
___ English Spiros uses is different to ___ English Svetlana uses.

Exercise 5.2   In Section 5.3.2 of this chapter we briefly looked at possessive -'s and said we were going to explore the complexity of this interesting construction further in an end-of-chapter exercise. Let's do this now. Let's start slowly by trying to work out which noun the demonstrative *this* applies to in *this squirrel's nuts*? *This* is singular, *squirrel* is singular, but *nuts* is plural; because *this* agrees with *squirrel* in number, we know that *this* is a determiner in a syntactic relation with *squirrels* and not with *nuts*. Once you have worked this out, try to determine what the function of *this squirrel's* is in the group of words headed by *nuts*. Note that we can replace *this squirrel's* with *his / her / its*. This fact makes *this squirrel's* equivalent to a determiner within the larger NP. In Section 5.3.2 we said that extending the possessive construction can become quite complex. Recall the possessive construction is recursive, which means we can have one such construction within another, as in *Val's cat's tail*. What's the head of the whole construction? And what is the function of each -'s above?

Exercise 5.3   An adjective can depend on a noun, but can it depend on another adjective? Take the example *a long stripy tail*. We have already established that *stripy* depends on *tail*. Does *long* also depend on *tail*, or does it depend on *stripy*? Compare this example with the other examples below

a long stripy tail
a very stripy tail
a stripy tail
a very tail
it is stripy
it is very stripy
it is long stripy

Exercise 5.4   Many but not all adjective phrases can appear in either attributive or predicative position. Try the following adjectives in either position: *asleep, blue, soft, polar, rustic, ill, rotten, future*, as in:

The future king of England is called either Charles or William.
*The king of England is / seems / becomes future.

What's peculiar about the 'adjectives' that can only be used attributively?

Exercise 5.5   Modify the words in bold with an adverb (phrase). What word / phrase or other-size units do the adverbs modify in these examples?

*Keith is _____ **sensitive**.*
*Aki Kaurismäki makes _____ **funny** films.*
*The cake was _____ **sweet**.*

I drive _____ ***fast.***
And spoke to Liz _____ ***recently.***
The solicitor saw the situation _____ ***clearly.***
Grandfather died in his sixties _____*.*
_____ *the alarm went off.*
Full-time students receive a student card _____*.*

Adverb phrases cannot only modify verbs but also adjectives, adverbs and whole sentences. In the latter function, they are called sentence adverb(ial)s. Sentence adverbials include *certainly, perhaps, unfortunately, actually, frankly, certainly* and many others.

Further reading
On phrase structure, see Huddleston and Pullum (2005) (especially Chapters 5 to 7); Greenbaum and Nelson (2009) (especially Chapters 2 and 3); Tallerman (2005) (especially Chapters 4 and 6); Aarts (2008); Hudson (2004); and O'Grady and Archibald (2008).

CHAPTER 6

Phrase structure 2

This chapter . . .

This chapter is almost exclusively dedicated to the most important element in every sentence – the verb and the phrases they head. In order to understand verbs and the way they interact with each other and other words they enter syntactic relations with, we first need to take a more in-depth look at how modality, tense, aspect and voice are expressed in English. We are then going to present some diagnostic tests that will help you identify phrases (the replacement test, the movement test, etc.). We will conclude by introducing different means of representing and identifying sentence structure, such as tree diagrams and other syntactic notations.

6.1 **Verbs**

Verbs establish the most important relations within sentences. The verb *pounce* in our example sentence from Chapter 5 (*Henry pounced clumsily on those sparrows*), for example, links the agent of the action, *Henry*, with the goal / target *on those sparrows*. Like nouns, adjectives, adverbs and prepositions, verbs are also heads; but verbs not only dominate the (verb) phrase they are related to, they are also the most important word in the whole clause. Verbs determine the meaning and grammatical character of the sentence. Not surprisingly, then, verbs tend to be obligatory.

> ### Activity 6.1
>
> The example below contains nouns, adjectives, adverbs and prepositions as heads of phrases.
>
> *Very quietly the kind man closed the door behind himself.*
>
> Try to find the three NPs, the AdvP, the AdjP, the PP and a VP and delete one at a time (don't forget that phrases can consist of one word only). Which ones can you delete without the sentence becoming ungrammatical?

Not much harm is done when we deleted the clause initial adverb phrase _AdvP_[*very quietly*] and the clause final _PP_[*behind himself*]. The man can still close the door even if he is not kind, so the adjective phrase _AdjP_[kind] is also optional. But after that we enter ungrammatical territory. The VP and all three NPs are obligatory. Removing the NP *himself* from inside the *_PP_[behind _NP_[himself]] is not good, having nobody who does the closing is unacceptable, *_NP_[the kind man] *closed the door*, and having nothing to close is also impossible, *_The kind man closed_ _NP_[the door], but without the verb *close*, we would have neither of the obligatory sentence elements. That's why we said that verbs determine the meaning and grammatical character of the clause. Because *close* creates the syntactic slot for the noun phrase [*the door*] and allows the prepositional phrase [*behind himself*], *close* is the head of the verb phrase _VP_[*closed* _NP_[*the door*] _PP_[*behind himself*]].

Every main clause therefore is headed by a verb phrase (VP), which is itself headed by a verb (V). Looking at it from a different perspective, a main clause always contains a V which is the head of a VP, which is the head of the clause. This is why we have said that the verb is the head of the clause / sentence, because it expresses the core meaning, and because it is the most crucial part of every sentence. To summarise the significance of verbs, we can say that

- Verbs are the most important words for syntax, because without verbs we don't even get simple sentences.
- Verbs determine the number of elements in a clause, as well as their roles (e.g. agent, patient, location etc.).
- Verbs typically occur as heads of verb phrases.

We established the morphological make-up of main or lexical verbs in Section 2.2.2. To recapitulate, they come in five different guises, i.e. the base form (e.g. *walk*), the *-s* form (e.g. *walks*), the progressive *-ing* participle (e.g. *walking*), the perfective *-ed* participle (e.g. *walked*) and the past *-ed* form (e.g. *walked*). In regular verbs, the *-ed* (morph) which is used to express past tense (e.g. *they walked to school last Thursday*) is identical in form to the *-ed* participle used to express perfective aspect (e.g. *they have walked to school* *all winter*). Yet it is only difficult to distinguish between the two morphemes and grammatical words in isolation, not in the context of a sentence. Why? How many (and what kind of) verbs are there in each of the two sentences:

1. *They walked to school last Thursday.*
2. *They have walked to school all winter.*

Example 1 contains only one lexical verb; example 2, on the other hand, contains one lexical (*walked*) and one auxiliary verb (*have*). In a clause in which the lexical verb follows an auxiliary, the *-ed* morph on the lexical verb will be the perfective *-ed* participle, *not* the past tense *-ed*.

6.2 Lexical and auxiliary verbs

In Section 2.2.4 we introduced the idea that some verbs can be used as both lexical and as auxiliary verbs. Distinguishing between the two contrasting uses was trickier then than it is now, because in Chapter 2 we only looked at individual word-forms. The word-forms, however, are identical for verbs that can function both as lexical and auxiliary verbs. The main syntactic relations these verbs enter, however, are different and this will help you distinguish between them in the next activity.

Activity 6.2

We said that English has roughly a dozen auxiliary verbs, the most common ones being *be*, *have* and *do*. Their contrasting use as lexical verbs and auxiliary verbs is illustrated by the following examples.

The winner did his best   *He is a loser.*
Have you not calmed down yet?   *He is clearly enjoying it.*
Did he win the race?   *Her mum had a stroke.*

In which of these sentences are the forms of *to be*, *to do* and *to have* lexical verbs and in which ones are they auxiliary verbs? Put the six example sentences in the appropriate columns.

Lexical verb	Auxiliary verb
_____	_____
_____	_____
_____	_____

As lexical verbs *be*, *have* and *do* are the only verb in the clauses in Activity 6.2. As such they go straight into noun (phrase) relations, as in

Figure 6.1

$_{NP}$[*the winner*]   *did* $_{NP}$[*his best*]

and

Figure 6.2

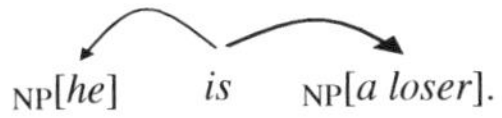

$_{NP}$[*he*]   *is* $_{NP}$[*a loser*].

As lexical verbs, *be*, *have* and *do* also carry tense themselves, as in *did*$_{PST}$, *is*$_{PRS}$ and *had*$_{PST}$. We will use *PST* and *PRS* in subscript to indicate present and past tense, respectively.

As auxiliary verbs, the first and foremost syntactic relations *be*, *have* and *do* enter are with other (lexical) verbs, as in *have . . . calmed, did . . . win, is . . . enjoying*. When used as auxiliaries, *be* and *have* and *do* **must** combine with a main / lexical verb, as in *We have eaten pizza again*. Activity 6.2 illustrates that when in a syntactic relation with a lexical verb, auxiliary verbs are characteristically used to mark tense (aspect, mood or voice).

The two most striking syntactic differences between auxiliary and lexical verbs, we said in Chapter 2, are illustrated by questions and negative sentences, which will be discussed in more depth in Chapter 10.

In questions, the auxiliaries invert with the subject; we therefore called this **subject-auxiliary inversion** (or *SAI*, as we called it in Section 2.2.4). This is, if the sentence contains auxiliary verb(s), then the leftmost auxiliary and the subject exchange place. In sentences that do not contain auxiliary verbs, like *He took the fine*, we have to add *do* to formulate a question, as in *Did he take the fine?* We call this '*do*'-**support**. In which of the following sentences in Activity 6.3 do you have to add *do*?

Activity 6.3

Turn the following sentences into *yes / no* (Y/N) questions:

a. *I am bothered.*
b. *He will take the mickey.*
c. *Many have been invited.*
d. *He seems annoyed.*

Sentences (a) and (b) are straightforward cases of subject-auxiliary inversion; so is sentence (c), but this example contains three verbs and therefore illustrates that the subject only inverts with the first tensed auxiliary; *been* and *invited* stay put, as in *Have many been invited? Seems annoyed* may look a bit like an AUX followed by a past participle, but is it? Can you say *Seems he annoyed?* No, we can't, we need *do*-support, as in *Does he seem annoyed?*

'Dummy' *do*, we said in Chapter 2, does nothing else but satisfy the grammatical requirement of regular English questions to contain an auxiliary verb. That's not quite true, actually. We simplified a bit in Chapter 2, because *Did he take the fine?* clearly shows that tense marking has shifted from the lexical verb onto the auxiliary verb (*took*$_{PST}$ vs. *did*$_{PST}$ ← take).

'Dummy' *do* is an odd case. It behaves like a modal verb in that it is always marked for tense and it is always followed by the base form of a verb. However, it also shares some characteristics with primary auxiliaries, in that it can show agreement with third-person-singular pronouns, as in *Does he seem angry?* Furthermore, unlike other auxiliaries, 'dummy' *do* cannot be preceded or followed by other auxiliaries.

In negative sentences, *not* gets inserted between the auxiliary and the main verbs, if the declarative counterpart of the sentence has both, as in *He has taken the fine* → *He has not taken the fine*. To make *He took the fine* negative, we once again have to add *do* to support the lexical verb, as in *He did*$_{AUX\ PST}$ *not*$_{NEG}$ *take*$_{INF}$ *the fine*. Note that tense has shifted from the lexical verb onto the auxiliary.

Activity 6.4

Negate the following sentences:

a. *The footballer was injured.*
b. *Many could believe his pain.*
c. *The public will demand his head.*

Can you use the contracted form *-n't* in all three cases?

Examples (a) and (b) in Activity 6.4 were easy: all you had to do is place the *not* between the respective auxiliary / modal and the lexical verbs. In both cases you could also cliticise the *not* onto the auxiliary to get the contracted forms *wasn't injured* and *couldn't believe*. Sentence (c) is also unproblematic. The *not* inserts straight between the auxiliary and the lexical verb, as in *The public will not demand his head*. When the auxiliary and the *not* contract, we get a phonological change to *won't*.

Equally important for the syntax of auxiliary verbs is the fact that it is auxiliaries, not lexical verbs, that 'carry' **negation**. We promised to introduce you to different means of representing and identifying sentence structure, such as tree diagrams and other syntactic notations. Here is an example for a dependency grammar called *Word Grammar* (Hudson 2010) which shows that the *not* is attached to the auxiliary *am*, and not to the lexical verb *referring*.

Figure 6.3

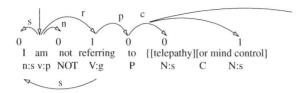

So far we have seen that auxiliary verbs are used to construct questions and negatives. We will add two other characteristics which distinguish auxiliaries from lexical verbs.

When used as auxiliary rather than lexical verbs *be*, *have*, and *do* also manifest **code**. 'Code' is used for this property because auxiliaries and *do* also represent or 'code' the omitted main verb in these constructions, as in

3. *Does Mary turn twenty-four today? Yes, she does.*
4. *Mary is turning twenty-four today, and so is Anne Belle.*

The base and progressive participle forms of the verb *turn* have been elided in the stranded second mention of the verbal complex. The auxiliary *is* and the third-person-singular form of *do* therefore display the phenomenon of code, i.e. the ability of auxiliaries to occur without the lexical verb.

Emphasis, the third property of auxiliaries we are looking into, is not a syntactic criterion, but a phonological one. It is nonetheless very useful, especially in situations when we want to stress the truth of a statement that has been called into question. For example, if Anne Belle is trying to deny that she is turning twenty-four today, we will say *Yes, she IS turning twenty-four today* and place emphatic or heavy stress on the auxiliary verb, not the lexical one. Auxiliaries can therefore add emphasis to a message.

The four characteristics that distinguish auxiliaries from main verbs form a quite NICE acronym (Aarts 2008: 42). It is auxiliaries (and not main verbs) that

- carry the Negative particle 'not',
- Invert with the subject,
- manifest Code,
- carry Emphatic stress.

The NICE properties of auxiliaries and modals are illustrated in the examples below.

Negation

Tom does   not   skate
Tom is   not   skating
Tom has   not   skated
Tom will   not   skate

Inversion

Does   Jerry   sneeze?
Is   Jerry   sneezing?
Has   Jerry   sneezed?
Will   Jerry   sneeze?

Code

Yes, Jerry   does.
Yes, Jerry   is.
Yes, Jerry   has.
Yes, Jerry   will.

Emphasis

Jerry does sneeze.
Jerry is   sneezing.
Jerry has   sneezed.
Jerry will   sneeze.

To summarise, the verbs *be*, *have*, and *do* can act as both lexical / main and auxiliary verbs. What distinguishes auxiliaries (and modals) from main verbs is that they can be used to construct questions and negatives, and to add emphasis to or give information about the mood or attitude of a speaker or writer (the latter is done by the sub-class of auxiliaries called *modals*). Auxiliaries and modals are sub-classes of verbs whose members are characteristically used to mark syntactic categories.

We have already worked with examples that contain more than one auxiliary / modal, e.g. *many have been invited*. Auxiliaries accumulate in sentences when we want to express meanings which involve more than one of the inflectional categories that can be expressed by verbs (introduced in Section 4.3). The English language, for example, gives us the opportunity to express the meaning of *I think he was invited at some point, but I am not sure if he is still invited* with *He may have been invited*. Short and nice, right? But it comes at a price: auxiliaries start piling up.

Do auxiliaries stack up recursively and more less randomly (like adjectives before nouns), or is there a method in the madness? There is. Depending on what they express, auxiliaries come in a strict order, which is illustrated in the examples below and explored further in the next section.

He shaves/d   present ($_{PRS}$) / past ($_{PST}$) tense
He can/could shave   modality / tense ($_{PRS/PST}$)
He can be shaving   modality / tense + progressive ($_{PROG}$) aspect

He could have shaved	modality / tense + perfective (PERF) aspect
He may have been shaving	modality / tense + PERF + PROG aspect
The customer may have been being shaved	modality / tense + PERF + PROG + passive voice

In order to work out how the modal, auxiliary and lexical verbs and their dependents relate to each other in sentences like *The customer may have been being shaved*, we need to look at some of the inflectional categories of verbs, i.e. modality, tense, aspect (and voice), in a bit more detail. If you are able to

- determine the form and function of all words in the above sentence, and
- tell
  - (a) when the event denoted by the verb happened (tense);
  - (b) if it happened at all or not (mood);
  - (c) if it is ongoing and / or viewed as completed or not (aspect);
  - (d) who did it (agent) and who experienced it (patient) (voice); and
  - (e) how these properties add up,

you can skip the next section.

6.3 Sequence of verbs

The sentence *The customer may have been being shaved* illustrates that a grammatical English sentence can contain up to five verbs. One of them, either a lexical verb or the copula, is always obligatory. The lexical verb is always the last one in a sequence of verbal elements; it can be preceded by up to four auxiliary verbs (including modals). The auxiliaries are optional and belong each to different sub-classes, as we will see below. It is very unusual for all four auxiliaries to appear in one clause, but if they do, they must appear in the sequence indicated in Table 6.1.

Table 6.1. *Sequence of verbs in VP*

	Aux1: MODAL	Aux2: PERF	Aux3: PROG	Aux4: PASS	Main verb
He	may	have	been	being	shaved

Table 6.1 illustrates that all four auxiliaries have different functions, and that we only need one auxiliary of any particular type. It is not possible for an English sentence to contain two modal verbs, or two progressive auxiliaries applied to the same lexical verb, as in *The customer may should have been being shaved*. But of course it is possible to have auxiliaries of the same type in

107

coordinate constructions, as in *You may and must have a shower* or *The customer may have been shaved and lotion may have been applied*. Notice that not all slots need to be filled in a sequence of auxiliaries. If the action denoted by the verbs has not been completed and if we are not even sure if it is happening at all, we would, for example, only use 1 + 3 (modal + progressive), as in *He may be cooking*. If we are sure something has been simmering away for a long time, we will select 2 + 3 (perfective + progressive), as in *The chef has been cooking Gulasch for hours*. Or if we want to focus on the dish rather than the chef, we would pick 1 + 2 + 4 (modal + perfective + passive), as in *The semolina may have been cooked by the chef*.

In a sequence of verbs, each auxiliary furthermore determines the form of the following verb, no matter whether it is another auxiliary or a lexical verb. The form of the main verb is determined by the auxiliary that precedes it, as we can see below:

The supporters must behave in the pub.	MOD determines base form of BEHAVE.
The fans have drunk the bar dry.	Perfective HAVE determines past participle form of DRINK.
They are calling for more snacks.	Progressive BE requires present –*ing* participle.
Pork pies will be served soon.	Passive requires past participle form of SERVE.

In combinations of auxiliaries, the first auxiliary determines the form of the second, the second determines the form of the third and so on, until the fourth determines the form of the lexical verb, as seen in Table 6.1, and illustrated below:

The supporters must have behaved in the pub.	MOD determines base form of HAVE, perfective HAVE determines -*ed* participle form of BEHAVE.
They have been calling for more snacks.	HAVE determines -*ed* participle form of BE; progressive BE requires -*ing* participle form of CALL.

Activity 6.5
Drawing on everything you already know about main / lexical verbs (Section 2.2.3), auxiliary and modal verbs (Section 2.2.4), tense (Section 4.3.1) and aspect (Section 4.3.2) and their respective form and order (this section), explain as clearly as you can the difference between:

> *Henry **pounces** on those sparrows.*   vs. *Henry **pounced** on those sparrows.*
> *Henry **is pouncing** on those sparrows.*   vs. *Henry **was pouncing** on those sparrows.*
> *Henry **has pounced** on those*   vs. *Henry **had pounced** on those sparrows.*
> *sparrows.*
>
> *Henry **has been pouncing** on those*   vs. *Henry **may have been pouncing** on*
> *sparrows.*   *those sparrows.*
>
> Aim at a comprehensive explanation. Comprehensive explanations include an analysis of samples of language on all linguistics levels, i.e. morphological, syntactic, semantic (meaning), pragmatic, discourse.

To summarise this section so far, not only is the form of every verb determined by the auxiliary that precedes it, the various types of auxiliaries also always occur in the same order in English. When you look back over all the examples on the last two pages, you will notice that modals are the first to occur in a sequence of auxiliaries. If there is no modal, tense is always marked on the first auxiliary. Our discussion of inflectional categories will follow the order in which they appear in a sentence. That is, we will start with modals and continue with tense, aspect and voice.

6.3.1 Mood: modal auxiliary verbs

Mood refers to distinctions in the form of the verb that expresses the attitude of the speaker to what is said. The most commonly expressed mood distinction is between imperative (commands, discussed in Section 9.3) and indicative (declarative sentences). Mood is expressed inflectionally in many languages, but in English there are no morphological markers for imperative and indicative. In English, mood is expressed by auxiliary modal verbs, which express possibility, necessity, obligation, etc.

In our brief introductory look at modals and modality in Section 2.2.4, we said that English modal verbs are used to describe an event in terms of whether it is necessary, possible, permissible, desirable and the like. Modality therefore is associated with the contrast between possibility and necessity. This involves two related contrasts, the one between factual and non-factual and the one between asserted and non-asserted propositions.

factual	vs. non-factual
The gardener grew flowers.	vs. *The gardener may / might have grown flowers.*

In the modal or non-factual version of this sentence the growing of flowers is presented as a more or less likely possibility, but not necessarily a fact, as in the non-modal factual reading.

asserted	vs. non-asserted

She sells up today. vs. *She must / can sell up today.*

The non-modal version is a positive statement or assertion. In the modal version of this sentence, *must* is a kind of directive, and *can* a permission (to sell up).

We also mentioned that modals express an expectation / evaluation or judgement on whether an event is likely to happen, or on human control over events. That is, modal verbs can be used in three types of meaning: *epistemic*, *deontic* and *dynamic*. Through epistemic modality the speaker is signalling degrees of knowledge, as in *She may / must / should be leaving soon.* Through deontic modality, the verbs mark the speaker's attitude to social factors of obligation and permission, as in *They may / must should talk it over*. Deontic modals, like epistemic modals, signal speaker's judgements, but while with epistemics the judgement is about the way the real world is, with deontics it is about how people should behave in the world. This means that the use of deontics is tied in with all sorts of social knowledge: the speaker's belief systems about morality and legality; and her estimations of power and authority.

Activity 6.6

Some sentences with modal verbs are ambiguous between an epistemic and a deontic reading. For each of the sentences below, try to imagine two contexts: one where the sentence might be used with an epistemic reading and the other a deontic reading.

a. *Alcohol may not be served to persons under eighteen.*
b. *You can go home now.*
c. *We could take the examination early.*
d. *You will not leave the island.*
e. *We should be at the hotel by nine.*

(*Saeed 1997: 136*)

To summarise, semantically we need to distinguish three different uses of auxiliaries / modals:

- Epistemic uses measure the likelihood or necessity of an event against our knowledge.
- Deontic uses indicate permission and / or obligation.
- Dynamic uses attribute certain abilities to individuals (e.g. *Eva can ride a bicycle*).

Most of the important morpho-syntactic characteristics of English modals have already been mentioned in Chapter 2: like all lexical and auxiliary verbs, modals have present and past tense forms (the exception is *must*), which do not relate to time but to the distinctions between possibility and necessity we have just explored. Nonetheless, modals are always finite and, like all tensed forms, they are the first to occur in a sequence of auxiliaries, as in *She must have been seeing him for several years*. Modals do not take typical verb endings: they don't take the agreement morpheme *-s* in the present tense when the subject of the sentence is third-person singular, and they also do not have participle forms. Syntactically modals require their complements to be in the base / infinitival forms.

Mood therefore is to modality as tense is to time: tense and mood are categories of grammatical forms, while time and modality are associated categories of meaning. We will look at tense next because our discussion of it in Chapter 4 covered only the inflectional basics.

6.3.2 Tense

As a way of tying this section to the previous one, we can say that tense is a morpho-syntactic way of referring to the time when some action, event or state takes place in relation to the moment of speaking (e.g. in the past, present or future). Of course, tense is not the only way of referring to time: we can use adverbials (like *yesterday*, *next week*, *in 1984*) to place an event in time. Tense is indicated by the form of the verb; it is marked inflectionally (i.e. by means of suffixes on the verb) in English. That's why tense got its first mention in Chapter 4. In English there are two tenses (present and past), both of which are related to distinctions in time. While English can refer to future events, it does not have a suffix indicating future.

The present tense is used to describe events and activities which include not only the present, but the past and the future as well: *all internal angles in a triangle add up to 180 degrees*; *we are both lecturers*; *it rains a lot in London*. As we have just seen, (regular) verbs have two forms for the present: the base form (*add* and *are* in the earlier examples), and the *-s* form (*rains*), which is used to show agreement with third-person-singular (pronoun) subjects (e.g. *he / she / it*). Plural and other subjects take the base form.

The present-tense morpheme, therefore, only shows when the subject of the sentence can be replaced with one of the three third-person-singular pronouns *he / she / it* (...). Only then do we get a morphological change to a word which reflects the characteristics of some other word it is in a syntactic relation with. We called this *agreement* in Chapter 4.

Agreement is a syntactic relation in which the inflectional form of a word or phrase is determined by the properties of another word or phrase (which is almost always a noun). We said that in English only agreement in person and number is expressed by inflectional morphology, as in *those*PL *sparrows*PL (where the PL subscript indicates *plural*). This also holds true for the agreement morphology that marks syntactic relations within a sentence; e.g. that *he* is the third-person-singular subject of *run* in *He runs back home*.

The past tense, on the other hand, places an action or situation in the past relative to the moment of speaking, or prior to some other event: *she typed Chapter 5 last week*; *tomorrow she will say that the weather was nice today*. The past tense is always marked in English, and with the exception of a small number of so-called irregular verbs (e.g. *he sold them a nice melon yesterday*; top half of the hour glass), it is always marked with the inflectional suffix *-ed* (past; bottom half of the hour glass).

Figure 6.4

Activity 6.7

If English only has two tenses (present and past), how is future time expressed in English? We have already given you one example (*she will say* in the paragraph on past tense), but can you think of others? Aim for as comprehensive a list as possible.

There is no shortage of ways of referring to the future with the English language, but there is no single inflectional category that marks verbs as future. Sentences 5–14 all clearly describe events and situations in the future, but you will fail to find a morpheme marking future in all of the following sentences, because there is none in English.

5. *I leave tomorrow.*
6. *She starts next week.*
7. *They will submit their essay in November.*
8. *I shall go to town later.*
9. *Jenny is going to give up smoking soon.*
10. *The actress is leaving in forty-five seconds.*
11. *We will be waiting for you.*
12. *I am going to visit France next year.*
13. *The programme is starting in ten minutes.*
14. *I shall be writing again next week.*

English does not indicate future tense by means of an inflection on the verb. (The term 'English future tense' is a misnomer, because if *tense* is the encoding of the notion of *time* in grammar and there is no grammatical way of encoding time in this language, there is no 'English future tense'.) Fortunately, English is not short of resources for expressing future events:

- using present tense (examples 5 and 6),
- using the modal auxiliary *will* (example 7), and the modal *shall* (example 8),
- using the (semi-)auxiliary *be going to* (example 9),
- using present progressive (example 10), and
- by various combinations thereof (examples 11 to 14).

Returning to the order of elements in a verbal sequence, the first or only verb is marked for tense (as well as for person and number). In example sentences 15 and 16, present and past tense are marked on the only verb. The present and past-tense markers are underlined.

15. *She types away.*
16. *She typed away*

Present tense is marked on the first verb in both sentences under example 17, so is past tense on both sentences under example 18. The finite or tense-carrying verbs are underlined again.

17. *She is typing away.*   *She has typed the manuscript.*
18. *She was typing away.*   *She had typed the manuscript.*

Can you remember what the circled forms are and what their function is?

6.3.3 Aspect: progressive BE and perfective HAVE

Tense helps us locate an event in time (present or past). **Aspect** refers to how the same event is viewed by the speaker / writer with respect to time. Aspect is a grammatical category (just like tense and mood), which means it is overtly encoded in English grammar (unlike future). Aspect is indicated by means of the presence of an auxiliary verb, which in turns determines the form of the following verb. Verbs have two aspects: *perfective* and *progressive*.

Perfective aspect looks at a situation / event from the outside, like an astronaut looking at earth from space. This perspective implies a focus on the situation as a whole, i.e. in its totality. English perfect is constructed with a form of auxiliary verb HAVE and a lexical verb in its *-ed* participle form. Looking at a situation / event as a complete whole (perfective aspect) is not only different from looking at a situation from within, with focus on its internal structure (imperfective, see next paragraph), but also independent of time. This is why the two sentences *She has typed the manuscript* and *She had typed the manuscript* are both perfective aspect, but different tense, as we saw in the previous section.

English progressive aspect presents a situation as ongoing, in progress. Clauses constructed with BE plus a lexical verb ending in the progressive morph *-ing* view what is expressed by the main verb as taking place over a stretch of time.

19. *He washed the car.*   (past non-progressive; complete)
20. *He was washing the car.*   (past progressive; incomplete)

We interpret the second sentence as: his washing the car took place over a period of time, it was an ongoing process. Note that both sentences are in the past tense, so time is not an issue. With aspect it is the internal temporal unfolding of an action / event that the speaker puts the focus on. From this point of view there is no difference between *He is / was washing his car*. In both cases, the action / event is described as in progress or ongoing.

In terms of aspect, *He is washing his car* (present progressive) therefore contrasts with *He has washed his car* (present perfective, complete).

To summarise aspect and to contrast it one last time with tense, we can say (with Huddleston and Pullum *et al.* 2005: 51) that aspect refers to how the speaker views the situation described in the clause with respect to its temporal structure or properties, not with respect to its location in time.

6.3.4 Voice: passive BE

The fourth auxiliary in a sequence of five verbs (in one clause) is involved in the construction of passive voice, and passive BE determines the form of the lexical verb immediately to its right, as we have seen in Table 6.1 (repeated below for convenience as Table 6.2).

Table 6.2. *Sequence of verbs in VP*

	Aux1: MODAL	Aux2: PERF	Aux3: PROG	Aux4: PASS	Main verb
He	may	have	been	being	shaved

The participle form of the lexeme SHAVE is a direct consequence of the passive BE preceding it (but the *-ing* ending on the grammatical word *being* is NOT part of the passive construction). For the answer to the question why passive BE is carrying the *-ing* suffix in the example in Table 6.2, see end-of-chapter Exercise 6.3.

In this chapter we take only a brief look at voice, because we will return to it once we have properly dealt with notions like thematic roles and grammatical functions in the next chapter.

The basic idea behind **voice** is that the action of a verb and the person(s) or thing(s) responsible for it can be conveyed in two ways: the active voice and the passive voice. **Active voice** is most common: it expresses the action of the verb, directly linking it to the person or thing carrying out the action. The person or thing carrying out the action will have the thematic role of agent. **Passive voice**, on the other hand, changes the focus of the sentence by reordering the elements / units (NPs) that express its constituent roles (e.g. agent, patient, experiencer, theme, etc.).

Activity 6.8

Turn the following active sentences into passive ones

a. *The public raised certain questions.*
b. *The police apprehended the judge.*
c. *The policeman saw the thief.*

For sentence (a) in Activity 6.8 you took the noun phrase to the right of the lexical verb and put it in place of the noun phrases to the left of the lexical verb, added a form of passive BE before the lexical verb, took the past tense morpheme *-ed* off *raise* and replaced it with the past-participle *-ed* suffix (which fortunately look the same!). Then you either embedded the noun phrase to the left of the lexical verb into a prepositional phrase and added it at the end of the clause or you didn't. From a grammatical point of view it doesn't matter whether you bothered with the second step or not, both *The question was raised by the public* and *The question was raised* are grammatical; in the latter version we, of course, lose the information of who raised the question, but this is deliberate in certain situations or text types, e.g. journalism.

So what you did is 'lose' the thematic / semantic role of the subject noun phrase. In the active voice sentence in example (a) in Activity 6.8, the NP[*the public*] had the active role of AGENT; it performed the action. In the passive sentence (example 21 below), the NP[*certain questions*], which is associated with the passive role of PATIENT (the entity undergoing the effect of some action), is made the subject. You followed exactly the same procedure for examples (b) and (c) in Activity 6.8. Syntactically all three sentences are identical.

21.	*Certain questions*	*were*	*raised*	*by the public*
22.	*The judge*	*was*	*apprehended*	*by the police*
23.	NP[*The thief*]	*was*	*seen*	PP[*by the policeman*]
		(passive *BE*)	(participle)	

We will return to the structural / syntactic differences between active and passive clauses in Chapter 9. For now we can summarise voice by saying that it changes the thematic / semantic role of the subject constituent, adds an auxiliary (passive BE) to the clause, and requires the lexical verb to be in its -*ed* participle form. Together, passive BE and the lexical verbs whose form it determines are always the last two verbs in a sequence of verbal elements.

6.4 The verb phrase

So far we have established that the verb is the most important word in the sentence, and that it heads a verb phrase. But what exactly is the VP made up of? Which sentence elements form part of it, and which ones don't? And how can we tell?

In this book we will go with Thomas (1993), van Gelderen (2002), Fabb (2005) and Burton-Roberts (2010) and assume that:

(i)   the verb phrase contains anything which follows the verb within the same sentence;
(ii) the verb phrase contains the auxiliary / modal verbs which precede the lexical verbs and the negative *not*.

One of the reasons we make these assumptions is to simplify representations of phrase structure in the form of tree diagrams, something we have reserved for the end of this chapter. In concrete terms this means that in the trees we will draw, all auxiliaries will be on the same hierarchical level, none of them higher up and none of them lower down than the others.

In many clauses, the verb phrase makes up most of the sentence. In accordance with assumptions (i) and (ii), everything after *he* is part of the verb phrase in example 24.

24. *He* VP[*may have been reading the newspaper to her*]

But the VP can be analysed further, as in

25. *He* VP[*may have been reading* NP[*the newspaper*] PP[*to* NP[*her*]]]

To show that the verb and the phrases which follow it together form the verb phrase, we will now move the verb's complements and adjuncts round, replace, delete or coordinate them. To demonstrate that the VP includes anything which follows the lexical verb within the same clause, we first move and replace the verb and anything that stays with it in these operations.

26. *Bela believes that he will conquer the world and* [*conquer the world*] *he will _.*

Example 26 shows that the noun phrase *the world* belongs to the verb (phrase) because it moves with it. The sentence even becomes ungrammatical if we move the verb without the NP[*the world*], as illustrated by sentence 27.

27. **Bela believes he will conquer the world and* [*conquer*] *he will _ the world.*

Sentence 27 illustrates that the VP needs to include the noun phrase complement of *conquer;* the NP[*the world*] is an obligatory element of the verb phrase VP[*conquer* NP[*the world*]].

Several exercises in this book have already asked you to delete optional words, phrases and even clauses. Which word / phrase in example 28 can be deleted?

28. *Bela believes he will conquer the world ineluctably and* [*conquer the world ineluctably*] *he will _.*

The adverb *ineluctably* can go. But example 28 also shows that, if we keep it, it forms part of the verb phrase. Why? Because the adverbial phrase AdvP[*ineluctably*] moves along with the verb *conquer* and the obligatory noun phrase NP[*the world*].

Notice that preposing as we have been using it does not support assumption (ii), i.e. that auxiliaries are part of the VP. In fact, it shows the opposite: for this test (for what is part of a verb phrase) to give good / appropriate results, auxiliaries and modals *must* be left stranded. This is what happened to *will* in examples 26 to 28, and what will happen to *has* and *been* in example 29.

29. *Bela says that he has been making films and* [*making films*] *he has been _.*

We even cause ungrammaticality if we, for example, include BE but not HAVE from our movement / preposing activities, as illustrated by example 30.

30.   *Bela says that he has been making films and [been making films] he has _.

Criterion (ii) can be argued for by simply saying that both auxiliaries, modals and *not* go under the VP because they are optional and 'only' express morpho-syntactic inflectional categories of the obligatory lexical verbs. A better argument for the inclusion of all auxiliaries and modals in the VP is the 'do so' test, illustrated in examples 31 to 33.

31.   Bela [conquered the world] and Boris did so too.
32.   Bela [conquered the world] slowly but Boris did so quickly ('did so' replacing V+DO]
33.   Bela [conquered the world slowly] and Boris did so too ('did so' replacing V+DO+Adjunct]

Note that this test does nothing else but delete the verb phrase and replace it with 'do so'. So nothing we aren't already familiar with, really. The only reason why we added sentences 32 and 33 is to show that the obligatory object NP[the world] and the optional AdvP[slowly] really do form part of the verb phrase (VP).

This section is dedicated to determining what a verb phrase is made up of, which elements belong within it, and which ones don't. We also experimented with preposing, replacement and deletion to help us answer this question. This question, however, not only emerges for the VP, but for all phrasal categories. In the following section we will look at some similar experiments which help us determine what other strings of words behave as recognisable groups with an internal structure, i.e. as phrases. This is the last prerequisite we need before we can start drawing trees. So how can we tell which group of words forms which kind of phrase?

6.5 Finding phrases

We have already conducted several small-scale 'experiments' on whether particular groups of words cluster together round a verbal head, i.e. on the verb phrase. Now we will use similar procedures to test whether other strings of words form phrases, too. Fortunately, we do not need a chemistry lab for this. We only need what we have been practising since Chapter 1: grammaticality judgements. The aim of our experiments will be to test what strings of words behave as phrases. Speakers should be able to manipulate these strings of words as a single chunk, these strings should have an internal structure, and they should fall into nameable sub-groups with significant common properties. How will we measure the success of these experiments? If we are dealing with something which isn't a phrase, the result of our experiment will be an ungrammatical sentence. We will provide you with guidelines for three different experiments: *substitution* (including deletion / ellipsis), *movement* (including clefting and pseudo-clefting) and *coordination*.

6.5.1 Substitution

One possible way of determining whether a string of words forms a unit is to show that it behaves like a word. Recall that a single word can form a phrase. What we are investigating is whether the string of words we are looking at can be substituted by a single word. If it can, the string will be a phrase. Remember that many words also have an internal structure (as discussed in Chapters 3 and 4), so, to be on the safe side, we will use roots of words for our experiments.

Activity 6.9

Our hypothesis is that if a string X can be replaced by a single word, this is some evidence that X is a phrasal unit. We are going to test this hypothesis by:

1. selecting a grammatical string X;
2. replacing X in kind by a root.

If the result is well formed, we conclude that X is a phrase.

Select grammatical strings from the following sentence and subject them to the substitution test. Try to make sure that X and its replacement are as similar in meaning as possible.

The woman in the green skirt will put a stamp of the library in your books today.

[*The woman in the green skirt*] *will put* [*a stamp of the library*] [*in your books*] *today.*

[*She*]   *will put* [*it/one*]   [*there*]   *today.*

This experiment works particularly well for noun phrases: if a string X can be replaced by a pronoun, this is some evidence that X is an NP. This test is therefore called *pronominalisation*. But we saw that we can also replace [*a stamp of the library*] with *one*: if a string X can be replaced by *one*, this is some evidence that X is a NP. This is called '*one*' substitution. We have already practised '*do so*' substitution in the previous sections. Does it also work here? Which string X can be replaced by *do so*? The string [*put a stamp of the library in your books today*] can be replaced by *do so*. This is some evidence that X is a VP. And because we assumed that the verb phrase contains the auxiliary verbs which precede the verb, we also include *will* in the VP.

Very similar to substitution is deletion or *ellipsis*, this is omission of understood material. If a string X can be deleted, this is some evidence that X is a phrase. This test works particularly well for all optional phrases, like the PPs PP[*with a green skirt*] and PP[*of the library*] and the adverbial phrase AdvP[*today*], but also for obligatory verb and noun phrases as in the exchange illustrated in example 34:

34. *A: Will the woman in the green skirt put a stamp of the library in your books today?*
    B: No, but the man in the black jumper will __(i.e. put a stamp of the library in your books today).

Phrases of the same type can furthermore frequently be swapped round, as in

35. NP[*The chemistry student*] *saw* NP[*the psychology tutor*] *at the rowing club*.

36. NP[*The psychology tutor*] *saw* NP[*the chemistry student*] *at the rowing club*.

It's not surprising that, if substitution works, *swapping* will work too, because swapping is really just doing two replacements at once.

Successful *substitution*, *ellipsis* and *swapping* indicate that the initial phrase X and its substitution share a distributional property. This is a characteristic of phrases which we will utilise in the next experiment.

6.5.2 Movement

Distributionally, phrases behave as single units of structure. We can therefore assume that, as single units, phrases may have the ability to appear in a variety of sentence positions. We hypothesise that, if a string X can be moved to another position, this is some evidence that X is a phrase. When we shift a phrase all the way to the left of a clause, we *topicalise* it, i.e. we draw attention to it by virtue of its unusual positioning.

37. AdjP[*Today*] *the woman will put a stamp in your books, not tomorrow*.
38. NP[*A stamp*] *the woman will put in your books, not a marker*.
39. PP[*In your books*] *the woman will put the stamp, not in your notepad*.
40. VP[*Put a stamp in your books*] *the woman will not rip out a page*.

These examples illustrate that topicalisation works well for AdvPs, NPs, PPs, but also VPs (VP preposing).

Another type of movement is called *clefting*, because what you do in this experiment is split clauses. This type of sentences are discussed in further detail in Chapter 10. This experiment takes the following format:

Activity 6.10

Starting from some acceptable string XYZ, we form the new string: *It* + form of the verb BE + XYZ + who/that + clause. Try it out on various phrases from the sentence

   Cara wants to look at your assignment after class.

If the result is acceptable, this is evidence that Y is a constituent of XYZ.

---

41.   *It is* NP[*your assignment*] *that / which Cara wants to look at.*
42.   *It is* PP[*after class*] *that Cara wants to look at your assignment.*
43.   *It is* NP[*Cara*] *who wants to look at your assignment.*

These examples illustrate that clefting works particularly well for noun and prepositional phrases. A related experiment, called *pseudo-clefting*, also works for VPs and AdjPs, as in the following sentences.

44.   *Mehmet will* VP[*serve fish and chips tomorrow*].
45.   *What Mehmet will do tomorrow is* VP[*serve fish and chips*].
46.   *Her colleagues are* AdjP[*afraid of being sacked*].
47.   *What her colleagues are is* AdjP[*afraid of being sacked*].

Can you extract the pseudo-clefting experimental guidelines from these two examples? OK, starting from a grammatical string XYZ, we form the new string *What* + X + form of BE + Y. If the result is grammatical, we've collected evidence that Y is a constituent of XYZ.

6.5.3 Coordination

In Chapter 2 we identified *and*, *but* and *or* as coordinating conjunctions. We are now going to employ them in an experiment that tests whether strings of words form phrases. We hypothesise that if a string X can be coordinated with a word (or phrase), this is some evidence that X is a word (or phrase) of the same category as the word (or phrase) it is coordinated with. This is because coordination joins similar elements.

   The coordination experiments can be conducted with all sorts of units.

Activity 6.11

Determine the coordinated units in sentences (a) to (f). Enclose them in square brackets and name them with the appropriate sub-scripts.

---

a. *The woman with the red and green skirt will end her shift soon.*
b. *The woman with the red skirt and the man with the blue jumper don't get on.*
c. *I like my pasta with no sauce and in a bowl.*
d. *They are teasing each other but fighting at the same time.*
e. *Clumsily and very heavily, Henry jumped on those sparrows.*
f. *He loves her or he hates her.*

The coordinated elements are adjectives / adjective phrases in example (a), noun phrases in (b), prepositional phrases in (c), verb phrases in (d), adverb phrases in (e), and clauses in (f). This experiment also teaches us that there are two constraints on coordination:

- only units of the same size can be coordinated, e.g. words, phrases or clauses; and
- only units of the same category can be conjoined, with the resulting string being also of that category, e.g. AdjP + AdjP = AdjP, PP + PP = PP, VP + VP = VP, NP + NP = NP etc.

Coordination is an extremely powerful tool because it never seems to fail. This is also important because if we can safely assume: 'if a string X can be coordinated with a word (or phrase or clause), this is evidence that X is a word (or phrase or clause) of the same category as the word (or phrase) it is coordinated with', words, phrases and clauses are psychologically real units of language. This brings us full circle and we can move on to notation.

6.6 Representing sentence structure

Sentence structure is not always immediately available (even in written language), so a special notation that would make it visible is a good idea. We have already been using one for quite a while, i.e. bracketing. We enclosed our phrases in square brackets and named them after their head (in subscript capital letters ending in P for 'phrase'). We have done this for individual phrases and have shown that phrases can be embedded in other phrases. It is particularly important that you close every bracket you open, otherwise the bracketing system is no longer meaningful!

So far we haven't bracketed a whole sentence. Let's do this with our example from the previous section:

$_S$[$_{NP}$[*The woman* $_{PP}$[*in* $_{NP}$[*the* $_{AdjP}$[*green*] *skirt*]]] $_{VP}$[*will put* $_{NP}$[*a stamp* $_{PP}$[*of* $_{NP}$[*the library*]]] $_{PP}$[*in* $_{NP}$[*your books*]] $_{AdvP}$[*today*]]].

We have been supporting the stationery industry for years by suggesting colour-coding to our students, i.e. red for VPs, blue for NPs, yellow for AdjPs, green for AdvPs, etc. The sentence *The woman in the green skirt will put a stamp of the library in your books today* isn't even particularly complex, yet it shows that brackets can turn rather dense when we deal with more complex structures. This is why we can use trees or other notation systems like the one illustrated below.

The structure of a clause like *Bela loves Gulasch* can be represented in diagram form as shown. This diagram already functions as a link to the next chapter, as it not only includes information about the categories of the various units (i.e. words, phrases, clauses, etc.), but also *shows* you information about their function (i.e. subject, predicate, object, etc.).

Figure 6.5

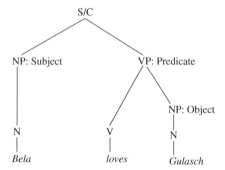

The units in the tree are given two labels: the first indicates their forms / categories, the second their functions.

This is what we know by simply looking at the tree:

- *Bela loves Gulasch* is a clause (or sentence).
- There are two main elements (phrases, constituents) at the higher level, functioning as subject and predicate.
- The subject precedes the predicate.
- The subject is an NP, and the predicate is a VP.
- The VP contains a verb and a (direct) object.
- The verb precedes the object.
- The object is an NP.

What follows are some rules of thumb for doing tree diagrams which are built on things you already know.

(1) Find the lexical verbs.

For each lexical verb there will be (i) one associated verb phrase and (ii) one associated clause. We said that we can easily identify how many clauses there are in the sentence by counting the number of lexical verbs.

(2)   Put S or C (for *sentence* or *clause*), somewhere in the middle of an empty page.

From here on, personal preference determines your method: you can start from the words and work your way up to the S/C node, or you can begin at that node and work your way down towards the actual lexical elements. Try it out on several examples to find what works best for you, but what you will need to end up with is an upside-down tree, with every unit (word, phrase, clause) labelled, named and joined to the overall structure. The following steps illustrate a top-down approach.

(3)   Draw two branches directly from S, and label them NP and VP.
(4)   Under NP, diagram the phrase functioning as grammatical subject.
(5)   Under VP, put separate labelled nodes for the verb and each of the phrases functioning as its complements.
(6)   Diagram each of those, one at a time.

In the following chapter we will discuss trees in a bit more detail, and illustrate how they can be used to represent different sentence structures.

6.7 Chapter summary

In this chapter we first went over the distinction between lexical, auxiliary and modal verbs again. This was deemed necessary because in exceptional cases up to five verbs can occur in a grammatical English sentence. We then established that the last one is always the lexical verb, and if there are several auxiliaries and one of them is a modal, the modal will be first to occur in the sequence of verbs. The modals furthermore express modality, and fulfil the requirement of every English sentence to have one tensed verb. The other auxiliaries have the following functions: they carry tense (in the absence of modals) and express perfective aspect, progressive aspect, and passive voice. But they do not do this on their own, but with the verb immediately to their right, whose forms they also determine.

We then looked at evidence for verb phrase and ways of establishing which words belong together as phrases. It turned out that substitution (including deletion / ellipsis), movement (including clefting and pseudo-clefting) and coordination are pretty reliable linguistic experiments for detecting phrasal categories. We needed to do all this before we could attempt our first structural representation of an entire sentence in the form of an upside-down tree.

Key terms

Aspect; *do*-support; ellipsis; negation; subject-auxiliary inversion (SAI); tense; voice.

Exercises

Exercise 6.1   Identify the type of auxiliary underlined in the sentences below (passive, perfective, etc.)

It <u>must</u> be your skin
I <u>do</u> not know
Peter <u>would</u> be able to help

Exercise 6.2   Construct sentences according to the following templates

- NP + VP,
- NP including a pre-modified AdjP + VP including a PP,
- Post-modified NP + VP including an AdvP,
- NP + VP including an NP,
- PP + NP + VP including two NPs, one of them pre-modified.

An example for a pre-modified NP followed by a VP including a post modified NP and a PP is

NP[*The* AdjP[*experienced*] *builder*] VP[*erects* NP[*scaffolding* PP[*with* NP[*netting*]]] PP[*around* NP[*the house*]]]

Exercise 6.3   In the main chapter text we said that the participle form of the lexeme SHAVE is a direct consequence of the passive BE preceding it, **but** the *-ing* ending on the grammatical word *being* is NOT part of the passive construction. Why is passive BE carrying the *-ing* suffix?
    There are two possible answers to this question.

- One is that it is a gerund, the hybrid noun / verb we introduced in Chapter 2, as in *Being at home (and not at work) would be wonderful.*
- The second possibility is that it is the *-ing* participle form of verbs.

Which one is it, and how can you rule one answer out completely? The answer lies in the syntactic relations *being* enters into.

Further Reading
On the structure of VP, consult Thomas (1993); van Gelderen (2002); Fabb (2005); and Burton-Roberts (2011). On NICE properties, consult Aarts (2008). On

constituency, see Radford (2004). The section on semantic argumentation is also inspired by Aarts (2008). On tense, see Comrie (1985) and Palmer (2001). On aspect, see Comrie (1976). On mood, modality and modal verbs, see Coates (1983); Palmer (1990); Collins (2009); Depraetere and Reed (2006); and Facchinetti et al. (2003).

Consolidation chapter 1

The first three linked tasks of this consolidation chapter aim at helping you distinguish

- language use which is really 'ungrammatical' according to standard English, as opposed to 'difficult to process' or 'nonsensical' (Task 1.1),
- uses which represent regional and / or social variation (Task 1.2), and
- uses which are ruled out by prescriptivists only (Task 1.3).

Task 1.1

Take a close look at sentences (a) to (j)[1] and decide which ones are grammatical, which ones are marginally grammatical (and should therefore be preceded by '?' to indicate uncertain acceptability) and which ones are ungrammatical (and should therefore be preceded by '*') in the variety of English you are most familiar with. Make sure you distinguish 'ungrammatical' from 'nonsensical' (which is a semantic concept) and / or 'difficult to process' (which refers to how easy / difficult it is to understand a sentence when you read / hear it).

a. *I will try to give up smoking this year.*
b. *Give up smoking I will certainly try to.*
c. *To give up smoking, I will certainly try.*
d. *I never heard a green horse smoke a dozen oranges.*
e. *He's muscular and a pretty good mat wrestler.*
f. *Go you to school.*
g. *Run youse to the telephone.[2]*
h. *Clive promised Claire to shave himself.*
i. *Clive promised Claire to shave herself.*

---

[1] Examples (a) to (d) and (g) are from Radford (2004); example (e) is from Pullum (2007); examples (h) and (i) are discussed in Hornstein and Polinsky (2010); and example (j) has been provided by Annabel Cormack.

[2] *Youse* is the plural form of *you* in many UK varieties of English. It corresponds to American English *y'all.*

j. *The claim that the link between convection heating and the time and energy which can be saved by baking biscuits in a convection oven rather than a conventional oven is not obvious at first sight is undoubtedly true.*

Huddleston and Pullum et al. (2002: 11) suggest that, when judging grammaticality,

> [t]he evidence we use comes from several sources: our own intuitions as native speakers of the language; the reactions of other native speakers we consult when we are in doubt; data from computer corpora ... and data presented in dictionaries and other scholarly work on grammar. We alternate between the different sources and cross-check them against each other, since intuitions can be misleading and texts can contain errors. Issues of interpretation often arise.

As you can see, English is not contained in any one's brain, dictionary or grammar book, so we need to rely on many different sources of information when making grammaticality judgements.

Task 1.2

Can you identify which non-standard UK dialects the following utterances originate from? Rewrite them in standard English and highlight what you have modified. Which word classes, morphemes and / or grammatical constructions are most frequently involved in the differences?

a. *I wasn't just sat at a desk, doing nothing.*
b. *This one is more easier to use.*
c. *They ran that fast, they fell over.*
d. *It's dead good.*
e. *There's people who's got arthritis.*
f. *See if you can mak it gan in the middle.*
g. *We'll lend someone else's.*
h. *We need them, to dry wirself.*
i. *Do it up ... geatt tight.*
j. *You cannae cook it on a fire.*
k. *... twenty mile away ...*
l. *And them will have to find jobs and all that.*
m. *It weren't going to be built.*
n. *It don't work.*
o. *We started first, isn't it?*
p. *We ain't got enough.*

(Data from Hudson and Holmes (1995))

Task 1.3

Formulate the prescriptive rules that would consider the sentences below wrong. Most of the 'usage' boxes in good dictionaries deal with prescriptive uses of language. Very good dictionaries have the advantage of explaining why these rules came into existence in the first place. Most of the time there are historical reasons that do not apply to current language usage.

a. *Data was collected over a number of years.*
b. *I lay.*
c. *I am disinterested in this TV show, I think I'll read a book instead.*
d. *I'll learn you to ride a bike.*

Task 1.4

Consider the phrase *all the other books*. Do you think it is grammatical? Play with it by systematically deleting one, two or three words at a time. Which combinations are grammatical, which ones are not? For example, if we delete the first word of the string, *the other books* is fine; if we delete the last word, it isn't: **all the other*. The results (grammatical or ungrammatical) have fairly little to do with the sequential positions in which the words appear, as *all other books* and *the other books* illustrate. Rather, the resulting grammaticality has more to do with the word class these words belong to.

The somewhat unusual thing about *all the other books* is that three of the words can be analysed as belonging to the same word class (which explains why we can delete one, two or all three of them in this particular example), and we can differentiate separate sub-classes (which is why they can co-occur).

Task 1.5

How many different words, word-forms, lexemes and grammatical words do each of the following example sentences contain?

a. *I cycled to work yesterday, and this morning the campaigners have cycled to Trafalgar Square.*
b. *Many prestigious banks have branches on the banks of the river Thames.*
c. *She cuts some cling film to wrap the cut of meat in; having cut it, she wishes her husband cut it all the time.*

Task 2.1

Underline all the non-words in this well-known poem by Lewis Carroll.

'Twas brillig, and the slithy toves
Did gyre and gimble in the wabe:
All mimsy were the borogoves,
And the mome raths outgrabe.
'Beware the Jabberwock, my son!
The jaws that bite, the claws that catch!
Beware the Jubjub bird, and shun
The frumious Bandersnatch!'
He took his vorpal sword in hand:
Long time the manxome foe he sought –
So rested he by the Tumtum tree,
And stood awhile in thought.
And, as in uffish thought he stood,
The Jabberwock, with eyes of flame,
Came whiffling through the tulgey wood,
And burbled as it came!
One, two! One, two! And through and through
The vorpal blade went snicker-snack!
He left it dead, and with its head
He went galumphing back.
'And, has thou slain the Jabberwock?
Come to my arms, my beamish boy!
O frabjous day! Callooh! Callay!'
He chortled in his joy.
'Twas brillig, and the slithy toves
Did gyre and gimble in the wabe:
All mimsy were the borogoves,
And the mome raths outgrabe.

- Make a list of all non-words in the poem, and assign them to word classes.
- What helped you assign these word forms to classes? Morphology? The position of the word in the sentence? Whether they are obligatory or optional? The type of words they are related to? Whether or not they are dominant words / heads of phrases or clauses? (Incidentally, do these questions ring a bell?)
- Order your word-class lists according to the number of non-words they contain. Which are the three longest lists?

- Which word classes are not represented in your lists of non-words at all? Why do you think that is?
- What's the umbrella term for all the word classes that 'accept' new words? And what is the one for those word classes that are not open to new members?

Task 2.2

Fill the blanks in the two sentences in (a) with **all** first-, second- and third-person-singular and -plural personal pronouns, and the blanks in the two sentences in (b) with **all** first-, second- and third-person-singular and -plural possessive determiners.

| a. | _____ *blinked his eyes* | _____ *held my tongue* |
| b. | *She blinked _____ eyes* | *We held ____ tongue* |

The exercise should yield two grammatical and ten ungrammatical sentences for both (a) and (b). Explain what causes the ungrammaticality (you should come up with two reasons, one to do with case, and one to do with co-reference).

Task 2.3

In the following data,

- identify and remove all affixes in the underlined words; then
- determine the word class of the base.

what's the word class of the words before you removed the affixes?

a. *They ducked when two ducks with their five ducklings flew over.*
b. *She ducks now.*
c. *They know that there is no point in ducking the issue.*

Task 2.4

In examples (a)–(h), are the underlined words adjectives or adverbs?

a. *My train arrived late.* AV
b. *I watched the late film.* ADJ
c. *We enjoy fast songs.* ADJ

d.   *He drives too fast.* AV
e.   *He goes to the pub daily.* A V
f.   *'The Sun' is a daily newspaper.* ADJ
g.   *I work best in a quiet room.* AV
h.   *This is the best present I've received.* ADJ

Task 2.5

Underline all prepositions and ⃝circle⃝ all conjunctions in the following extract.

The majority of tropical shores, in contrast, are not backed by dune systems ... but are colonized by fast-growing vegetation ... This may be because the sand is more often kept damp by rain, and hence is in general more stable. In spite of the predominant juxtaposition of sandflats and sand dunes on temperate shores, the two environments have seldom been considered together. The sandflats are regarded as the province of marine biologists, while the dunes are investigated by terrestrial biologists. This unfortunately means that the junction of the two is often neglected. To some extent it must be admitted that this also reflects the relatively sudden change in conditions between flat and dune.

(ICE-GB:W2A-022)

Are there cases where you are not sure to which of the two classes a word belongs? Fish them out and try to work out what these examples have in common.

If you are not sure, go back to the relevant sections on prepositions and conjunctions in Chapter 2, and to the diagnostic tests for phrases discussed in Chapters 5 and 6. And here is an additional hint: it is likely that you are looking at a conjunction if the word in question heads a group of words that is bigger than a phrase.

Task 2.6

Do the underlined words in the text below function as adverbs or as prepositions?

a.   *The escaped dogs randomly ran around.* AV
b.   *Go up the street and keep to the left. Around the corner you will find a shop. Behind the shop is a garage. But make sure you don't get left behind.* AV P
c.   *He drove off the carriageway.* AV
d.   *Climb up quickly, and sit by me.* AV P

What helps you decide? Morphology? The position of the words in the sentence? Whether they are obligatory or optional? The type of words they are related to? Whether the underlined words are the heads of phrases or clauses?

Again, do these questions ring a bell? They are the five questions we said (in Chapter 5) we would be asking again and again when analysing the structure of phrases and sentences.

Task 2.7

In Chapter 2, we briefly looked at some preposition-like elements that form a close idiomatic relationship with verbs. We said that these elements are then called *particles* and the resulting verbs are called (phrasal) verbs. To get a grip on this type of verbs, from the list in the box below, select the phrasal verb that best replaces the underlined verb in sentences (a) to (h).

> *make up, draw up, give up, look up, speed up, blow up, sum up, catch up, stir up, come up*

a. *After fire engulfed it, the building <u>exploded</u>.*
b. *After you have read the chapter, <u>summarise</u> it in two paragraphs.*
c. *Can you <u>walk faster</u> and catch up with them?*
d. *Before you write an essay, you should <u>prepare</u> an outline.*
e. *The marathon runner <u>abandoned</u> his effort.*
f. *Every time this student is late for class she <u>creates</u> a wild and unbelievable story.*
g. *Some people always <u>cause</u> trouble.*
h. *The keen student <u>searched for</u> some important study materials.*

This task should have been easy for native speakers of English, but more difficult for non-native speakers. If you have not acquired English from birth, you have to learn these idiomatic uses of verbs like single lexical items.

To get additional practice on the syntax of verb + preposition + (extended) noun phrase sequences, take a good look at sentences (i) and (j) and decide in which one *up* is the verb's particle (with the extended noun phrase as the verb's object), and in which one it is a preposition (and thus the head of a prepositional phrase which provides additional information about the direction of the running).

i. *He ran up big hills.*
j. *He ran up big bills.*

If you find this difficult, reverse the order of the preposition and the noun phrase, as in

k. *He ran big bills up.*
l. **He ran big hills up.*

The two analyses are quite easy to distinguish. If it is possible to reverse the order of the preposition-like element and the noun phrase (as in (k)), the preposition is the verb's particle and the noun phrase is the verb's object. If it is not possible to reverse the order preposition-like element and (as in (l)), we have scrambled the word order of a prepositional phrase, and the preposition is the head of the prepositional phrase (and not a particle).

Task 3.1

How many morphs and allomorphs represent the plural morpheme, and the past-tense morpheme in English? Base your answers on the examples under (a) and (b). You will have to rely on orthographic and phonetic information, i.e. you will have to say the following words out loud:

(a)

pictures	*pots*	*boxes*
tissues	*cups*	*buses*
blinds	*books*	*suitcases*

(b)

pictured	*scraped*	*potted*
bussed	*rocked*	*waited*
sneezed	*stuffed*	*tasted*

Put your answers in the following table:

Morpheme	Morph	Allomorph (phonetic form)
{PLURAL}		
————	————	————————————
————	————	————————————
{PAST}		
————	————	————————————
————	————	————————————

Task 3.2

Like in Activity 1.4, sort the following words into two groups: one in which the letter sequence *un-* represents a morpheme (i.e. an indivisible unit which is either meaningful in itself or marks a grammatical function), and another one in which *un-* does not have any identifiable grammatical or semantic value.

> *uncover, uncle, untidy, under, undulate, unjust, undress, universe, unleash*

Task 3.3

Is *ric* in *bishopric* a suffix?
What about *feck* in *feckless*? Is it a prefix? Is it a suffix?

Task 3.4

Identify the morphological processes involved in the underlined words.

a. *I've been to so many holy places in Thailand that I'm actually templed-out.*
b. *The government has been trying to demagogue the issue of immigration.*
c. *Hong Kong is very far from London, and it took me a few days to dejet-lag.*
d. *This sample belongs to an unoaked variety of wine.*
e. *I am busy quality-assuring the modules for next year.*
f. *We are looking for REF-able publications.*
g. *Every woman's wardrobe should include an LBD.*
h. *My USB is not working properly.*
i. *Mike doesn't get stuck in the detail, he's a getter-on.*
j. *My new classmate is very sitnextoable.*
k. *We are planning a family but want to go on a babymoon first.*
l. *The economic recession brought staycations back into fashion.*

Task 3.5

What – morphologically speaking – happened to the poor *hamburger* before it could become a *cheeseburger*? Clue: identify the root, which in this case is a common noun designating a place name in Germany. Then check if that root is still there in *cheeseburger*.

A similar morphological process brings about the following joke:

My mum is an alcoholic, my Dad a workaholic, and I'm a Catholic.

Task 3.6

What's odd about the following examples? They all seem to contain comparative forms of the adjective *bad*. But do they? And are they all grammatical? Which sentence contains the ungrammatical form? Which one is *not* a comparative?

a. *More bad news are coming from Indonesia.*
b. *Worse news are coming from Indonesia.*
c. *Badder news coming from Indonesia.*

Do sentences (a) to (c) mean the same thing?

Task 3.7

Which morphological processes yield the forms related to *hand* and *log* in examples (a) to (d)? Use a two-step approach: first determine the word class of the different lexemes of HAND and LOG; then describe the morphological processes used to derive the forms in (b), (c) and (d).

a. *My hand is dirty*
b. *I have to hand out my registration to the authorities*
c. *My handouts get good feedback from the students*
d. A: *Have you logged this on the web?*
   B: *No, I haven't created a web-log yet.*
   A: *Do you mean you haven't got a blog? Then you're no blogger.*

Task 3.8

In Chapter 3 we looked at compound nouns. In this task we want to determine

- whether the forms *lived*, *hearted*, *natured* and *winded* under (a) are free or bound morphemes;
- which word class each word in the compounds under (a) and (b) belong to; and
- which word class the compounds themselves (as wholes) belong to.

This task may be easier if you embed the words into grammatical sentences you construct yourself. The following example illustrates the process on the example *user-friendly* from the (a) list.

You are the user of this book, and we intend this exercise to be approachable/friendly to you; you can then say that this exercise is user-friendly.

a. *fool-proof, good-natured, long-lived, seaworthy, far-sighted, under-developed, world-wide, kind-hearted, user-friendly, overwhelming, long-winded, outspoken*
b. *underline, freeze-dry, manhandle, over-rate, whitewash, down-size, blacklist, sidestep, upgrade*

The notion of *head* (which we developed in relation to phrases) can also be applied to morphology. Like in syntax, the head of a word is the element that determines the properties of this word. Which word in the compounds listed under (a) and (b) is the head of the compound? For instance, *user-friendly* is composed of a noun (*user*) and an adjective (*friendly*): the resulting compound is an adjective, so the head is *friendly* and not *user*. Try to describe this consistency as a linguistic rule. Informally speaking, we can say that _____. What you should have ended up with is called the *English right hand head rule* (RHHR, Williams 1981).

Task 4.1

For each word in the following example, underline all *roots* with a single line, all *bases* with an interrupted line and all *stems* with a squiggly line.

As the nature and function of the brain has become better understood, the power of conventional computers has similarly increased to the point where simulations of highly interconnected brain-like systems have become possible and inevitable. In addition, the emergence of new techniques of implementation of the high connectivities seen in brains ... have spurred interest in the study of brain-like architectures ... The artificial neuron usually takes the form of a processing element with a large number of inputs which are summed to produce an excitation. The single output is then produced by applying a nonlinear activation function to the excitation.

(ICE-GB:W2A-032)

Task 4.2

For each sentence, underline derivational affixes and circle inflectional affixes

a. *Staying warm during winter is easier when you are a duck.*
b. *The youngest daughters are being awarded the highest degrees of honour.*
c. *His helplessness was really infuriating.*
d. *The humidifier in my office cabinet has broken down, but the rest of the humidifiers in the building are working perfectly.*
e. *My club is a sad place.*

Task 4.3

Are the underlined morphemes in sentences (a) to (g) derivational or inflectional? If they are derivational, state whether they are meaning-changing or word-class-changing. If they are inflectional, state what grammatical category they encode.

a. *Jeremy drink-s the beer very quickly.*
b. *The beer-s are going down very well today.*
c. *He drinks fast-er than his friends.*
d. *His friend the sing-er doesn't approve of his drinking.*
e. *The kill-er murdered the hamster with a hammer.*
f. *Eleonora has passed her driv-ing test.*
g. *The sheepdog was chas-ing the goat.*

Task 4.4

Why are the asterisked examples in (a) to (c) ungrammatical if they

(i) look very similar to the ones immediately above them, and
(ii) involve the same morphological processes?

   Work on this task without any hints first. If you don't get anywhere, use the guidelines below the examples.

a.	i.	*right*	*rightist*	*rightists*
	ii.	*right*	*rights*	**rightsist*
b.	i.	*foot*	*football*	*footballs*
	ii.	*foot*	*feet*	**feetball*
c.	i.	*sleepwalk*	*sleepwalked*	
	ii.	*sleepwalk*	**sleptwalk*	

(Examples Cornelia Hamann)

   If this task proved difficult without guidelines, start by dividing all the words in the middle and rightmost columns into morphs. Identify which morphological categories the morphs belong to. Then check which morphological process is applied to which morph.

   Does the ungrammaticality of the asterisked example words indicate that these morphological processes have to be applied in a particular order?

   The morphological jungle of English is not very deep in comparison with other languages. If you emerged from our guided tour intact, you will have found that the examples in this exercise illustrate that derivational processes have to apply before inflectional ones. This holds true for all known languages and therefore creates a linguistic universal.

But how universal is this universal, given the following example (which is not a one-off, by the way)?

'We kept our heads and there were no <u>sendings-off</u>,' he added.

(Daily Post North Wales, 28 December 2011)

Task 4.5

How many morphemes are there in the following words? Identify the morphological forms which realise each morpheme, using the 'proper' notational form as illustrated for *walked* and *doors*.

{WALK}	{PAST}		{DOOR}	{PLURAL}
walk-	ed		door-	s

walked	watched	were	sang
doors	staplers	fish (pl)	geese

Watched and *staplers* are the straightforward examples and they work according to the same principles as *walked* and *doors*.

Morphologically, however, *were* and *sang* can be analysed in the same way as *walked*, and *fish* and *geese* can be analysed the same way as *doors*. Let's look at the individual examples:

were =	{BE}	{PAST}
fish =	{FISH}	{PLURAL}
geese =	{GOOSE}	{PLURAL}

The problem with *were* is that it bears no phonetic relation to *be*. This is known as **suppletion**. Other examples of suppletion are *good / better, bad / worse*. Can you think of more English examples of suppletion? _____

As for *sang*: *sing* and *sang* are clearly phonologically related to each other; the central vowel has changed (vowel mutation). This is called **ablaut** (a term coined by a person you may more readily associate with fairy tales, Jacob Grimm, but who was also a good linguist). Ablaut forms past tense not by adding a suffix but by changing the stem vowel. Ablaut is very common in Germanic languages; the few English forms which are based on ablaut are a reminder that English also belongs to this family.

Can you think of more English past tense forms with ablaut? _____
_____ .

In short, when we see a change to the vowel in the root of the word and that change indicates a grammatical property (e.g. past tense) we call that **ablaut**.

Another word in our list looks like ablaut: *goose* → *geese*. Unfortunately that's not ablaut but a second type of vowel alternation called **umlaut**. Umlaut is a phonological process whereby, in a certain phonetic environment, a vowel that is formed towards the back of the mouth (like /ʊ/) gets assimilated to a front vowel (like /ɪ/). Umlaut explains not only *goose* → *geese*. Can you think of other English examples of umlaut? _____

The last example, *fish*, illustrates that the same form can be used both as a singular and as a plural word, that is to say, there is no overt marker (be it the addition of -*s*, or a change of vowel) that indicates that in e.g., *two fish* the noun is plural.

Task 4.6

We have just seen that for some nouns it isn't that easy to determine whether they are singular or plural. We can utilise the notion **agreement**, which we introduced in Chapter 4, to help us determine the number (grammatical category) of such nouns.

In the following sentences, determine which noun phrase the underlined verbs have to agree with, and then delete the incorrect verb form.

a. *The set of examples from the Cambridge corpus is / are very complex.*
b. *The examples from the set in section 5 listed below is / are very difficult to analyse.*
c. *The sheep were / was rounded up by the sheepdog.*
d. *The thesis was / were submitted by the student.*

Task 5.1

What are the heads of the marked phrases? The sentences after the semicolon are there to help.

a. *Homer ate [an entire box of jelly doughnuts]; Homer ate it.*
b. *Bart [stayed after school to write lines on the blackboard]; he stayed.*

c. *[Eva's favourite saxophone player] is Houston Person; he is Houston Person.*
d. *Snowball the cat went [to Kitty Heaven]; Snowball the cat went there.*
e. *Maggie Simpson [shot Mr Burns]; she shot him.*
f. *Chief Wiggum cracked open the walnuts [with the butt of a loaded revolver]; Chief Wiggum cracked open the walnuts with it.*
g. *Marge Simpson has [the biggest, bluest hair you ever did see]; Marge Simpson has hair; Marge Simpson has it (etc.).*
h. *[George's blue tie] is in [my best friend's car]; it is (in?) there.*

(Examples from O'Grady and Archibald 2008)

Task 5.2

In the sentences below:

- bracket the noun phrase/s;
- identify their heads;
- write down a pronoun which could replace the entire phrase

a. *Kate's mum is coming tomorrow.*
b. *Where's my beloved pair of slippers?*
c. *The best things in life are free.*
d. *Mary can't stand jazz.*
e. *The angry men in the pub were shouting really loudly.*

Task 5.3

What are the heads in the following phrases? Put square brackets round all phrases (or you may want to draw trees); underline the heads of the phrases and label the brackets (or nodes in your trees).

a. *that wide tunnel*
b. *a small scruffy box-room*
c. *the gorgeous high-diver on the cover of the Olympic magazine*
d. *Anna's red dress*
e. *her best friend's bicycle*
f. *That old worn-out jumper made from the cheapest Oriental fibres*
g. *the obsolete computer sitting on the desk*

With this task we are stepping it up a bit; we are taking linguistic analysis a bit further than we did in Chapters 1–6. Most probably, you struggled with three things in this exercise (particularly if you decided to draw trees).

The first difficulty is how to analyse the possessive -'s clitic in (d) and (e). This isn't that hard. Try the replacement test, i.e. what can you replace *Anna's* and *her best friend's* with in (d) and (e)? With *her* in both cases (or with *his* in (e), if the friend is male). What's the function of *her* and *his* in the resulting NPs [*her red dress*] and [*his bicycle*]? Both function as determiners. We will therefore put *Anna's* in the determiner space in a bracketed noun phrase and / or a tree.

Our second problem is where to put *red* in a tree. We discuss a proposed solution on the companion website.

Did you have any another problems? One may have been what to do with *box-room*, *high-diver* and *worn-out*. What do these words have in common? They are all _____ . This can be dealt with in a variety of ways. We reserve the tree for *box-room* until we discuss coordination. For now, just stick these words under a node which specifies which word class they belong to, i.e. N for *box-room* and *high-div-er*; and Adj for *worn-out*.

Task 5.4

Identify the pre-modifiers and post-modifiers in the bracketed NPs.

a. [*The good supervisor*] *is originally from Eastern Europe.*
b. *For war veterans, the Victoria Cross is* [*a sign of distinction*].
c. *Parasols protected Victorian ladies from* [*the harsh sun*].
d. *Before that, straw hats were used as* [*a protection from the sun*].
e. [*Ladies who suffered from sunstroke*] *were recommended long cold baths.*

If you have been on the companion website to check the position of pre-modifying adjectives like *red* in a tree, you are already familiar with one way of representing [*the harsh sun*].

How would you fit optional post-modifiers into a tree? Model your answer on how we dealt with optional pre-modification in the suggested answers to Task 5.3 on the companion website.

Task 5.5

Bracket the prepositional phrases in each of the following sentences and underline the preposition.

a. *The boy kicked the ball through the window.*
b. *All those intellectuals at the bar are not drinking beer.*
c. *The marathon ran across six boroughs.*

Task 5.6

Decide if the NP [*this morning*] is optional or obligatory in (a)–(d). If you think it is optional, put it in round brackets (which is the linguistic convention for indicating optional material); if it is obligatory, put it in square brackets.

a. *This morning the sun is shining.*
b. *He is arriving this morning.*
c. *This morning is gloriously sunny.*
d. *The game is this morning.*

Task 6.1

In each of the following sentences underline every auxiliary verb (don't forget that this includes modals) and label them.

Example: *He will be knocked out by that pill.*
              MOD PASS

a. *It should be a good game.*
b. *The customer will be staying in her seat.*
c. *My ideas were being discussed in public.*
d. *She should have been studying all night.*
e. *Patricia has had a headache all day.*
f. *They must have gone by now.*

Task 6.2

In Chapter 6, we discussed the NICE properties which distinguish main verbs from auxiliaries. In this task we will practise **N** for negation.

Use the contracted form *-n't* to make each sentence below negative. In some sentences you will need to make morpho-syntactic changes to allow for the presence of the negative particle. Which are these sentences? Why did you have to make changes?

a. *Protesters were occupying the streets of London.*
b. *A wave of indignation swept over the country.*
d. *Revolution had been televised before.*
e. *Bankers and financiers would soon be humiliated.*
f. *A new deal will be arrived at.*

143

Task 6.3

We continue consolidating the distinction between main and auxiliary verbs through NICE properties with *I* for inversion. This time, turn sentences (a) to (e) into *wh*-questions asking for the leftmost NP and underline the auxiliary involved.

a. *The brain stem is responsible for basic life functions.*
b. *The manager dealt with the problem effectively.*
c. *The colour of the petals is essential for flower pollination.*
d. *The largest orchids are those from Cuba.*
e. *But the florist avoids the need for constant cross-pollination.*

Task 6.4

Identify whether the underlined verb in each sentence is the base form, *-s* form, past form, *-ing* participle or *-ed* participle.

a. *Cats were held in high esteem among the ancient Egyptians.* (__)
b. *Egyptian law protected cats from injury and death.* (__)
c. *The Egyptians used to embalm the corpses of their cats.* (__)
d. *They put them in mummy cases made of precious materials.* (__)
e. *Entire cat cemeteries have been unearthed by archaeologists.* (__)
f. *The Egyptians were impressed by the way cats can survive high falls.* (__)
g. *They originated the belief that the cat possesses nine lives.* (__)
h. *Dread of cats first arose in Europe in the Middle Ages.* (__)
i. *Alley cats were often fed by poor, lonely old women.* (__)
j. *During the Inquisition, women were accused of witchcraft.* (__)

(Greenbaum & Melson 2009)

Task 6.5

Is the underlined auxiliary a modal, perfective *have*, progressive *be*, or passive *be*?

a. *The employment agency should be contacting you soon about the job.*
b. *My insurance company has been informed about the damage to my roof.*
c. *The band has been heavily influenced by The Beatles.*
d. *I can be reached at my office number.*

e.   *The committee is holding its next meeting later this month.*
f.   *The remains were accidentally discovered by a team of palaeontologists.*
g.   *Who has been disturbing my papers?*
h.   *The dot com boom had finally collapsed.*
i.   *You can't have forgotten it already.*
j.   *I am relying on you.*

Task 6.6

In Section 4.3.3 we noticed that present tense and perfective aspect (which implies that an event is viewed in its totality) don't go well together. Take a critical look at tense and aspect in English now: in examples (a) and (b) below, which sentences portray the event as closed / completed? Is it sentences (i)? Or is it sentences (ii)?

a.   i.   *She has written a book.*
     ii. *She wrote a book.*
b.   i.   *I've known her for years.*
     ii. *I knew her for years.*

Could you come to a conclusion? Is it possible that English simple past is also perfective?

CHAPTER 7

Functional analysis

This chapter . . .

In this chapter, we will look at functional relations between phrases and the role verbs play in assigning these functions. We will show that some sentence elements are optional (adjuncts), whereas complements (i.e. subjects and objects) are part of the argument structure of the verb. We will introduce you to different types of complements (as well as to some adjuncts) and to procedures which will enable you to carry out a functional analysis of sentences. You will then be able do something which is not only crucial in human language production and comprehension, but also in computer-generated language use and machine translation: identify the argument structure of verbs (i.e. valency / transitivity).

7.1 **Structure, form and function**

Can you put square brackets round all the noun phrases in the following two sentences?

1. *Parker kicked the ball.*
2. *The boy sneezed last night.*

You will have noticed that both sentences have the same structure, consisting of a NP, followed by a verb, which in turn is followed by another NP. We can see that this similarity has consequences for the way we understand the sentences. For instance, we can see that the first NPs in 1 and 2 (*Parker* and *the boy*) both describe individuals who are performing the activity denoted by the verbs (i.e. *kicking* and *sneezing*). They are agents of the action. The second NPs in (1) and (2) (*the ball* and *last night*), on the other hand, do not share the same characteristics: while we can say that the ball is being kicked (the ball is the entity undergoing the effect of the action, the patient), we cannot say that *last night* is undergoing the sneezing. Despite their similarity in both shape (i.e. they are both NPs) and position (they both occur after the verb), the meaning and function of these NPs are clearly different. How can we capture this distinction?

So far we have mainly been concerned with the *form* of phrases, and a little bit with the semantic / thematic roles they fulfil in Chapter 6. We used terms such as *noun phrase, verb phrase, prepositional phrase* and others. We have established that calling a particular string a NP, for instance, tells us that its most important word is a noun, and that the string can be replaced by a pronoun. But this type of structural analysis does not tell us anything about the *function* the NP is performing in a particular sentence. This is what we are going to look at in this chapter. Grammatical functions do not describe what a certain string is, but rather what it is doing in a certain context. The main grammatical functions are **subject, predicate, object** and **complement**.

As you may have noticed, part of the problem is that phrases of the same kind, for example noun phrases, are not tied to performing the same function. In sentences 1 and 2 above, four NPs are performing three different functions: *Parker* and *the boy* are subjects, *the ball* is a (direct) object, and *last night* is an adjunct. This may sound strange and far from ideal in that it could create confusion, but it actually makes a lot of sense: after all, many things in life have more than one function. We use books for reading, but we can also use them to prop a door open (having said that, we hope that you do not put this book to that use). And just like phrases can perform more than one function, functions can be carried out by different types of phrases, much like using glue, nails or tacks to hang a poster on a wall.

We can rely on the formal characteristics of a string to determine whether it is, e.g., a PP or an NP. For a structural analysis, no context is necessary. Determining whether a particular NP is functioning as subject or object, however, cannot be done in isolation: we have to have context (of occurrence); we have to have access to the sentence / clause in which the phrase occurs.

7.2 **The basic sentence structures**

Chapter 6 dealt with the centrality of the verb in clause structure. We saw that it is the verb that assigns functions and role relations to the other sentence elements. It is useful to think of the structure of an English sentence as consisting of a number of thematic positions. The necessary number and types of these positions are determined by the verb. The English language has a handful of basic sentence structures which are presented in the Table 7.1. We will discuss each individual pattern separately in the next sections. To be able to read the table summarising the different complementation patterns you need to know that *S* stands for *Subject*, *V* for *Verb*, *DO* for *Direct Object*, *IO* for *Indirect Object*, *OC* for *Object Complement*, and *SC* for *Subject Complement*.

7.3 **Subjects, predicates and verbs**

As we have seen in Chapter 6, an English sentence is usually made up of a NP which is followed by a VP. In unmarked cases (that is, in cases where the speaker / writer does not wish to fore- or background a constituent), this first NP is the **subject** of the sentence (S in Table 7.1). Whatever is not the subject, we call the **predicate** of the sentence. The predicate consists of a VP, which is headed by a verb. We will identify the function of the verb as *V*. (Some linguists prefer to call the function of the verb *predicator*: we choose not to do this so as to avoid confusion with the term *predicate*). In Table 7.1, every single complementation pattern contains at least a subject and a verb. S and V are the basic elements in clause structure. The verb can be followed by different configurations of complements and adjuncts, of which we will have more to say in the following sections. Let's consider the subject next.

Table 7.1. *Standard complementation patterns in English*

	Complementation pattern	Verb type	Examples
1	S + V	Intransitive	*Mary blushed*
2	S + V + DO	Transitive	*Peter built a boat*
3	S + V + IO + DO	Ditransitive	*Judas gave Jesus a kiss*
4	S + V + DO + OC	Complex-transitive	*Many people called him a traitor*
5	S + V + SC	Copulative	*Paul looked miserable*

7.4 The subject

Some languages use inflectional morphology to identify a particular NP as the subject of a sentence. The English language used to do this, too, but, as we briefly mentioned in Chapters 3 and 4, it abandoned all its case marking, and Modern English relies almost entirely on position to mark grammatical functions. In normal circumstances, the subject NP in English is the first NP in the sentence, which means it is found 'before' or to the left of the verb. Can you identify the subjects in Activity 7.1?

Activity 7.1

Enclose the subject noun phrase of sentences (a) to (c) in square brackets.

a. *The astronaut landed on the moon with a loud crash.*
b. *The man on the moon wasn't pleased.*
c. *Last Monday, he registered a complaint.*

If you think that the head noun of one of the three sentences is optionally pre- or post-modified by another phrasal category, also put square brackets round this group of words and label it with the appropriate subscript.

We trust you correctly identified *the astronaut* and *the man* as subjects, but did you include *on the moon* in the subject noun phrase? We have to, because the PP optionally post-modifies *the man*, and together they form the subject $_{NP}$[the man $_{PP}$[on the moon]]. Although *last Monday* is the first NP in sentence (c) (and would thus fit our positional description of subjects), it is not the subject. Why not? For the same reason that *last night* in sentence 2 at the beginning of this chapter is not very important: it can be deleted without resulting in an ungrammatical sentence, so it is an adjunct.

You may have been taught that the actor, agent or doer of the action described by the verb is the subject, and we have used the role of agent, too. This way of identifying subjects relies on meaning as opposed to formal properties; it is a valid and powerful tool in a majority of cases. If we apply this criterion to the sentences in Activity 7.1, we see that its predictions are actually fine: the doer of the landing is *the astronaut*, the one not pleased is the *man on the moon*, and the person doing the registering is *he*. But what about the examples in Activity 7.2?

> ## Activity 7.2
> Enclose the subject noun phrase of sentences a–d in square brackets.
>
> a. *It is raining cats and dogs.*
> b. *Look, there is a man at the door.*
> c. *It is unusual to hear him complain.*
> d. *Close the window.*

The difficulty with these sentences is that it is not clear who is doing the activity denoted by the verb. The subject of sentence (a) is *it*, but who or what does *it* refer to? And our positional criterion is not much help either, as sentence (b) illustrates. In sentence (b), neither of the two sentence elements before the verb is the subject, and we need to look to the right of the verb *is* to identify *the man* as the subject of sentence (b). The same logic applies to sentence (c) as applies to sentence (a), and sentence (d) is a bit unusual: it is the only construction type in English where the subject is always implicit (i.e. not overtly expressed) and always refers to the addressee. We have already mentioned this construction type in Chapter 4 and said that it is a command in the imperative mood. We will come back to imperatives in Chapter 9.

Besides our notional and positional criteria, there are other tests for ascertaining whether a particular string is functioning as the subject of a sentence. For instance, unlike many other languages, subjects are obligatory elements in English sentence structure. This is why we have called S and V the basic elements in clause structure. Normally, English requires an overt, explicit subject in every clause (with the exception of imperative sentences, as just mentioned). Have you noticed that occasionally native speakers of, for example, Italian and Spanish don't bother spelling out the subject pronoun of English sentences? They may do this because it's not necessary in their mother tongue.

Formally speaking, the function *Subject* is mainly performed by NPs. There are other elements that can also perform the subject role (other phrase types as well as clauses); we will discuss the latter in Chapter 8.

We have a nice test to see which NP is the subject (especially when first-person-singular, or third-person-singular agents are involved). The test involves replacing the noun phrases with pronouns. When a pronominal NP is functioning as subject, it carries nominative / subject case, as opposed to accusative / object case. Remember that in Chapter 2 we had to split the table for personal pronouns in two because the nominative and accusative form of these pronouns differed in the first-and third-person singular.

Table 7.2. *Case-marked pronouns*

	nominative	accusative
First pers. sg.	*I*	*me*
Third pers. sg.	*he / she / it*	*him / her / it*

We can use this to our advantage now that we are trying to identify subjects, which, as we said, have to be in the nominative case form; consider:

3. *I chased the pigeons off our balcony.*
4. **Me chased the pigeons off our balcony.*
5. *Asterix chased the Roman soldiers.*
6. *He chased the Roman soldiers.*
7. **Him chased the Roman soldiers.*
8. *Asterix chased Obelix.*
9. *He chased him.*
10. **Him chased he.*

We can also use *agreement* (an inflectional property, first discussed in Chapter 3 and Section 4.4) to see whether a NP is or isn't the subject of a clause.

11. *My dog likes juicy pies.*
12. **My dog like juicy pies.*

Omitting the *-s* ending on the verb (which indicates not just the tense, but also third-person-singular person) causes ungrammaticality, which shows that there is indeed a relationship of agreement between the verb and the subject. Note that this agreement in number and person only holds in present-tense sentences between the subject and the verb (and not between the object and the verb, as illustrated by the ungrammaticality of **I likes him.*)

The next three characteristics of canonical subjects involve rearrangement / dislocation / movement of clausal constituents. The first one we have already mentioned in a different context in relation to auxiliary verbs in Chapter 6. It involves *yes / no* questions, that is, questions which demand yes / no answers (as opposed to open or content questions, which normally start with *wh*-words). In Y/N questions, subjects invert with the first auxiliary if there is one, as in

13. *Mary married John.*
14. *Did Mary marry John?*
15. *The farmer could work all day.*
16. *Could the farmer work all day?*

17. *The students have been busy all night.*
18. *Have the students been busy all night?*

Turning the declarative sentences into questions requires the subject to swap positions with the auxiliary. We called this rearrangement of obligatory sentence elements *subject-auxiliary inversion* (SAI, for short) recently in Chapter 6, but it first made an appearance in Section 2.2.4.

A related test involves the use of *tag questions* (which will be discussed in more detail in Section 9.2.3). Subjects are duplicated and replaced by pronouns in this type of structure, as in:

19. *Mary had a little lamb, didn't she?*
20. *Its fleece was white as snow, wasn't it?*
21. *It followed her to school one day, didn't it?*

Only pronouns that are co-referential with the subject can appear in tag questions. Pronouns that are co-referential with the object of the sentence render ungrammatical tag questions, as illustrated below:

22. **Mary had a boyfriend, didn't he?*
23. **It followed her to school one day, didn't she?*

The final test for subjecthood involves the use of an operation called passive voice (first introduced in Chapter 6, and to be explored in more depth in Section 9.5). This operation actually makes reference to functional categories such as subject and object. Passive voice takes the subject NP of the active sentence and places it within an optional prepositional phrase headed by *by*. Only subject NPs can be moved in such a manner.

24. *Mary forgave Paul.*
25. *Paul was forgiven by Mary.*

Activity 7.3 and the end-of-chapter exercises have been designed to give you additional practice in putting the different criteria to the test. They involve extraordinary cases of subjecthood, and it would be a good idea to make every single sentence run the gauntlet of all our tests.

Activity 7.3

Identify the subject in the following examples. Enclose it in square brackets.

a. *There are great sales on the High Street.*
b. *Smoking is bad for you.*
c. *The footballer was injured.*

> d. *Don't just stand there!*
> e. *It is important to tell the truth.*
> f. *In comes the bride.*
> g. *That Monday he overslept again.*

The answers to Activity 7.3 can be found in the next section.

7.5 The predicate

We used Activity 7.3 to draw your attention to the fact that the subjects of sentences can have either not much or no independent meaning of their own (as *there* and *it* in sentences (a) and (e)), can start life out as non-agentive objects (like *the footballer* passive subject in sentence (c)), can be implicit (as in the imperative sentence (d)), can be placed to the right of the verb (as *the bride* in (f)) for rhetorical effect, or can be not the first noun phrase in the sentence (as *he* in sentence (g)). Activity 7.3 has led us onto *predicates*. A **predicate** consists of a sentence from which its subject has been 'removed' one way or another. This also showed us that predicates tend to convey the majority of the information contained in a clause. In this light, subjects serve an indexical purpose, identifying a particular referent (e.g. *the Prime Minister*, *the man on the Clapham bus*, *my father*, etc.) about which some information is going to be produced, something is going to be predicated.

Predicates always contain a verb. Recall that verbs are central, pivotal elements to clause structure, so much so that many grammatical sentences can actually consist of only a single verb (e.g. *Help*; *Shoot!*). Besides the verb, there are other elements which also appear as part of the predicate. We distinguish between *complements* and *adjuncts*, based on their syntactic behaviour; that is, on the functions they perform and not on their phrasal make-up, as we will see in the next section.

7.6 Complements and adjuncts

If the verb is central to sentence structure, it is even more so in the predicate, determining not just which elements are required, but also how many are required. This characteristic of verbs is so important that lexical verbs can be classified according to this behaviour, that is, according to the number and type of complements they allow and require. Depending on the complements they require, we can distinguish five groups of verbs (intransitive, transitive, ditransitive, complex-transitive and copular).

Activity 7.4

In this activity we only want to establish how many elements the verbs in the following sentences require. We will look at the 'what kind of' question later.

In a first step, delete all the words or phrases that are optional in that the sentences stay grammatical once you have deleted them.

In a second step, count how many obligatory sentence elements / phrases there are in the predicate (i.e. exclude the subject from your count)

a.   *Meggy plays the guitar really well.*
b.   *The delivery man hands me my parcel.*
c.   *In my dreams I sleep.*
d.   *Oh my god, he wants to become an accountant!*

We see from Activity 7.4 that it is also essential to distinguish between optional and obligatory elements in the predicate. Those elements which are required by the verb are called **complements**, a term which in this book includes direct objects, indirect objects, subject complements and object complements. At the same time, the verb allows other elements to appear in the predicate, without actually demanding that they do. Those elements which do not require licence from the verb to occur in the predicate are called **adjuncts**, and are typically optional elements. The optional elements from Activity 7.4 are *really well* (in sentence (a)), *In my dreams* (in sentence (c)), and *Oh my god* (in sentence (d)). We see that these elements are quite different: they belong to different phrase classes (which ones?) and serve different functions in the sentence. What they all have in common is that they can be removed from the sentence without making it ungrammatical. They are optional; they are adjuncts. We will briefly return to adjuncts is the next section, but our focus is on obligatory **complements** of verbs in the next section.

7.7 Complementation patterns

In the Activity 7.4, you established that some verbs need the assistance of complements to express a complete meaning. Verbs can be sub-classified according to the type and number of complements they need, which is known as their **valency** or **transitivity**. In classifying verbs by their transitivity, we have no use for adjuncts, as these are optional elements, which is another way of saying that they can be omitted without the grammaticality and central meaning of the sentence being radically affected. The following examples illustrate the transitivity requirements of *sneeze*, *give* and *put*.

26.   *Amy sneezed.*
27.   *Simon gave his wife a kiss.*

28. *Simon gave his wife.
29. *Simon gave a kiss.
30. Shahanara put her laptop on her desk.
31. *Shahanara put her laptop.
32. *Shahanara put on her desk.

We can see that verbs like *sneeze* do not require additional elements in order to make sense; whereas *give* requires not just one but two elements (the NPs *his wife* and *a kiss*) to express a complete predication, and none can be omitted. A similar case is that of *put*, which also requires two elements, but one is a NP and the other a PP.

We start our discussion of complementation patterns with verbs like *sneeze*.

7.7.1 Intransitive verbs and adjuncts

Verbs which do not require complements in order to express a complete meaning are called **intransitive** verbs. This group includes verbs such as *disappear*, *laugh*, *sneeze*, *stand*, *sleep*, *agree*, *exist*, *lie* and many others. And it is not only the case that they do not require them: they actually forbid their occurrence! And this is why some of the sentences below are ungrammatical:

33. The doorman laughed.
34. *The doorman laughed the car.
35. *The doorman laughed Bill.
36. *The doorman laughed a dog.

Adjuncts, as we have already noted, are optional elements which can occur in sentence structure, regardless of the verb's transitivity pattern. Unlike complements, they are not required by the verb, which means they can be added or removed without resulting in ungrammaticality. Typically, adjuncts provide additional meanings connected to the when, where, how or why of the situation (i.e. time, place, manner, etc.), but not what or who.

Other characteristics of adjuncts include: (i) their tendency to be realised mainly as AdvP and PP (note that *really well* and *in my dreams* from Activity 7.4 are exactly this, an $_{AdvP}$[*really well*] and a $_{PP}$[*in my dreams*]); (ii) they can be recursive or 'stackable', i.e. there is no upper limit to the number of adjuncts a sentence might take (remember that we came across the word 'recursive' in Chapter 5).

Activity 7.5

Let's stack a few adjuncts up.

The sun shone _____

How about *The sun can shine very brightly on the house at lunchtime*, for example? What kind of phrases are *very brightly*, *on the house* and *at lunchtime*? They are one adverb phrase and two prepositional phrases respectively. And what is their function in the sentence? They specify the manner, place and time of how, where and when the sun shone on the house.

The third main characteristic of adjuncts is (iii) their mobility, which refers to the potential of adjuncts for occurring at different locations in the sentence (even before the subject!). Let's try this out again. Depending on what we want to focus on, we have some alternative arrangements available:

37. *At lunchtime the sun shone very brightly on the house.*
38. *On the house the sun shone very brightly at lunchtime, not on the barn.*
39. *Very brightly the sun shone on the house at lunchtime, not dimly.*

If, however, we strip this sentence of all its adjuncts, we end up with a very short sentence: *The sun shone*. We can represent the structure of sentences with intransitive verbs using trees in the following manner:

Figure 7.1

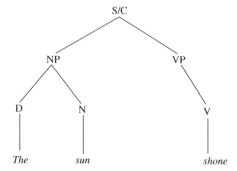

What this upside down tree tells us is that we have got a sentence (S) or clause (C) that consists of a noun phrase (NP) and a verb phrase (VP). Because *shone* is an intransitive verb, it is quite content on its own under the VP node. The NP, on the other hand, consists of a determiner *the* (D) and a noun *sun* (N). Of course, we can 'hang' optional adjuncts like AdvP[*very brightly*], PP[*on the house*] and PP[*at lunchtime*] on the tree so that it doesn't look as spindly any more. This sums up quite nicely what adjuncts are: optional, stackable and moveable ornaments that are not essential for the sentence structure.

The remaining complementation patterns are more complex (and tree diagrams representing their structure will consequently also be more complex) and have more specific transitivity demands: we start with the next easier one: transitive verbs and their required complement, the direct object.

7.7.2 Transitive verbs and direct objects

Unlike intransitive verbs, transitive verbs need a complement in order to complete their meaning. Moreover, they do not need any old complement; they need a noun phrase that functions as a direct object. These verbs cannot stand alone. Consider what happens in the absence of a DO:

40. *The farmer's wife cut the three mice's tails.*
41. **The farmer's wife cut.*

The sentence becomes ungrammatical.

If subjects refer to the doer (agent) of the action described by the verb, direct objects tend to refer to those people / things which undergo the activity denoted by the same verb (patient). This means that in *Tom chased Jerry*, *Tom* is the subject (the one doing the chasing) and *Jerry* the direct object (the one undergoing the chasing). Here we are appealing to meaning, a notional criterion which we have seen is not successful all the time. Fortunately, we have other tools in our toolbox.

Direct objects are very typical complements. For starters, they are obligatory: as we have just seen, omitting them brings about ungrammaticality. Positionally, DOs tend to occur near the verb. Generally speaking, DOs are also NPs (just like subjects). When DOs are realised by a pronoun, however, the pronoun carries accusative / object case (not nominative case, which is reserved for subjects).

Activity 7.6

Replace the proper nouns in the following sentence with pronouns:

Idefix chased Obelix and Asterix.

The pronominalisation test clearly shows us that we must use accusative case object pronouns like *him* (or *her*, or *them*) in object position, and nominative case pronouns like *he / she / they* in subject position. We cannot use object pronouns in subject position; and neither can we use subject pronouns in object position.

42. *He*$_{\text{NOM}}$ *chased them*$_{\text{ACC}}$.
43. **Him*$_{\text{ACC}}$ *chased they*$_{\text{NOM}}$.

Apart from pronominalisation, we can also use passive voice to check whether something is or isn't a DO. If you recall, passive voice not only moves the subject but also takes the direct object and turns it into the subject of a passive-voice sentence. This operation is not possible with adjuncts.

The passive version of *He*$_{\text{NOM}}$ *chased them*$_{\text{ACC}}$ clearly illustrates what's going on: when the object becomes the subject, its case changes from accusative to nominative, as in *They*$_{\text{NOM}}$ *were chased by him.*

We can represent the structure of transitive verbs using trees in the following manner:

Figure 7.2

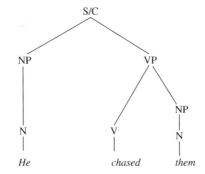

This tree is less spindly than the one representing the structure of a sentence with an intransitive verb; it doesn't contain any adjuncts either. How can we 'read' it? Note that the top of the tree is identical to the one for the intransitive verb *shine* in the previous section. Therefore the beginning of the reading is identical: This upside-down tree tells us that we have got a sentence (S) or clause (C) that consists of a noun phrase (NP) and a verb phrase (VP). The pronoun *he* constitutes the subject noun phrase in this case (because we do not have a determiner). But because *chased* is a transitive verb, it is not happy on its own under the VP node; it requires an NP representing somebody or something that can fill the other (semantic or thematic) role it assigns: that of the person or thing being chased, here realised by the (pro)noun *them*. Remember that single words can constitute phrases, but because we could also have ₙₚ[*the short Gaul with the red trousers and the really fat one with the unflattering stripy trousers*] instead of ₙₚ[*them*], linguists sometimes use the following notational system. This time we also label the functions the individual phrases categories fill.

Figure 7.3

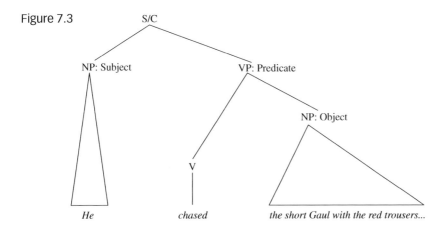

The advantage of this triangle notification system is that there is no way we can or would want to fit the monster ₙₚ[*the short Gaul with the red trousers and the really fat one with the unflattering stripy trousers*] in the tree; we therefore represent the NP with a triangle. The diagram thus deliberately omits some information that is irrelevant here: it does not show anything about the internal structure of the two NPs. For the slim and slender ₙₚ[*he*] the triangle notation wouldn't be necessary, but as both *he* and *the short Gaul …* are phrases, we can represent them the same way.

Note that no function is assigned to the clause itself, because it is not part of any larger syntactic constituent. The other units are given two labels: the first indicates their form / category, the second, their function. We have just conducted the first full functional and structural analysis of an English canonical sentence, i.e. a sentence with a S(ubject)V(erb) O(bject) structure.

Before we move onto the next complementation pattern, let's look at a slightly trickier case.

Activity 7.7

Do a full functional and structural analysis of the next two sentences. Are both of them grammatical? What is the transitivity type or valency pattern of *jump*?

a. *The thoroughbred jumped the hurdle.*
b. *The thoroughbred jumped.*

For sentence (a) in Activity 7.7 we can either represent the full structure, as in

Figure 7.4

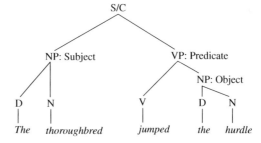

Or we can use the triangle shorthand notation, if the internal structure of the NPs is not the focus of our attention, as in this case:

Figure 7.5

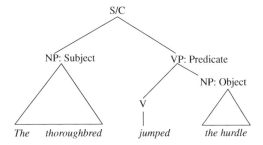

The sentence (b) in Activity 7.7 can be presented as

Figure 7.6

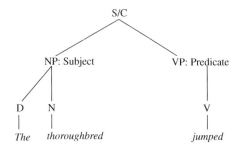

So what does this analysis tell us? It tells us that the very same verb can under certain conditions be intransitive, as in the latter case, or transitive, as in *The thoroughbred jumped the hurdle*.

7.7.3 Ditransitive verbs and indirect objects

'Ditransitive' refers to those verbs which require not one but two verb complements or objects in addition to the subject. To distinguish between the two objects, we call the one of them 'indirect object' (IO). IO are usually NPs, and must be followed by a DO, as in *He gave* NP[*his mother*] NP[*a kiss*]. Like in this example, the IO usually describes a recipient or beneficiary of the action denoted by the verb. IOs also share several characteristics with DOs, such as a) being largely NPs, b) carrying object case if pronominal, and c) potential for becoming the subject of a passive-voice sentence. These features are illustrated below:

44. *Trish gave* NP[*Francis*] NP[*an apple*].
45. *Trish gave him/*he an apple*.
46. *Francis was given an apple by Trish*.

Indirect objects can also be expressed as noun phrases embedded in a prepositional phrase headed by *to* (in the case of recipients) or *for* (in the case of beneficiaries). In this case the PP containing the indirect object noun phrase follows the direct object, e.g.

47. *Jenny wrote* IO NP[*Tom*] DO NP[*a letter*].
48. *Jenny wrote* DO NP[*a letter*] PP[*to* NP[*Tom*]].
49. *Francis sent* IO NP[*Trish*] DO NP[*a card*].
50. *Francis sent* DO NP[*a card*] PP[*for* IO NP[*Trish*]].

Ditransitives can be represented in tree structure in the following manner:

Figure 7.7

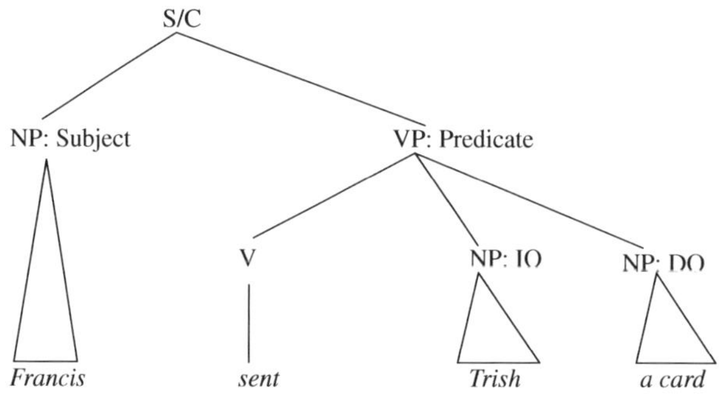

Can you 'translate' the tree diagram into linguistics prose? Model your answer on the 'reading' of a tree representing a transitive sentence and add the second object that is required by ditransitive verbs.

To summarise so far, some verbs are happy with just a subject; verbs that do not require an object are called *in-transitive*. Note that the prefix *in-* here has the same meaning as in *in-edible* or *in-sane*, i.e. it means 'not' and therefore intransitive means 'not transitive'. Verbs that are transitive require one (direct) object, as in *I arrange the flowers*. Without the direct object, the sentence becomes ungrammatical. The same holds true for ditransitive verbs. As the prefix suggests, *di*-transitive verbs require two objects to form a grammatical English sentence. The only thing you have to remember so far (if you haven't come across the term 'transitive' before) is that transitive refers to the type and number of complements verbs need. The rest you can deduce from your knowledge of English (or Latin) morphology. This is going to change a bit now because we are going to introduce a different type of verb complement.

7.7.4 Copulative verbs and subject complements

Just like transitives, copulative verbs require a complement. Unlike transitives, though, that complement must not be an object, but rather a subject complement, which we can define as a complement (i.e. obligatory element) which refers to the subject. More specifically, the subject complement predicates something about the subject, often attributing a property to the referent of the subject NP. Fortunately for us, copulative verbs are a closed set, which effectively means that there is only a handful of them and no further additions are possible. Copulative verbs are *be*, *become*, *yield*, *seem*, *appear* and a few others. The most frequently used copulative verb is *be*, which is called copula (from the Latin noun for 'link'). Copulative verbs do not describe actions as such but only perform a linking function, that is, they link the subject of a sentence with the subject complement in the predicate. Subject complements take a number of forms, for the most part being NPs, PPs, or AdjPs, as we can see below

51. *My bicycle is in ruins.*
52. *You seem tired.*
53. *Chloe is a dancer.*

In example 53, *a dancer* is in typical DO position, that is, it is the first (and only) NP after the verb. How can we tell this NP is actually not a DO? Shall we get our linguistic toolkit and open our battery of tests? Which one would you select? Replacement? Subject Auxiliary Inversion? Substitution? Passivisation? Clefting? We suggest passivisation because direct objects but not subject complements can passivise. Let's try it.

54. *Chloe punched the customer.*
55. *The customer was punched by Chloe.*
56. *Chloe is a dancer.*
57. **A dancer is been by Chloe.*

The infelicitous result of passivisation in example 57 indicates that the noun phrase *a dancer* indeed fulfils the function of subject complement in the sentence *Chloe is a dancer*, and is not a direct object. Note that *the customer* is indeed a direct object in sentence 54, as the result of passivisation in example 55 shows.

Activity 7.8

What functions does the noun phrase *a dancer* fulfil in the following sentences?

a. *A dancer has to train at least five hours per day.*
b. *He gave her a statue of a dancer for her birthday.*
c. *Walter hit a dancer with his bike.*
d. *She became a dancer in her second career.*
e. *He sent a letter to the dancer every day that she was in hospital.*

In sentence (a) of activity 7.8 the ₙₚ[*a dancer*] is clearly the subject, but what is it in sentence (b)? It forms part of the direct object, but it is a modifier to the head noun of the direct object NP[*a statue* PP[*of* NP[*a dancer*]]]. That was mean, wasn't it? The answer to sentence (c) (as a linguistic activity) is easy: *a dancer* is the direct object. In sentence (d), on the other hand, *a dancer* is a subject complement. In sentence (e) it is the indirect object and follows the direct object because it is embedded in a PP[*to* NP[*a dancer*]]. Well done, if you got all the different functions of the noun phrase *a dancer* right. Note that in our analysis of the function of *a dancer* we have completely ignored all adjuncts in sentences (a) to (e) in Activity 7.8, although there are quite a few of them, e.g. the PP[*at least five hours per day*], PP[*for her birthday*], PP[*with his bike*]; PP[*in her second career*], NP[*every day that she was in hospital*].

Activity 7.9

What's the function of the PP[*in Paris*] in the following sentence
   We are in Paris.

In Paris is clearly a prepositional phrase and indicates a kind of location. It therefore fulfils two characteristics of adverbials. But is it an adjunct? Well, it is required by the verb, and is thus not optional but obligatory. Linguists have different names for these structures, such as *adverbial complement*, *prepositional object* and even *obligatory adverbial* (although this is a contradiction in terms). Activity 7.9 highlights that we always need to begin our analysis with the most important question: is the sentence element / phrase we are looking at obligatory or optional? In other words, is it a complement or an adjunct?

Tree representations of sentences containing a subject complement are identical in structure to trees representing what kinds of predicates? Transitive ones.

Figure 7.8

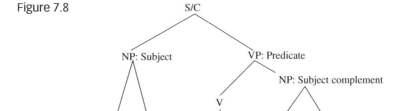

Only one other complementation pattern is possible in English: the one of complex-transitive verbs which take an object and an object complement.

7.7.5 Complex-transitive verbs and object complements

The final type of verbs we will consider here is that of complex-transitive verbs. These require two elements, a (direct) object followed by a complement which predicates something of the referent of the direct object. More simply put, the object complement describes an attribute of the DO. In the example below, who is an idiot?

58.   *I called him an idiot.*

He is, right? The object pronoun *him*$_{ACC}$ and the $_{NP}$[*an idiot*] refer to one and the same person. As is the case with any type of object, the DO in complex-transitive complementation can also be passivised. An interesting fact is that the co-reference between the OC and the DO survives passivisation.

59.   *They made <u>him</u> president.*
60.   *<u>He</u> was made president.*

Note, however, that it is the direct object and not the object complement that can passivise!

61.   *They made him <u>president</u>.*
62.   **President* was made him.*

The next Activity is very similar to the last one, so you shouldn't fall for it this time.

Activity 7.10
What's the function of the prepositional phrases in the following two sentences?

a.   *The revolution drove them <u>into exile</u>.*
b.   *Put the car <u>in the garage</u>.*

The PPs are complements again. And what do they complement? The direct object *them* in sentence (a) and the direct object *the car* in sentence (b). Therefore they are object complements.

Tree diagrams for sentences with complex transitive verbs are about as complex as those for ditransitive verbs, and the only thing that distinguishes them is not their structure but their functions.

Figure 7.9

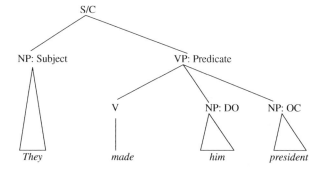

165

7.8 Chapter summary

In this chapter we have looked at the centrality of the verb in English clause structure from a slightly different, namely functional, angle. We have seen how it is actually the verb that determines not only which phrases need to occur, but also how many phrases are required. The obligatory elements called upon by the verb to complete its meaning are called complements, and their occurrence (in number and kind) is often used for classification purposes (intransitive, transitive, ditransitive, copulative, and complex transitive). We also discussed the additional meanings provided by adjuncts, which are optional and omissible elements and more peripheral than complements in that they are certainly not mentioned in a verb's transitivity requirements.

Knowing what a phrase is (e.g. PP, NP, VP) is a first step for the structural analysis, but we also need to know what function the phrase performs in a particular context. To help us distinguish between these functions, we introduced a number of tests (passivisation, subject-auxiliary-inversion and others) useful for determining whether a particular noun phrase is or isn't a subject, object or other complement. Finally, we showed how trees can be used as a descriptive device to illustrate the different transitivity patterns in sentence structure. What we haven't done yet is show you how adjuncts are linked into trees. We will do this in the end-of-chapter exercises and provide the answers on the companion website.

Key terms
Complement; adjunct; subject; predicate; direct object; indirect object; subject complement; object complement; intransitive; transitive; ditransitive; complex-transitive; copular.

Exercises

Exercise 7.1   Underline the subjects in the sentences below

Mary had a little lamb.
Pop goes the weasel.
Have you any wool?
The grand old Duke of York had ten thousand men.
All the King's horses and all the King's men couldn't put Humpty together again.

Exercise 7.2   Underline the direct object in the sentences below

Row your boat.
Mary had a little lamb.
Little Jack Horner was eating a Christmas pie.
Jack and Jill fetched a pail of water.
If you see a crocodile, don't forget to scream.

Exercise 7.3   Complete the following examples by adding an adjunct

_____ *Mary had a little lamb.*
Row your boat _____.
Three blind mice are running _____.
Little Jack Horner sat _____.
The grand old Duke of York marched them _____.

Exercise 7.4   State the function of each underlined phrase in the extract below.

I am forever blowing <u>bubbles</u>, pretty bubbles in the air _____
They <u>fly</u> so high, nearly reach the sky   _____
And like my dreams <u>they</u> fade and die   _____
Fortune is <u>always</u> hiding   _____
I've looked <u>everywhere</u>   _____

Exercise 7.5   Construct sentences according to the following templates

S + V
S + V + SC
S + V + DO + OC

Exercise 7.6   Draw a tree for the sentence *Meggy plays the guitar really well* (we came
across it in Activity 7.4, remember?). Start by drawing a tree for the
obligatory sentence elements, then decide what *really well* modifies. Based on
that decision, try to hang the adverbial phrase *really well* on the tree.

Further reading
More on functions can be found in Quirk *et al.* (1985); Leech *et al.* (1982); Huddleston
and Pullum *et al.* (2002), and Aarts (2011). See also Aarts and Aarts (1982).

CHAPTER **8**

Coordination and subordination

In this chapter . . .

So far we have dealt with the most important basic categories (words, morphemes, phrases, clauses) and structures of the English language. In this chapter we will look at the different ways English has of expressing more complex information, starting with *coordination* (of phrases but also of clauses). We will then move on to consider other types of complex structures, which are called *subordinate clauses*. Subordinate clauses can be grouped according to several characteristics. One way of classifying them is according to the finiteness of their verbs (if they have one); another way is according to their function in the sentence and / or what they modify. We will look at subordinate clauses in that order.

8.1 **Sentences and clauses**

Earlier in this book (Chapters 1 and 3) we noted that communicating with one- or two-word utterances is rather limiting, as we all know from talking with two- to three-year-old children. Slightly older children and adults operate in language using sentences. So far, and especially in Chapter 7, we have dealt with simple sentences, that is, sentences where the grammatical functions (e.g. subject, object, etc.) were not performed by clauses. Sentences may also consist of more than one clause. This is usually the case when the information we want to relay is more complex than a simple SVO pattern would allow, and this is where coordination and / or subordination take place. We can hear you asking: 'But how do we know how many clauses there are in a sentence?' The answer is very straightforward: just count the lexical verbs. One lexical verb, one clause; two lexical verbs, two clauses; three lexical ... you get the idea. The crucial thing here is that only lexical – but not auxiliary or modal verbs – count. That's one of the reasons why we spent a considerable amount of time talking about this distinction in the previous chapters. Another way of putting it is to think that a clause is a sentence within a sentence. Let's try it out.

Activity 8.1
How many verbs, lexical verbs and clauses are there in the following sentences?

	No of Vs	lexical Vs		No of clauses
a. *I must have left my mobile phone at work.*	_____	____	→	_____
b. *I have to go back and get it.*	_____	____	→	_____
c. *If I go back, I'll be late for my Kurdish class.*	_____	____	→	_____

Sentence (a) contains three verbs altogether, but only one lexical verb (*left*). Consequently sentence (a) consists of only one clause. Sentence (b) also contains three verbs (*have*, *go* and *get*), two of which are lexical verbs (*go* and *get*), so sentence (b) consists of two clauses. The subject, although it refers to the same person, has to be repeated in sentence (c) (any idea why?). In this same sentence, the column for Vs should have a 3 in it, the column for lexical verbs, a 2 (*go* and *be*), and so should the column for the number of clauses. Is this what you've got? Sentence (a) is one main clause, sentence (b) consists of two coordinated clauses, and sentence (c) contains a subordinate clause.

To introduce quick definitions, **subordination** involves the use of a clause as a constituent part of a larger clause, whereas **coordination** involves the joining of two or more sentences (or phrases), without any one element being dependent from the other. Look at the examples below.

1. *The ant worked away.*
2. *The grasshopper only sang.*

3. *The ant worked away but the grasshopper only sang.*
4. *The grasshopper only sang but the ant worked away.*

Examples 3 and 4 involve a linking of sentences 1 and 2 by means of *but*, an element we have called a **coordinating conjunction** in Chapter 2. (Which other coordinating conjunctions could we have used?) The two sentences have now become (a larger) one, but both still maintain their syntactic independence; they are grammatically well-formed units in their own right, as we know from examples 1 and 2 (bear this in mind for the next two minutes). When two or more clauses are combined in such a manner, we called the result a *compound sentence.*

Consider example 5. How many lexical verbs does it contain?

5. *The grasshopper complained because it was hungry.*

In example 5, we can identify two lexical verbs (*complain* and, yes, *was* is a lexical verb in this case. How do you know it is not an auxiliary verb? If you are not sure why, go back to section 6.2). We can therefore assume that *The grasshopper complained because it was hungry* is more than one clause. However, there is a sense in which the two parts in which the sentence can be divided (*the grasshopper complained* and *because it was hungry*) are not 'equals', as was the case with the clauses in coordinated structures. The second part (*because it was hungry*) is not an independent sentence. It could perhaps make sense in a particular conversational situation (e.g. as in answer to a question), but not out of context. Without the preceding clause (*the grasshopper complained*), we even have trouble working out who is hungry, i.e. who *it* refers to.

When one sentence 'loses' its syntactic independence and becomes dependent on another clause, we call it a *subordinate clause*. The relationship between a main and one (or more) subordinate clauses is more hierarchical and complex than the one between two coordinated clauses and we therefore call the resulting structure *a complex sentence*. The main difference between coordination and subordination is the nature of their 'joining': while coordinates maintain their independence and are equal partners in a longer sentence, a subordinate sentence is dependent on a main clause for its existence, that is, it is embedded into a larger structure as a minority partner or stakeholder.

What compound sentences and complex sentences have in common is that both their constituent clauses can have their own subjects, objects, etc. This is largely a consequence of all coordinated clauses (and almost all subordinate clauses) having a lexical verb. We saw in Chapter 7 that lexical verbs select their own subject and complements (depending on their meaning). This additional level of analysis is illustrated for both compound and complex sentences in the examples below:

6. *The ant worked away but the grasshopper only sang.*
   [[S + V] *but* [S + V]]
7. *The grasshopper complained because it was hungry.*
   [S + V [*because* S + V + SC]]

As you can see, it would be misleading to speak of the subject of sentence 6 or the subject of sentence 7, in that there are two subjects in these sentences (as well as two verbs). Two subjects are not always necessary (as example (b) from Activity 8.1 illustrates), but often two verbs are (with very few exceptions, see Exercise 8.1).

Another thing compound and complex sentences have in common is that they are both *recursive*, that is, both subordination and coordination can (in theory) go on and on and on . . .

8. *You said [that Mary believes [that Peter claimed [that Noam wrote [that . . .]]]*
9. *I enjoy reading, writing, swimming, sleeping, dancing . . .*

The only restriction on the recursiveness of coordinate and subordinate structures is the limited memory capacity of our brain, which has to deal with these sentences. And there is most definitely a limit to that, as we all know. These limits, together with the added complexity that subordinate clauses impose on the computational resources of our poor human brains, can be beautifully shown in psycholinguistics experiments. There is a wealth of evidence that some (subordinate) sentences are difficult to process (see Exercise 8.2). We will now turn to discuss coordination in more detail.

8.2 Compound sentences: coordination

In English we can coordinate linguistic units of various sizes: words as in *press and enter*, phrases *the green laser beam and the blue strobe light*, and sentences. Coordination in all these cases takes place at various different levels in a tree. The result of coordination at the topmost or clause level are *compound* sentences. The overt presence of the coordinating conjunctions *and*, *or*, *but* are clear indication that coordination is taking place at some level.

Coordination is intrinsically different from subordination in terms of the typical syntactic properties of the resulting compound sentence. We have hinted at some of these properties in the preceding discussion, and we will now provide you with a more detailed overview. First of all, coordination (unlike subordination) operates by joining elements of equal syntactic status.

This means that each component is not dependent on the presence of another. In their monumental *Cambridge Grammar of the English Language*, Huddleston and Pullum et al. (2002) express this idea by claiming that coordination is a non-headed construction, that is, their components cannot be distinguished as *head* vs. *dependent*. We introduced these two notions in Section 5.2. Heads, we said there, are words which largely determine the meaning and grammatical character of groups of related words. The other words are called *dependents*. Applied to coordination at the clause level, this means that neither clause determines the meaning and / or grammatical character of the other one, nor indeed of the compound sentence.

Another important syntactic property of coordination is the fact that grammar has got nothing to say about the maximum number of coordinates allowed (the minimum is clearly two). Coordination can repeat itself time and again, the only limit again being a pragmatic one, that is, one taking into account ease of processing and human memory.

10. *Tim sang, Mary cried, Judith sighed, Eva wrote, the bird slept …*

Now, coordination is a syntactic operation linking equal elements of various sizes (words, phrases, clauses), which means that, within a coordinated structure, neither element is higher up the syntactic hierarchy than the other/s. This condition also applies to the *kind* of elements that can be joined together: these must be similar in their syntactic make-up, e.g.

11. *[Peter] and [in the park] went for a swim
12. *We don't agree with [their politics] or [while they're drunk]

Examples 11 and 12 illustrate that linking a NP and a PP, or a NP and a clause is not allowed. We have already taken advantage of this syntactic property of coordination. Can you remember when? Yes, exactly, in Chapter 6 (specifically, in Section 6.5.3), when we conducted a few experiments on whether strings of words formed phrases. We hypothesised that if a string X can be coordinated with a word (or phrase), this constitutes evidence that X is a word (or phrase) of the same category as the word (or phrase) it is coordinated with. We concluded from the experiment that this works most of the time. However, consider the following example. Label the word(s) enclosed in square brackets with the appropriate subscripts.

13. *He felt [sad] and [in need of a drink].*

Coordination, in this case, does not result in ungrammaticality, despite the fact that the coordinated elements are syntactically dissimilar, i.e. $_{AdjP}$[*sad*] and $_{PP}$[*in need of a drink*]. The two phrases have different heads, which result in one of them being an AdjP, while the other one is a PP. Their syntactic function, however, is the same: both are subject complements. This shows us two things. It shows why both a structural analysis (as introduced in Chapters 5 and 6) and a functional analysis (as introduced in Chapter 7) have to be carried out to arrive at a full understanding of a sentence; and it demonstrates yet another syntactic property of coordination, that the resulting coordinated structure must have the same function (not form) of their coordinated parts.

The next section looks at some tell-tale signs of coordination.

8.3 Markers of coordination

We have already been working with the most common markers of coordination, the coordinating conjunctions *and*, *but*, *or*. They link units of equal status. The type of coordination which uses overt markers of coordination in between coordinates is called *syndetic* coordination. This is perhaps the most common pattern.

There are other coordinating conjunctions which serve to strengthen the role of *and*, *or*, *but*: these are called *correlative conjunctions*, and they occur along with *and*, *or*, *but*.

14.   *Both* [Adam] *and* [Eve] *realised they were naked*.
15.   *Either* [we discuss this now] *or* [we do it next week].
16.   *Not only* [are they tired], *but also* [they have been ill for the whole of last week].

Apart from these overt markers of coordination, there are other elements with a coordinating function. A more subtle, less overt way in which coordination can be carried out is through punctuation. We can link coordinated clauses using commas or semi-colons.

17.   *The ant worked away, the grasshopper only sang, Aesop wrote.*
18.   *The ant worked away; the grasshopper only sang; Aesop wrote.*

In examples 17 and 18, commas and semi-colons are used to separate / join coordinates; so punctuation can also serve coordinating purposes. When there are no lexical markers of coordination, we call that *asyndetic coordination*.

Activity 8.2
How is asyndetic coordination done in spoken language?

Exercise 8.1 at the end of the chapter may tempt you to rely on punctuation or pauses and falling intonation (the spoken language equivalents of commas and semi-colons) to determine the number of clauses contained in the example sentences, so take care when you get there.

Activity 8.3

The *Oxford comma* refers to a particular use of the comma as coordinator between the last element (in a list or enumeration) and an overt coordinator, as illustrated below:

a. *Tom, Mary, Peter, and Lawrence went to the party.*

Many think this use is pretentious and unrequired, in that the overt coordinator can actually perform the linking function perfectly on its own. But consider the following:

b. *I would like to thank my parents, Homer and Marge, who have given me constant support.*

Example (b) is ambiguous between an appositive reading and an enumeration. That is, when reading example (b) for the first time, we intuitively imagine a Simpson sibling speaking, and *Homer and Marge* are in **apposition** to *my parents* (i.e. *my parents, that is to say, Homer and Marge*). However, there is another possible meaning, where the speaker is thanking four different people, that is, 'my parents', as well as two other people called 'Homer' and 'Marge'.
Consider now example (c):

c. *I would like to thank my parents, Homer, and Marge, who have given me constant support.*

The presence of the Oxford comma (i.e. the one after 'Homer') makes the appositive reading impossible, and it can only be read as an enumeration: in (c) the speaker is clearly thanking four people, with no identity claimed between 'my parents' on the one hand, and 'Homer' and 'Marge' on the other.

  The presence or absence of the Oxford comma can be useful for disambiguating between different meanings, without actually relying on contextual or intonational information (falling intonation or pause). The Oxford comma thus conditions the interpretation of the sentence as being an enumeration.

(NB: Remember the term **apposition**? We first came across this term in Chapter 5. Here is a hint: which name can replace the whole group of words *the white cat with a stripy tail?*)

There is a third, largely stylistic, kind of coordination. It's called *polysyndetic* and refers to structures in which conjunctions are repeated in between every coordinated element, as in

19. *The rescued man thanked the paramedic again and again and again.*
20. *Dylan would rant and rant and rant and rant.*

This type of coordination has mainly an emphatic purpose, and is normally associated with perseverance, repetition, etc.

8.4 **Coordination at different levels**

So far we have mainly discussed coordination at the level of the clause. In our examples and discussion, however, we have hinted at coordination taking place at other levels. The remainder of this section provides an orderly treatment of coordination at different levels, including phrases and clauses.

Coordination can take place at the phrase level. Example 21 links three NPs:

21. [*The chickens*], [*the cows*], *and* [*many dogs*] *were under the rain.*

What is coordinated in the example 22?

22. *Mary* [*works in a bank*] *and* [*studies Linguistics*].

The units linked in example 22 are verb phrases, if we want to use a structural description, or predicates, if we want to use a functional one. Coordination, however, can also take place deep inside a phrase. We can, for example coordinate modifiers to a N.

23. [*Warm*] *and* [*cold*] *drinks* (AdjPs).
24. *The* [*rank*] *and* [*file*] *were restless.*

Activity 8.4
The following example sentence is interesting from a linguistic point of view.
The rank and file were restless.
Does the determiner (i) refer to both nouns, or (ii) are we dealing with a process of coordination similar to compounding (see Chapter 3)?
What's the difference between these two possibilities? How many lexemes does interpretation (i) contain? How many lexemes are there if we assume interpretation (ii)?

Rank and file is an idiomatic expression which behaves like a single lexeme, like a compound noun, and the determiner therefore refers to both nouns as a unit. The reading **The rank and the file* is not possible.

The main topic of the first half of this chapter, however, was coordination of clauses, as in:

25. *My dog was barking like mad but I couldn't hear anything.* (clauses)

The main thing to take home with you from this chapter so far is that in coordination the two (or more) conjoined elements are equals; equals either in terms of function, as the two subject complements in *He felt* [*sad*] *and* [*in need of a drink*], or in terms of type and structure (e.g. two adjective phrases). As long as these requirements are met, coordination can take place at any level (word, phrase or clause levels).

This wasn't bad so far, was it? But don't let coordination deceive you. How to analyse and represent coordination is one of the biggest nightmares for most syntactic theories. We will raise some of them in the exercises at the end of this chapter, where we will also draw trees for coordinating structures.

8.5 Complex sentences: subordination

Complex sentences have exactly the same grammatical / functional elements (subject, object, etc.) as simple sentences. The only difference between them is that in complex sentences one (or more) of these functions is realised as a clause (rather than a phrase). This sounds worse than it is. Let's look at a few examples. Examples 26 and 27 below consist of exactly the same elements: a subject (S), a verb (V) and a direct object (DO). The only difference between the two is that in example 26 the direct object is realised as a noun phrase, whereas in example 27 it is realised as a clause (with a lexical verb and other elements required by that verb).

26. *He told him* [*a lie*].
    S + V + IO + DO(NP)
27. *He told him* [*that Paolo can't play football*].
    S + V + IO + DO(CL)

The complex example 27 contains an embedded clause which acts as its object. How do we know that [*that Paolo can't play football*] is the direct object of *He told him …*? Well, the sentence becomes ungrammatical if this element is missing; so it has to be a complement of the lexical verb. We know it's not a subject complement because it does not modify the subject; it is clearly not an object complement because it doesn't modify the direct object *him*; so it has to be an object itself. How do we know that it is a clause? Well, it has a lexical verb *play*, a subject *Paolo* and an object *football*. When we analyse the subordinate clause in example 27 (repeated below as example 28), we realise that it has got all the tell-tale signs of a clause: a subject, a verb and an object.

28. *Paolo can't play football.*
    S + V + DO

Complex sentences contain an embedded or subordinate clause which acts as one of its sentence elements (or as part of one). What other markers of subordination are there?

8.6 Markers of subordination

How can we identify a subordinate clause when we see one? There are two main ways. The first one involves the presence of certain overt markers of subordination, subordinating conjunctions. The second way of identifying a complex sentence is by looking at the form of the verb. We will discuss these methods in that order.

8.6.1 Subordinating conjunctions

Most (but not all) subordinate clauses are introduced by a conjunction, especially if the verb in the subordinate clause is finite / tensed. *That* in example 27 above is a marker of subordination and thus very useful for identifying the following unit as a clause-size one. Unfortunately, *that* can be left out without rendering the sentence ungrammatical.

29.   *He told him [Paolo can't play football]*.

The job of a subordinating conjunction is to mark that the clause it introduces is a dependent or subordinate one. Words which always introduce a subordinate clause are *if* and *whether* (these are also sometimes called complementisers) but many other words can function as subordinating conjunctions, too. For example *after, although, as, because, before, since, till, unless, until, when, where, while, except that, provided that, as long as.*

Activity 8.5

Which word class do the underlined words belong to? Are they all introducing embedded clauses?

a.   *Before I asked her, she knew nothing.*
b.   *Before my question, she knew nothing.*
c.   *I will wait until he gets home.*
d.   *I will wait until tomorrow.*

   In examples (a) and (c), the underlined words are conjunctions which introduce subordinate clauses with a subject, a finite verb and another obligatory sentence element. But what do they head in the examples (b) and (d)? They introduce a noun phrase which they head to form a prepositional phrase. Activity 8.5 therefore illustrates that it is important not to mix up certain subordinating conjunctions with prepositions which share the same form.

8.6.2 VP form: non-finite and verbless clauses

The second way of identifying a complex sentence, we said, is by looking at the form of the verb. If the verb in a potential clause is non-finite (i.e. if it's not marked for tense), then the clause is definitely a subordinate one. There are three non-finite verbal forms (see Section 2.2.2):

- the base or infinitival form (with or without *to*),
- the *-ed* participle form, and
- the *-ing* form.

Each one of these forms gives rise to a non-finite type of subordinate clause:

30. *He decided* [*playing football as a professional*] *was beyond his ability.* (*-ing* part)
31. [*Reconciled to his limitations*], *he became a football referee.* (*-ed* part)
32. *He always wanted* [*to be on a football pitch*]. (infinitive with *to*)
33. *His career helped* [*realise that dream of his*]. (infinitive without *to*)

These subordinate clauses are more difficult to recognise than fully fledged embedded clauses, but they are not too bad because they still meet the main structural criteria for clause status. That is, despite the fact that they do not have a subject, they still contain a lexical verb in a non-finite form (*realise* in example 33 and *to be* in 32 are infinitival; *reconciled* in 31 is an *-ed* participle, and *playing* in 30 is an *-ing* participle form). It only gets tricky when the subordinate clause contains no verb at all, whether finite or non-finite, as in

34. <u>With a heavy heart</u>, *Peter followed suit.*

Occasionally, non-finite and verbless clauses are nice to us. If they want to help us identify them as clauses, they give themselves away by either containing subjects, as in

35. *He stumbled,* [<u>his legs</u> *shaking*].
36. *Peter sighed,* [<u>his dreams</u> *in tatters*].

or a subordinating conjunction, as in

37. [<u>Though</u> *sad and devoid of hope*], *Peter walked up the aisle.*

But which one of the two clauses in sentences (34) to (37) is the subordinate one? Don't play the lottery, instead use the syntactic characteristics for main vs. subordinate clause status that we have already established. Recall that while a main clause must contain a finite verb, a non-finite clause can either contain a finite, a non-finite or no verb at all.

If we apply these criteria to sentence 35, we can easily and with 100 per cent certainty identify *his legs shaking* as the non-finite subordinate clause. The same test reveals in sentence 36 that *his dreams in tatters* is the subordinate one. The subjects don't help in these cases as all clauses have one (*he*, *his legs* and *Peter* and *his dreams*).

It may also help if you think of non-finite and verbless clauses as reduced clauses, i.e. clauses without a subject and at times even without a verb. Like before, we can help ourselves by utilising all the structural information we have, comparing it with a fuller, finite clause, and recovering understood elements from the context. This particularly helps with verbless clauses such as sentence 36. When we introduce a verb, the relationship between *his dreams* and *in tatters* becomes more transparent. We have already identified *his dreams* as the subject of the verbless clause, but what is *in tatters?*

38. *His dreams were in tatters.* (S + V + SC)

In tatters modifies the subject, it is a subject complement.

Note, furthermore, that non-finite and verbless clauses tend to function largely as adjuncts, so you can delete them without rendering the complex sentences ungrammatical.

8.7 Subordinate clause types

At the beginning of Section 8.5 we defined complex sentences as syntactic structures consisting of two clauses in which one (or more) of the main clause's functions are realised by a clause (rather than a phrase). We can therefore also identify, describe and classify clauses according to the functions they perform in clause structure: we can distinguish between clauses that function as phrasal elements (post-modifiers of noun and adjective phrases or complements of prepositional phrases, see Section 8.8.2), or as sentence elements (such as subjects, objects, subject complements and adjuncts, see Section 8.8.1). We will look now at relative clauses (see also Section 10.1), nominal relative clauses and *that*-clauses. We'll start with relative clauses.

8.7.1 Relative clauses

Relative clauses function as post-modifiers to a noun. Nouns, we decided after some deliberations in Chapter 5, are the heads of noun phrases, and NPs can fulfil many different functions in clause structure, such as subject, object, complement and adjunct. Relative clauses therefore can be found in many different positions in a sentence, basically any position that allows a noun which acts as the head of an NP. So we can't say 'relative clauses tend to be placed at the beginning, the middle or the end of a sentence', but we can say relative clauses are placed after the noun they modify, and as you are good at recognising nouns, this distributional criterion of relative clauses works well. In terms of function, the relative clause has the same function as the noun phrase whose head it modifies.

Relative clauses are frequently introduced by the relative pronouns *that*, *who*, *which* or *whose*. These pronouns, however, can under certain circumstances be omitted from relative clauses, as in:

39. *The house (that) I live in is small.*
40. *The appointment (which) we missed cannot be rescheduled.*

When you come across the term *zero-relative clause* in some other textbooks, you can associate them with relative subordinate clauses in which the relative pronoun has been left out.

Zero relative clauses are to be distinguished from *reduced relative clauses*. Relative clauses can undergo the same reduction or shrinking process we discussed more generally for all subordinate clauses in Section 8.6.2: not only can the relative pronoun be deleted, but the lexical verb can also be stripped of its tense, giving rise to a non-finite relative subordinate clause (usually *-ed* or *-ing*), as in:

41. *Seeds sown in winter rarely prosper*
42. *The song playing on the radio is odious*

Before we move on, a quick question. What's the function of all (finite and non-finite) relative clauses we have looked at in this section so far? Remember that relative clauses take on the function of the noun phrase they are part of.

Activity 8.6
And what are the functions of the relative clauses in the following sentences?

a. *I drank ammonia, which tasted awful.*
b. *Samantha paid the money she had earned over the last few weeks to the finance office.*
c. *Craig paid the money to the cashier whose wife he went to school with.*
d. *He has a beauty that will age well.*

If you don't immediately go 'all relative clauses in Section 8.7.1 are within subjects', you may want to get to the answer one step at a time. You will need to take five steps:

Step 1. Identify the subordinate clause.
Step 2. Identify the noun it modifies.
Step 3. Identify the noun phrase headed by the noun.
Step 4. What function does that NP have in the main clause?

The relative clause has the same function as the NP it modifies. In arriving at the answer, everybody takes the same five steps, only experienced linguists do this so quickly that it seems like a single step. You can do this, too: with practice you will be able to skip one step at a time and arrive 'straight' at the correct answer. The end-of-chapter exercises will help you get there.

8.7.2 Nominal relative clauses

Nominal relative clauses, as their name suggests, are a good link between relative clauses and nominal clauses, i.e. clauses that function as sentence elements. Let's unpack one and you will see why.

43.   *I wish I could do whatever I wanted.*

As suggested in step 1, first we identify the subordinate clauses. How many of them are there in example 43? There are two: *I wish* $_{C1}$[*(that)* I could do $_{C2}$[*whatever I wanted*]]. We have re-introduced the conjunction for the first subordinate clause, and underlined both elements introducing each subordinate clause. OK, in this case we have to introduce a step 1b. Which of the two subordinate clauses is the relative one, i.e. which one modifies a noun? This is a tricky one because we need to reconstruct the noun from the context. In other words, we can see the *whatever* in our second subordinate clause expresses two things:

whatever I wanted = the thing/s $_{C2}$[*that I wanted*]]

Now that we've got the noun *thing/s*, we are ready to take step 3: identify the noun phrase headed by *thing/s*.

whatever I wanted = $_{NP}$[*the thing/s* [*that I wanted*]]

For step 4 we have to return to the full sentence *I wish I could do whatever I wanted*, or at least to the reconstructed *I wish I could do* $_{NP}$[*the thing/s* [*that I wanted*]]. What's the function of $_{NP}$[*the thing/s* [*that I wanted*]] in the larger subordinate clause, i.e. in C1? It's the object. *Whatever I wanted* therefore functions as the object of *I could do* [*whatever I wanted*]. Replace it with *it* or anything *it* can stand for, e.g. $_{NP}$[*the sudoku*], $_{NP}$[*my make-up*], etc., and it becomes clear. Can you think of an example of a relative clause with a nominal function?

We thought not. Our example 43 illustrates that nominal relative clauses are a different kind from relative clauses: while relative clauses post-modify Ns, nominal relative clauses (as their name indicates) are nominal in function, i.e. they behave like NPs. They are easily identifiable by being introduced by *what (ever)*, *who(ever)*, *where(ver)*, *how(ever)*.

8.7.3 *That*-clauses

Activity 8.7

What's the difference between the use of *that* in the following subordinate clauses?

a. *The dog that bit me was mad.*
b. *We believe that responsibility is a good thing.*

Can you replace *that* with *which* in both cases? If not, why not?

To be able to approach the question posed in Activity 8.7 in a meaningful way, we first need to agree on what constitutes the subordinate clauses in sentences (a) and (b). [*that bit me*] is the subordinate clause in example (a) and [*that responsibility is a good thing*] is the subordinate clause in example (b), and intuitively we know that we can replace *that* with *which* in sentence (a); but not in (b). How can we systematically identify the differences between these subordinate clauses? We are going to use some standard tests from our tool box.

We can try omissibility, which always reveals obligatory vs. optional sentence elements. The deletion test shows that the subordinate clause in sentence (a) can be deleted, consequently [*that bit me*] is an optional modifier. What does it modify? Well, the subordinate clause is adding information about a *dog*, which is the head of an NP. This is typically the function of a relative clause. As we have seen in Section 8.7.1, relative clauses are often introduced by relative pronouns such as *that*, *which*, *who* and others. And as we will see in Chapter 10, these relative pronouns have a function to perform within the structure of the subordinate clause. The *that* in sentence (a) refers to *the dog*; if we replaced *that* with *which*, the *which* will also refer to *the dog*.

On the other hand, the subordinate clause in sentence (b) cannot be deleted, and is thus an obligatory complement. But what kind of complement is it, and what does it complement? It's a complement of the lexical verb *believe* of the main clause. *Believe*, therefore, is a transitive verb which requires an object. Subordinate clauses like the one in sentence (a) function as nominals, and can often be introduced by *that*, which is why we call them *that*-clauses. However, this type of *that* is called a *complementiser* (or subordinating conjunction). This type of words does not perform a function within the subordinate clause; rather it simply serves to signpost the subordinate clause. Unlike in sentence (a), the *that* in sentence (b) does not refer to *the dog*, which is why we cannot replace it by another referring word such as *which*.

To summarise, *that*-clauses are subordinate clauses which (i) are introduced by the subordinating conjunction *that*, (ii) are obligatory elements in clause structure, and (iii) are nominal in function, that is, they serve as subjects, objects and other sentence elements, as we shall see next.

8.8 Subordination at clausal and phrasal levels

8.8.1 Clauses in sentences

Regardless of their type and make-up, subordinate clauses perform certain functions. They either modify the head noun of a noun phrase (then they are called _____) or they are obligatory elements which behave like NPs (and we call those _____), or they sit uncomfortably between relative clauses and the nominal clauses we are going to look at now (then they are called _____).

An alternative way of looking at subordinate clauses is in terms of the functions they take on at sentence level. They can function as subjects (S), direct objects (DO), subject complements (SC) or adverbials (A); most frequently they function as optional sentence elements, i.e. adverbials. These uses are exemplified in Activity 8.8, but we leave it up to you to determine which function is illustrated by which set of examples.

Activity 8.8

Start by identifying the subordinate clauses and put them in square brackets, then determine their functions (e.g. S, O, A), and finally decide what type of clause you are dealing with, that is, is the clause finite or non-finite? If non-finite, is the verb in infinitive form (with or without *to*), or in its *-ing* or *-ed* participle form? And is it a *that*-clause, a relative clause, or a nominative relative clause?

All examples under one number serve the same function, but they are different types of clauses. Your answers can take the following format:

In examples (1a) to (1d), the subordinate clause (enclosed in square brackets) functions as a _____ and the clause is a _____ (e.g. non-finite *-ed* clause).

1a. *I believe that lions are dangerous.*   2a *Drinking pineapple juice is horrible.*

1b. *They decided to sell the house.*   2b *That she pretended to care was really sad.*

1c *The employees need kicking.*

1d. *I imagine what will happen.*

3a *My decision is to become a millionaire.*

3b *My dad's job was building containers.*

3c *The truth is that he loves her.*

3d *That's what she's been trying to tell me.*

2c *Whoever told you that is right.*

2d *To suffer in silence can be hard.*

4a *Don't forget to scream if you see a crocodile.*

4b *Because the roads are closed, I couldn't go.*

4c *She died while waiting at the level-crossing.*

4d *Hidden behind a bush, I could not see her.*

In examples (1a) to (1d), the subordinate clauses [*that lions are dangerous*], [*to sell the house*], [*kicking*] and [*what will happen*] function as direct objects. Example (1a) is a *that*-clause, (1b) is a non-finite infinitive clause with *to*, (1c) is a non-finite *-ing* clause, and (1d) a nominative relative clause.

All subordinate clauses in the examples under 2 function as subjects. [*Drinking pineapple juice*] is a non-finite *-ing* clause (2a), [*That she pretended to care*] is a *that*-clause (2b), [*Whoever told you that*] is a nominal relative clause (2c), and the last example (2d) contains the non-finite infinitive clause [*To suffer in silence*], which is again with the infinitive marker *to*.

The examples in 3 are a bit more difficult, but all of them function as subject complements. We've got one infinitive clause with *to* [*to become a millionaire*] in (3a); one *-ing* clause [*building containers*] in (3b), one *that*-clause [*that he loves her*] in (3c); and one nominal relative clause [*what she's been trying to tell me*] in (3d). The last example, (3d), is particularly difficult because the finite verb of the main clause (*is*) is cliticised to the subject, and out of context as these examples are presented, the subject *that* is semantically as empty as it can be.

The last set of examples, however, was easy. All subordinate clauses function as adverbial elements and express a wide range of meanings: [*if you see a crocodile*] is a finite conditional clause; [*because the roads are closed*] is a finite causal clause; [*while waiting at the level-crossing*] is a temporal non-finite *-ing* clause; and [*hidden behind a bush*] is a non-finite *-ed* clause indicating location.

8.8.2 Clauses in phrases

Besides their function in clause structure, clauses can also function as modifiers to phrases, with relative clauses being the typical case illustrating this. Recall that relative clauses post-modify the head noun of a noun phrase. There is no grammatical reason why clauses do not normally pre-modify phrases, but perhaps the burden these structures would place on human language processing is the most likely explanation why clausal pre-modification doesn't exist (at least not in English). In short, when modifying phrases, clauses are found as post-modifiers, as the following examples illustrate.

Post-modifier in NP

44. *The postman [who was bitten by the dog] is better.* (relative clause)
45. *I didn't get the chance [to be in class].* (*to*-inf)
46. *The policy covers expenses [incurred in the process].* (*-ed* clause)

Postmodifier in AdjP

47. *I am aware [that your society is very active].* (*that*-clause)
48. *Don't be afraid [to experiment with other flavours].* (inf)

Complement in PP

49. *I am not interested in [doing sports].* (*-ing* clause)
50. *I have to think about [what to get her].* (nominal relative clause)

8.9 Chapter summary

In this chapter we have looked at different ways in which speakers and writers combine and condense information while still following the basic sentence patterns of English. We discussed how different syntactic operations (coordination and subordination) are put to use. We said that **coordination** is a process by which linguistic elements/units of various sizes are joined as equals. This is only possible because the two conjoined units are equal in one way or another: either they are units of the same type (e.g. two main clauses, two AdjPs, two heads of phrases), or function (two subject complements, for example).

By starting with coordination, we tried to ease you into clause combining, and then it gradually got more complex. The complexity of subordinate clauses arises from the fact that they can be anything from 'full' clauses (with a subordinating conjunction, a subject and a tensed verb) to radically reduced ones (either without a subordinating conjunction, or a subject, or a tensed verb, and if they are particularly mean, even without a verb). The other reason why complex sentences (i.e. those containing a subordinate clause) live up to their name is the fact that they can fulfil several quite distinct functions: they can either take over from noun phrases as subjects, direct objects and subject complements, or function as adverbials; they can be post-modifiers in noun phrases, modify noun phrases (then they are called relative clauses) and adjective phrases or complements in prepositional phrases. Because we need to describe both the form and the function of subordinate clauses, we ended up with a rather complex classification system. The exercises at the end of chapter give you more practice.

What we need to say now is that very often coordination and subordination tend to co-occur. We have seen these two patterns as separate things for ease of presentation, but speakers and writers take full advantage of *both* when constructing their messages. In other words, a sentence may be both compound and complex.

51.   [*Mary thinks* [*that Peter is wrong*] [*because he looks smug*]], *but* [*I know* [*he is right*]].

Key terms
Coordination; subordination; finite; non-finite; relative clause.

Exercises

Exercise 8.1   How many clauses are there in the following two sentences?

An amazing variety of flowers were displayed in the garden, every one of them a slightly different shade from the one next to it.
If anything, it was more difficult than I expected it to be.

We are sure you got the answer right (two clauses in each sentence is the right answer) but we suspect you may have used the punctuation mark as a crutch, right? This is very dangerous, as punctuation is not a reliable indicator of clause status. What is a safer way of determining the number of clauses in a sentence? Counting lexical verbs, as we suggested in Section 8.1. Does this test work in the case of the example sentences above? No, it doesn't, because *every one of them* is slightly different from *the one next to it*, and recall there are verbless clauses out there too! What other linguistic criteria indicate that we are dealing with clauses in these cases?

Exercise 8.2   *The cheese the rat ate was rotten.*
Ha, we sprung this sentence on you. It's not that easy to understand, is it? How can you make it easier to process for the human brain? Yes, adding a relative pronoun like *that* helps. (Think about this next time you write an essay. Your tutor will appreciate it.)

The cheese the rat the cat chased ate was rotten is almost impossibly complex. It is a so called *doubly centre-embedded sentence* and frequently causes the human language processor (the brain) to break down. Another structure that is difficult to understand has got a very appropriate name. Consider the sentence below:

The cotton shirts are made from comes from India.

These are called *garden-path sentences*. Did you get led up the garden path? Inserting what type of word would have saved the neurons in your brain all the excess mileage? *That*, for example.

How do we know that these structures are very difficult for us to process? Well, we intuitively know it, but it can also be measured. It takes humans milliseconds longer to tick the right answer out of the following two options in psycholinguistic experiments

The shirts come from India.
The cotton comes from India.

Exercise 8.3   There is a very well-known prescriptive rule in English which states that you should not start sentences with *and* or *but*. Can you think of the reasons behind this recommendation?

Exercise 8.4   Normally, the order of coordinated elements can be altered, e.g.

Tom and Mary went to the park.
Mary and Tom went to the park.

Is that always possible? Why / why not? Consider the following:

We had fish and chips for lunch.
He put on his best suit and went to church.
She ordered a pint and a half.

Exercise 8.5   What type of elements (Ns, NPs, clauses, etc.) are being coordinated in the sentence below?

John played Scrabble; Mary Sudoku; and Peter a record.

Notice that the verb *played* is actually omitted (i.e. it is contextually recoverable) from the second and third conjoins. For this reason examples like these are often described as *gapped coordination*.

Exercise 8.6   Bracket all the coordinated structures in the following sentences.

Batman and Robin and Fred and Ginger came to the party.
Susan is skipping and Mary is drawing in the playground, but Kim is ill.
Would you like fish fingers or fish and chips for your dinner?

This exercise shows you that coordination can also be layered, i.e. a coordinated structure can work as a coordinate within a larger one. We are going to use Fred and Ginger again in our next exercise, to illustrate the various different ways in which coordination can be structurally represented in the form of tree diagrams.

Exercise 8.7   How would you go about drawing a tree for the sentence *Ginger and Fred danced*? The three main possibilities suggested in the literature are as follows:

Figure 8.1

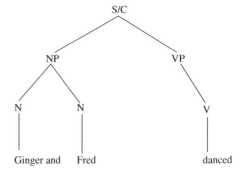

Figure 8.2

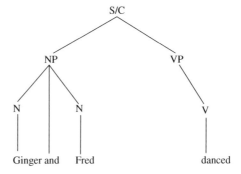

Figure 8.3

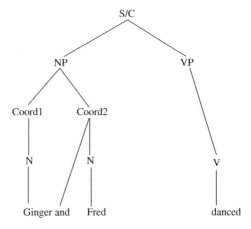

Further reading

On coordination and subordination, Huddleston and Pullum et al. (2002); Huddleston and Pullum (2005) (especially Chapter 14); van Gelderen (2002); and Radford (2009) (especially Chapter 5). Coordination is discussed in depth in Heiman and Thompson (1998).

CHAPTER 9

Clause types

In this chapter . . .

Up until now most of the example sentences we have used in our discussion have been active, positive and declarative. But English is not limited to that type of sentences. We can ask questions, utter commands, negate statements as well as be sneaky and hide away (grammatically, that is) the person who is responsible for an activity (by using passive voice). We will now have a closer look at how these sentence types differ from default declarative sentences in terms of the elements they contain and the order in which they appear.

Different sentence types are classified largely on the basis of their syntactic behaviour, properties and structure. Simply by looking at their form, we can tell whether a sentence is declarative, interrogative, imperative or exclamative. Of course the different types of clauses also differ in terms of the functions they perform in communication, but one and the same function can frequently be carried out by different clause types as Activity 9.1 illustrates.

Activity 9.1

Describe what functions the following sentences perform.

a. *I'm going to miss the train?*
b. *I never miss the train.*
c. *You must not miss the train, dear.*

The rising intonation of example (a) (indicated by the question mark) shows that it is being used as a question. Example (b) means almost the same thing as *I don't miss trains*, and example (c) expresses (nicely) an order or advice, yet all three examples from Activity 9.1 are declarative active main clauses. For this reason we will groups clauses according to their syntactic structure and not their function.

We will discuss declarative, interrogative and imperative clauses in this chapter, and will reserve exclamatives for Chapter 10. And that is not all: you will have noticed that we will also be discussing negative, passive and other, more marginal, types of sentences. Let's begin with a recap on declaratives.

9.1 Declaratives

Declarative sentences are the most frequent type of sentences. They normally make an informative statement:

1. *West Ham United won the FA Cup in 1964, 1975 and 1980.*

The default SVO order of English sentences is based on declarative sentences: the subject comes first, followed by the verb, and then the object (if any). We have discussed this pattern in previous chapters: it is the yardstick against which all other sentence patterns are measured. In other words, the sentence types discussed in the following sections all depart in different ways from the default SVO order typical of English declarative sentences.

9.2 Interrogatives

Interrogative sentences are normally used for asking questions, requesting information from others.

2. *Did West Ham United win the FA Cup in 1980?*
3. *What did West Ham United win in 1980?*

Interrogatives are easily identified because a part of the predicate (usually the auxiliary) appears before the subject. What is the subject in the sentences above? Notice that *did* and *what did* precede it. Yes, the subject is indeed *West Ham United*.

We can classify interrogatives based on the kind of information they seek. *Did West Ham United win the FA Cup in 1980?*, for example, questions the entire clause. It asks whether the entire declarative sentence (or proposition) is true or false. The expected response is either confirmation or disconfirmation of the whole proposition; in this case whether it is true or not that *West Ham United won the FA Cup in 1980*. Normally the answer comes by means of a simple *yes* or *no*; and this is why these sentences are called **yes / no interrogatives** (or Y/N interrogatives, in short).

In *What did West Ham United win in 1980?*, on the other hand, information is only sought about a particular part of the sentence, in this case the object $_{NP}$[*the FA Cup*]. This second type of interrogative is called a ***wh*-interrogative**, largely because these types of questions tend to be headed by *wh*-words (e.g. *when, who/m, what, which, where, why* and also *how*). These interrogatives do not expect a *yes* or *no* answer, but rather a fuller response. We will discuss this type in more detail immediately below.

9.2.1 *Wh*-interrogatives

These interrogatives are also known as *open interrogatives* or *constituent interrogatives*. These two labels focus on different components / parts of the behaviour of *wh*-interrogatives: open interrogatives refer to the fact that the expected answer to a *wh*-interrogative does not belong to a closed set (as is the case with Y/N interrogatives); constituent interrogatives refer to the fact that the *wh*-word is used to seek information about a particular unit or phrasal constituent of the clause. We already used this property of *wh*-interrogatives in Chapter 6, when we were confronted with the task of identifying phrases. One diagnostic test that helped us work out which words behave as a group involves asking for the information expressed by the phrase by means of a *wh*-pronoun. This test not only reveals that a word or a group of words behaves as a phrase; it also provides us with important information about the function of that phrase. Let's look at this in a bit more detail.

In *Who won the FA Cup in 1980?*, *who* is (or heads) the noun phrase that functions as the subject of the clause (recall that phrases can consist of just one word, but that word must be the head of that type of phrase. If you are struggling with this, go back to Section 2.1.4, where we identified *who* as an interrogative pronoun, and to our discussion of heads in Section 5.2). The structural analysis of the sentence *Who won the FA Cup in 1980?* therefore identifies NP[*who*] as a noun phrase, and the functional analysis identifies this noun phrase as the subject of the interrogative clause NP[*Who*] *won the FA Cup in 1980?*

In *Which football team won the FA Cup in 1980?*, on the other hand, the *wh*-element *which* is the determiner of the noun phrase NP[*which team*]. This noun phrase also functions as the subject of the sentence NP[*Which football*] *team won the FA Cup in 1980?*

These examples show that the group of words headed by the *wh*-word is normally a phrase in sentence structure, i.e. in the examples above, the subject. (That's why we can use *wh*-interrogatives for diagnostic tests to identify phrases and the function they have in sentences.) But *wh*-phrases need not be the subject, they can also have different functions, as in examples 4 and 5. What's the function of *what* and *when* in examples 4 and 5?

4. [*What*] *did West Ham United win in 1980?*
5. [*When*] *did West Ham United win the FA Cup?*

In example 4, the *wh*-phrases functions as the direct object; in example 5 it functions as an adjunct. How do we know this? We can easily delete the *when* from example 5 without it becoming ungrammatical (*Did West Ham United win the FA Cup?*) which shows us that *when* is an optional element in this sentence, and thus an adjunct. Example 4, on the other hand, becomes a completely different type of question when we remove the *what*: it actually becomes a Y/N question. When a diagnostic test results in such a drastic change (like a change in clause type), you know that something is wrong. In this case, we have lost the obligatory verb complement, i.e. the object represented by *what*.

You may have noticed that the above examples all start with a *wh*-phrase, but this is followed not by the verb itself, but by the first auxiliary. We have called this operation *subject-auxiliary inversion* (or SAI for short) as far back as Section 2.2.4. Subject-auxiliary inversion is a typical characteristic of *wh*-interrogatives: the order of their constituents differs systematically from that of declarative clauses in that they begin with an interrogative phrase, which is followed by an auxiliary, and only then does the subject make an appearance. The subject is followed in turn by the main verb. The notable exception to this rule is when the *wh*-word is functioning as the subject of the interrogative (as in <u>*Who won the FA Cup in 1980?*</u> and <u>*Which football team won the FA Cup in 1980?*</u>). Then no SAI is required, and the order of sentence elements is similar to that of declaratives (i.e. SVO).

Activity 9.2

Can you ask for two different sentence elements with one single *wh*-question?
Try asking for *the dog-owner* and *the park* in one question:

The dog owner went to the park.

Now try asking for *the girls* and *five apples* in one *wh*-question:

You gave five apples to the girls.

What do you notice about the structure of these 'double' *wh*-interrogatives?

Yes, it is possible to ask for *the dog-owner* and *the park* in one question, as in *Who went where?* and it is equally possible to ask for *the girls* and *five apples* in one *wh*-question, as in *How much did you give to whom?* These 'double' *wh*-interrogatives, however, also show that (in English) only one interrogative can be fronted.

The main point about interrogative *wh*-words is that they stand in for / replace missing information, the information the speaker / writer asks of their addressee. Structurally *wh*-interrogatives differ from declarative clauses in that the *wh*-phrase and the finite auxiliary are fronted. Note that the fronted *wh*-word keeps its grammatical function when fronted.

What's the function of *what* in example 6?

6. *What did Mehmet give the girl _ ?*

What is the direct object, *the girl* is the indirect object and *Mehmet* is the subject. (Turn the *wh*-interrogative into a declarative and you'll see.)

7. $_{NP}$[*Mehmet* $_{VP}$[*gave* $_{NP}$[*the girl*] $_{NP}$[*the key*]]].

The *wh*-word doesn't get a new function when it is fronted; it doesn't, for instance, become the subject: the subject in our example sentence is still *Mehmet*. Instead, the *wh*-word seems to replace the phrase it stands for, so that *what* has the same function as the direct object *the key* in the bracketed declarative version of the *wh*-question.

Some authors have claimed that the *wh*-phrase is associated with an informational gap in the sentence. We will discuss the relationship between the *wh*-phrase and its corresponding 'gap' in Chapter 10.

The end-of-chapter exercises include some examples of *subordinate wh-clauses*. We can hear you go 'Oh no!', but the strange thing is, they are easier than main *wh*-clauses, but you'll need to go to exercise 9.1 to find out why.

9.2.2 Y/N interrogatives

Which part of the on-screen question is elided (or omitted) in the following cartoon?

The elided part of the question is the VP / predicate *be upgraded*. Once we've filled in the ellipsis (and we do this so quickly in everyday language that we don't even notice it), we realise that the interrogative in the cartoon calls into question the whole proposition *Can you be upgraded?* The expected response is a simple *yes* or *no* (or equivalent). *Can you?* furthermore illustrates that Y/N interrogatives always begin with a verb, whether auxiliary or main. Other examples are

8. *Did West Ham United win the FA Cup in 1980?*
9. *Are West Ham United the winners of the 1980 FA Cup?*

Notice that in the first sentence, SAI takes place: the auxiliary dummy *do* is placed in front of the subject, while in the second example, it is the main verb *be* which inverts with the subject. But what do we do when we've got more auxiliaries in one sentence, as in example 10?

10. *We have been given tickets for an Arsenal match.*

If you don't believe us, you will ask:

11. *Have you (really) been given tickets for an Arsenal match?*

It's only the first of a sequence of auxiliaries that swaps place with the subject in Y/N questions.

To summarise, Y/N questions ask whether something is the case or not. They differ from declarative clauses in that their subject and the finite auxiliary (or dummy *do*) from the predicate are inverted.

9.2.3 Other types of interrogatives
Alternatives
Do you know this joke?

DAD: *Shall we meet in Brussels or Paris?*
SON: *Yes.*
DAD: *Yes what?*
SON: *Sorry, yes, sir.*

Get it? Or has language changed so much that this joke is no longer funny? There are several components to this joke. One is that the son interprets his father's 'Yes what?' as a reprimand, apologises for being impolite and addresses his father with the term that is / was used by children to fathers (among members of some social classes). The father, on the other hand, just wants an answer to his alternative interrogative question, i.e. shall he buy a ticket to Brussels or to Paris?

Alternatives are just a slightly more special case of Y/N interrogatives: they have the same structure and expect an answer from a limited, closed set of alternatives (*yes* and *no* are also a limited, closed set of alternatives). In alternatives, however, a range of possible answers is provided in the wording of the interrogative, and the addressee is only asked to choose the most appropriate alternative (*Paris* or *Brussels* in the joke). What are the alternatives in the following two examples?

12. *Is your car the red, the blue or the black Peugeot?*
13. *Are you travelling by bus, train, or driving?*

The first example is an straightforward example of coordination from which the addressee is asked to select the appropriate $_{AJ(P)}$[*red*], [*blue*] or [*black*]. What are the possible answers to the question in example 13?

14. *I am travelling by bus.*
15. *I am travelling by train.*
16. *I am driving.*

This example shows one of the complexities involved in coordination. If the difficulties involved in the analysis of this coordination example are not immediately apparent to you, put square brackets around the coordinated elements and try to label them for structural, i.e. phrasal (NP, PP, VP), and functional categories (adjunct, object, predicate). Then you will become aware of some of the complexity involved in structurally representing coordination in almost any theoretical framework (see end-of-chapter exercises for Chapter 8).

Activity 9.3

Are the following sentences *wh-*, *Y/N*, or alternative interrogatives?

a. *Is it me, or has it just gone very dark in here?*
b. *Could you pass the salt?*
c. *Who did what to whom?*
d. *Are you sure he didn't do it?*
e. *What seems to be the problem?*

In Activity 9.3, example (a) is an alternative, (b) and (d) are Y/N, and (c) and (e) are *wh*-interrogatives.

Declaratives

At this point, declaratives are a useful reminder of what we are doing in this chapter: we are looking at clause types which depart in different ways from the default SVO order of canonical declarative sentences.

Declarative interrogatives are interrogatives only because of the purpose they serve. Formally and structurally, they are indistinguishable from declarative sentences: that is, they do not evidence SAI, and they do not employ *wh*-words, i.e. they are garden-variety SVO clauses.

17. *You walked to school?*
18. *He could read when he was three?*

We can only tell that these sentences are interrogatives because of the (rising) intonation used by the speaker, usually represented by a question mark in writing. Otherwise they have the default SVO order of English declarative sentences.

Tags

Tag questions perform important functions in discourse. Some (early) language and gender researchers, for example, claimed that tag questions like *This book is interesting, isn't it?* indicate uncertainty / insecurity on part of the (female) speaker. More recent research has shown that tags also have different and more diverse functions. That's another reason why it is important to identify tags by their structure (so that you can study their function in discourse, if you wish to do so).

Tag questions are literally and metaphorically peripheral elements in clause structure. They are literally peripheral because they attach themselves to the right periphery of sentences which are not in themselves interrogatives. They are structurally peripheral because their relationship to the declarative clause they are attached to is neither one of coordination nor one of subordination (as discussed in Chapter 8). Structurally, tag questions take the form of Y/N interrogatives, i.e. the subject and the finite auxiliary are inverted. In fact, they consist of hardly anything else. Huddleston and Pullum (2005) call tags *truncated interrogative clauses* because they consist only of an auxiliary verb and a pronominal subject. All other elements are omitted because they are retrievable from the main clause, as in

19. *This book is interesting, <u>isn't it? Isn't</u> $_{NP}$[it]*
$_{NP}$[this book] $_{ADJP}$[interesting]?

This example illustrates that the subject and auxiliary in a tag replicate the subject and auxiliary of the declarative clause it is attached to.

Another characteristic of tag questions is that they usually evidence *reverse polarity*, that is, they are negative if the main sentence is positive, and positive if the main sentence is negative, as in example 20. However, some tags have constant polarity, especially when the intended meaning is one of disapproval or disbelief

20. *They aren't in serious trouble, aren't they?*
21. *You could make it up, could you?*

Activity 9.4

In the following examples, which other words are acting as tags?

a. *It's hot in here, innit?*
b. *So I told her, right?*
c. *Not bad, eh?*
d. *We've seen this before, no?*
e. *So I go to this party, yeah? And this girl is there, yeah?*

Rhetorical

Hath not a Jew eyes?
Hath not a Jew hands, organs, dimensions, senses, affections, passions?
If you prick us, do we not bleed?

If you tickle us, do we not laugh?
If you poison us, do we not die?
And if you wrong us, shall we not revenge?

Act III, scene i: lines 55–63

This is possibly the most famous set of rhetorical questions from world literature. The speaker is Shylock, the author is Shakespeare and the play is *The Merchant of Venice*. What structure do rhetorical questions have? And what function do they have?

Rhetorical questions are interrogatives because they have the form of Y/N- or *wh*-interrogatives; but unlike all other questions they do not expect a response. The speaker / writer is not seeking information; she / he tends to know the answer, and so does the addressee. These interrogatives are a rhetorical device whereby the speaker presents something as obvious, and expects the addressee to agree with the proposition expressed. This has the effect of engaging the audience and building a sense of shared beliefs – or not. This depends how critical / uncritical / accepting the audience is. That's why rhetorical questions are a topic in critical discourse analysis, language and the media, language and politics, and stylistics. Other rhetorical questions are:

22. *Why me, god?*
23. *Is there anything better than a beer after a football game?*
24. *How stupid is that?*
25. *Relaxed much?*
26. *Who in their right mind would drive that car?*
27. *Can't you read the sign?*
28. *Who knows?*
29. *Ain't that the truth?*
30. *Didn't he do well?*

Activity 9.5

What about questions (a) to (e) below? Are they rhetorical interrogatives? If yes, why? If not, why not?

a.   *How many times do I have to tell you to be quiet?*
b.   *Why don't you go jump in the lake?*
c.   *Why don't you shut your face?*
d.   *Are we there yet?*
e.   *Can you pass me the salt?*

In Activity 9.5, we can see that, while examples (a) to (e) are quite clearly questions, they are not seeking information and are thus not interrogatives.

Echo questions

As their name indicates, these questions echo the preceding sentence. Consider the exchange below:

31. *A: Peter fired Paul*
     B: Peter fired who?

Speaker B has either not understood who was fired, or is simply surprised by the fact that Paul was fired and thus demands confirmation.

Echo questions look like *wh*-questions, with the difference that the *wh*-words in echo questions are never fronted, and thus SAI is not required. In the following exchanges, the echo questions are those uttered by speaker B.

32. A: *My dog is watching TV.*
     B: *Your dog is what?*
33. A: *Is Mary coming to the vernissage?*
     B: *Is Mary coming to the what?*
34. A: *Why did they leave Peter behind?*
     B: *Why did they leave who behind?*
35. A: *Occupy Ormskirk!*
     B: *Occupy what?*

What clause types are the echo questions contrasted with? They are juxtaposed with a declarative in 32, a Y/N question in 33, a *wh*-interrogative in 34 and an imperative in 35. Imperative clauses are what we will look at next.

9.3 Imperatives

Imperative sentences are used to express, for example, orders, requests, threats, advice, invitations, etc., as in:

36. *Shut the door.*
37. *Mail this to the mitigating circumstances committee.*
38. *Do that and I'll kick your head in.*
39. *Be careful please.*
40. *Come in.*

Formally, they can be characterised according to three main criteria.

(i)   They depart from the default SVO order in that they are the only type of clause in English that does *not* require an overt subject. This is because the subject of an imperative is almost always 'you' (i.e. the context-bound addressee), whether in the singular or the plural.

While imperatives do not require an overt subject, they can still have one.

41. *You(,) pipe down.*

As example 41 illustrates, when the second-person (singular or plural) subject is spelt out in an imperative, it results in a much more forceful, emphatic command, suggestion, etc. In Activity 9.6 we look at other imperatives with subjects.

Activity 9.6

What's the subject in the following two sentences? Describe the subjects in terms of first-, second- or third-person singular or plural.

Somebody say something.
Nobody move.

The sentences in Activity 9.6 have a third-person pronoun as a subject, which, depending on the context, can be either singular or plural. These examples therefore illustrate that, in certain situations, imperative sentences can have overt subjects.

With a few exceptions, however, imperatives depart from the default SVO order in that they are the only type of clause in English that does not require an overt subject. What are the other two formal characteristics of imperatives?

(ii) The verb in imperative sentences is in its untensed / non-finite base form (see Chapter 2).

42. *Give me some chocolate, please!*
43. **Gives me some chocolate, please!*
44. **Gave me some chocolate, please!*

(iii) Imperatives form their negative forms by means of dummy *do*.

45. *Don't look down.*
46. *Don't you shush me.*

This characteristic applies even to the main verb *to be*, as in *Don't be silly!*

Activity 9.7

Why did we say 'even' above? Make Y/N and *wh*-interrogatives and negative sentences from the following sentence:

You are silly.

The copular *be* is quite exceptional in that it only requires *do*-support in imperatives, but not in other clause types in which dummy *do* is frequently needed.

The main verb *to be* never requires an auxiliary, neither in questions nor in negation, only in the imperative. Notice further that if the imperative sentence has an overt subject, then it must follow the dummy *do*, as in *Don't you be silly!*

Imperatives present further restrictions. Modal verbs, for example, cannot occur in imperative sentences (why?).

47.   *Shall be on time.*

However, emphatic *do* and (passive) *be* are OK.

48.   *Do shut up.*
49.   *Don't be moved by her lies.*
50.   *Be on time.*

Activity 9.8
Is *Don't be jumping to conclusions* grammatical in the variety of English you speak?

Depending on where you are from, your answers may differ considerably. In most UK varieties, imperative clauses with auxiliaries in progressive aspect are definitely marked (as opposed to unmarked or not outstanding), if not ungrammatical. In Southern US varieties and AAVE (African American Vernacular English), on the other hand, imperatives with progressive auxiliaries are nothing unusual.

9.4 Positive and negative sentences

'Why even talk about negative sentences?' we hear you say. 'They are easy!' Sure, they are easy to recognise because of their meaning, but structurally they have some quite distinct features, i.e. features that distinguish them from positive declarative sentences.

The term *polarity* refers to the dimension along which positive and negative sentences are differentiated. In English, negative sentences are overtly marked by the presence of certain negative elements (particles like *not* and *no*, adverbs like *never*, etc.). If you are not sure whether a sentence is positive or negative, you can employ the tag question test. Recall that these occur very frequently in reverse polarity configuration, so that if a sentence is positive, the tag would be negative and vice-versa.

51.   *The superglue is completely dry, _____ ?*
52.   *The phone isn't working, _____?*

Don't forget that there are exceptions to this test, given that reverse polarity is not the only possibility for tag questions (see Section 9.3).

Positive sentences are turned into negatives by means of the addition of *not* after the first or leftmost verb in the sequence, whether main verb or auxiliary. These are cases of *verbal* negation.

53. *She cannot dance all night.*
54. *My house isn't small.*
55. *She hasn't been driven to the shops.*
56. *They will not/won't go far.*

Notice that some auxiliaries have different morphological forms (*will / won't*) and that in examples 54 and 55 the *not* is contracted and attached to the first verb in the sequence of verbs. Grammatically this *not* is still an independent morpheme, but phonologically it depends on a 'host'; i.e. it has become a **clitic**. (See exercise 9.2 for the only auxiliary which refuses to host the contracted *not*. We first came across it in Section 2.2.4.)

Positive sentences, however, can also be negated by other means, not with negative *not* applied to the verb, but with words which belong to the word class of adverbs, e.g.

57. *She gave <u>nothing</u> away.*
58. *<u>Nobody</u> moved.*
59. *There are <u>no</u> special circumstances.*

These are cases of *non-verbal* negation. Note that these adverbs trigger subject-auxiliary inversion when used clause-initially, as in:

60. *<u>Never</u> have I seen such a mess.*
61. *<u>Rarely</u> does he speak out about it.*
62. *<u>Scarcely</u> were they out of sight than the noise started up again.*
63. *<u>Hardly</u> had he begun to speak when the door opened.*

SAI is a good indicator that these negative clauses have something in common with interrogatives, the other main non-SVO clause type discussed in this chapter. And again we can test that these adverbs indicate negativity because they require positive tag questions:

64. *It never happened, <u>did it?</u>*
65. *It hardly matters, <u>does it?</u>*

We will now let you work out some other structurally distinct features of negative clauses yourself. In Activity 9.9, we address the question whether all positive sentences have corresponding negative ones (and the other way round).

Activity 9.9

What are the opposites of the following?

They have some too
They don't have any either
I have just seen him
He didn't do it at all
She didn't lift a finger to help
Don't ever do that again
Don't bother doing it then
You needn't do it

What determines whether positive sentences have corresponding negative ones (and vice versa)?

In the Activity 9.10, we look at what happens in the case of negated interrogatives.

Activity 9.10

Describe the structure of the following negated interrogatives in relation to their positive declarative counterparts. How would you explain to a non-native speaker how to ask for something that is not the case / has not happened?

Has he not paid you the money?
Have you not seen this film?
Do you not like apple pie?
Which plants didn't you water?
Which plants did you not water?

After all this you will be glad to hear that positive sentences are the most frequent ones, as we know from corpus linguistics (see Biber et al. 1999: 168ff.). One generalisation we can make about negative sentences is that the *not* is always placed after the leftmost verb in the sentence, but that it cannot appear after the rightmost verb in the sentence. What do we do if the left- and rightmost verbs are one and the same, i.e. there is only one verb? Then there is no space for *not*, and we need an extra verb (an auxiliary verb, to be precise) to create a place that is structurally appropriate for *not*. Where to put negation in a tree is an issue we leave to colleagues teaching higher-level syntax modules. Now, take a deep breath for the end spurt of this chapter. Passives are not easy, but they are important because they can be used to manipulate you (or any addressee for that matter).

9.5 Active and passive sentences

The vast majority of sentences and examples in this book so far have been active, but we have also come across passive ones already. In the monster verb group from Chapter 6 *The customer may have been being shaved* (modality / tense + PERF + PROG + passive voice) we said that the last *be* (the one from *be-ing*) and the *-ed* on the main verb together are the morpho-syntactic indicators that we are dealing with a clause in the passive voice. Passive sentences are marked and their unmarked (or default) counterparts are active.

Active sentences are clauses in which the subject and the agent (the doer of the action) coexist in one and the same NP, which is usually located before the verb. However, English offers an alternative arrangement (for transitive sentences, i.e. those with a direct object), whereby the subject (function) and the doer of the action (role) disassociate: this has the effects of (i) making the subject not the doer of the action but rather the one who is undergoing the action (i.e. the patient, hence *passive*); (ii) putting new information later in the sentence; (iii) making the doer of the action an omissible element in clause structure. These effects of passive constructions can be used for a variety of purposes, for example, as we mentioned at the end of Section 9.4, for manipulating audiences.

How do passive sentences do this? Or, asked differently, why do speakers / writers use passive sentences? A speaker / writer may want to avoid mentioning the person (or thing) responsible for the action denoted by the verb because:

- (s)he does not know who that person is (e.g. *My car was scratched*), or
- their identity is retrievable from prior discourse or preceding text (e.g. *The scooter scratched my car. My car was scratched because it was parked awkwardly*) or irrelevant (e.g. *He was sentenced to life imprisonment*), or
- (s)he chooses to focus on the results of the action rather than on the agency (e.g. *Books must be returned within a week*).

These are all very benevolent suggestions; the more sinister one is that the speaker / writer knows who the actor is, but doesn't want to present him / her in a disadvantageous light by associating him / her with an action that has negative consequences for someone, as in *Mobile phones have been hacked for years*.

In political discourse and the media, passive constructions can therefore be used to transport ideologies. However, passive constructions can only do this if you don't recognise them and are unaware of the possible effects they can have. So let's see if you can recognise passives.

Activity 9.11

Are examples (a) to (f) active or passive sentences?

a. *The carer has taken the old woman to the supermarket.*
b. *The walls were decorated with heavy tapestries.*
c. *The old woman is taken to the supermarket by her carer.*
d. *The fingernails were filed to perfection.*
e. *The old woman is scrubbing away under the shower.*
f. *The carer has filed the old woman's fingernails.*

Sentences (a), (e) and (f) are active; examples (b), (c) and (d) are passive. The sentences in Activity 9.11 illustrate that there is no specifically passive form of the verb in English. The two morpho-syntactic features that distinguish passive clauses from active ones (namely the presence of a form of the auxiliary *be* and the *-ed* or past-participle form of the verb) both occur separately in different constructions. Forms of the auxiliary *be* also occur in progressive aspect constructions like example (e) of Activity 9.11, and the *-ed* participle form occurs also in perfective aspect constructions like sentence (f) of Activity 9.11 (for progressive and perfective aspect see Section 2.2 and especially Section 6.3.3). So neither the *-ed* form of a verb nor the presence of the auxiliary *be* (in one form or another) alone indicate a passive construction in English. Only when these two forms occur together in one clause do we have a passive construction as in sentences (b), (c) and (d) in Activity 9.11.

Activity 9.12

Turn the active sentences from Activity 9.11 into passive ones.

a. *The carer has taken the old woman to the supermarket.*
e. *The old woman is scrubbing away under the shower.*
f. *The carer has filed the old woman's fingernails.*

Recognising the auxiliary *be* in its various guises is less difficult than distinguishing the *-ed* participle from (i) the past tense morpheme *-ed* on verbs and (ii) adjectives that end in *-ed*. If you are not sure you recognise the difference between *-ed* forms of verbs and adjectives ending in *-ed*, make sure you do Exercise 9.4.

Active sentences are more frequent than passive ones not only in this book but in general. Their frequency varies with different genres and text types. For instance, in technical, scientific papers, passive voice sentences are over-represented, and amount to around 25 per cent of all verb phrases used in academic prose (see Biber et al. 1999: 475ff.)

Activity 9.13

Consider the following extract from an instructional text taken from the British version of the International Corpus of English. Underline all passive verbs. What effect do you think the writer is pursuing?

No student will be admitted to any course until he has paid the requisite fees... No student is allowed to register or study concurrently for more than one examination ... Students ... are required to state their status when applying for admission to the School. Students of the School who are reading for degrees of the University ... are registered by the School as Internal Students of the University. As such they are bound by the Regulations of the University. The principal provisions of the Regulations ... are described in the following sections ... All applications for admission to full-time courses ... should be made through the Universities Central Council on Admissions ... and all completed application forms should be sent there.

[ICE-GB:W2D-007]

Highlight the forms of BE and verbs in their *-ed* participle forms that helped you identify the passive constructions.

To summarise, passive constructions have the following morpho-syntactic characteristics:

- Only active transitive clauses (i.e. clauses with an object) can be passivised.
- The resulting passive sentence is intransitive because:
  (i) the object (of the active sentence) has been promoted to subject (of the passive sentence), while
  (ii) the subject of the active sentence is either deleted, or demoted to an adjunct PP headed by *by*.
- A passive clause contains both a form of the auxiliary *be* and the main verb in past participle (*-ed*) form.

What passive constructions have in common with interrogatives and the other clause types discussed in this chapter is that (i) their structure deviates from the default SVO order of active declarative clauses and (ii) sentence elements are dislocated and fronted. In Y/N questions the auxiliary is placed in front of the subject; in *wh*-questions, the *wh*-word / phrase is placed clause initially; and in passives, the verb complement that can't be deleted, i.e. the object, is put in the earlier subject position. Every syntactic theory aims to capture these commonalities; in generative transformational grammar they are captured under the notion of *movement* operations; in non-tranformational approaches, they tend to be handled as *long-distance dependencies*.

9.6 Other clause types

In this section we will illustrate and briefly discuss other clause types whose syntactic relations with main sentences is not very clear, and have thus been considered to be peripheral to sentence structure.

9.6.1 Reporting clauses

These short clauses serve to identify the author of a particular phrase which is being reported. When the words of the speakers are being quoted verbatim (i.e. in direct speech), reporting clauses can occur either before or after the reported extract.

66. *'My shoes are killing me,' said Posh.*
67. *David said, 'So are mine.'*

Notice that reporting clauses do not occur in indirect speech, i.e. when the words are not reported as actually uttered.

68. *Posh said that her shoes were killing her.*

Example 68 above illustrates a clear example of subordination , i.e. *Posh said* is not a reporting clause.

9.6.2 Parentheticals

Parenthetical sentences bear some resemblance to subordinated sentences in that a complete sentence is inserted 'parenthetically' into another. However, as their name indicates, this type of sentence is separated from the larger sentence by means of parenthesis or dashes:

69. *By the time the luggage has come through (and planes are always delayed anyway) we will be very hungry.*
70. *During the last five years – and I take the figures quite arbitrarily – the GNP has gone up by 40 per cent.*

This separation puts a stop to any potential grammatical relation between the parenthetical and the 'host' sentence, and gives the impression of a secondary thought, or an aside.

9.6.3 Comment clauses

These are very short clauses (usually consisting of nothing more than a subject and a verb) which, much like parentheticals, are inserted into a sentence. They include the following: *I assume, I guess, I should think, I must admit*, etc.

71. *We could, I suppose, share a cab.*
72. *It's too late, I'm afraid.*

Unlike parentheticals, though, comment clauses are useful for expressing how the speaker / writer views what they are saying. In other words, the speaker / writer is simultaneously conveying a message and commenting upon its content.

9.6.4 Fragments

We use the term *fragments* to refer to incomplete sentences, i.e. sentences where an element is missing, for instance, sentences without a verb, a subject or an object. Despite any apparent difficulties, communication is not impeded by these omissions. In particular, spoken language is a prime location for fragments, especially as responses to questions:

73. A: *How are you?*
     B: *[I am] Bored to death.*
74. A: *When is your essay due?*
     B: *[It is due on] Monday.*

Activity 9.14

Newspaper headlines are not always complete sentences: verbs (especially *to be* and auxiliaries*)* and determiners are omitted, tenses simplified, and short words preferred over longer ones. Due to their fragmentary nature, headlines may not be comprehensible at first sight.

 Row over aid cuts

Notice that there is no verb, but we can still make sense of the fragment by providing one:

 There has been disagreement on the subject of reduction in aid.

Newspaper headlines are thus fragments because, despite omissions and idiosyncrasies, they can be interpreted as fully grammatical sentences.

9.6.5 Non-sentences

We make a distinction between fragments, where the potential structure of the sentence is retrievable from contextual information, and non-sentences, which not only are devoid of any structure but also tend to appear in a verbal contextual vacuum (i.e. without preceding context). Non-sentences tend to be found in notices, signs and billboards, and convey simple, immediate information.

75. *Emergency Exit*
76. *No Loitering*
77. *Speed Bump*
78. *Sale*

Non-sentences are also very frequently found in spoken English; some examples include *hello*, *hi*, *bye*, *ok*, *thanks*, *right*, *sure*, etc.

9.7 Chapter summary

In this chapter we have looked at how Y/N interrogatives, *wh*-interrogatives, imperatives, negative and passive clauses differ from the default SVO order of canonical declarative positive active clauses. We said that in **Y/N interrogatives** the subject and the tensed auxiliary invert (subject-auxiliary inversion); the same thing happens in most **wh-interrogatives**. These interrogatives, however, also feature a clause initial *wh*-word or phrase which asks for the information the speaker is seeking. The *wh*-word replaces the sentence element that will (hopefully) be provided by the addressee in their declarative answer, as in *What will Raewyn get soon? Raewyn will get her diploma soon.* English **imperative** clauses also depart from the default SVO order in that they do not require an overt subject, their verbs are in their untensed / non-finite / base form, and imperatives form their negative forms by means of dummy *do*. Most **negative** sentences are formed with the negative word / particle *not*. This *not* is very peculiar about where in an English sentence it needs to occur: it only wants to appear after the leftmost verb in the sentence and most definitely not after the rightmost one. If not between two verbs, the *not* isn't happy and makes the clause ungrammatical. If it has an auxiliary to its left, on the other hand, it is so happy that it even cliticizes onto it (i.e. it uses the auxiliary as a phonological host). Only **active** transitive clauses can be put into **passive** voice. This has the effect of turning the object (of the active sentence) into the subject (of the passive sentence), while the active subject is either demoted (and added to the sentence in a PP), or deleted altogether. The characteristic verb forms of passives are a form of the auxiliary *be* and the past participle (*-ed*) form of the verb.

Key terms
Y/N questions; wh-questions; imperative; negative; active voice; passive voice.

Exercises

Exercise 9.1   In Section 9.2.2 we tried to entice you to look at the end-of-chapter exercises by promising you that subordinate *wh*-clauses are simpler than *wh*-main clauses. Here are a few pairs of subordinate and main *wh*-clauses. What's the difference between them? Put square brackets around the subordinate clauses to help you identify what's going on.

a. *Ilana always knows which remedy she should give me.*
b. *Which remedy should she give me?*
c. *The porter asked why my door wasn't locked.*
d. *Why isn't your door locked?*
e. *When Atila would get his glasses worried her.*
f. *When would Atila get his glasses?*

If you're a native speaker of English, using *wh*-questions in main and subordinate clauses comes so naturally that perhaps you don't see why one may be easier than the other. Ask a non-native speaker, though, and they will tell you that in subordinate *wh*-clauses you have to make fewer changes to the default SVO pattern. What are they?

Exercise 9.2   List all modal verbs and all forms of the auxiliary *to be*. Which form of which auxiliary refuses to host the contracted form of *not*?

I will go home now. → *I won't go home now.*
They are singing. → *They aren't singing.*

This phenomenon is so strange that it's got its own name. It's called the *amn't* gap: only certain British dialects (Irish English, Scots English) do not seem to have that gap.

Exercise 9.3   At the beginning of Section 9.5 we said English offers an alternative to SVO for sentences in which the agent role is performed by the subject, and in which there is also an object.
    This alternative arrangement in which the subject (function) and the doer of the action (role) disassociate are passive clauses. But can all transitive sentences be put into the passive voice? Carry out a structural and functional analysis of the sentences below (to ascertain that these sentences are indeed transitive (i.e. have an object) and then try to put them in the passive.

James has a new car
Paul resembles Anthony
The colour suits you

Exercise 9.4   In Section 9.5 we said that recognising the -*ed* or past-participle form of verbs is potentially the trickiest bit about identifying passive constructions and promised you an additional exercise. Here it is. Every one of the following clauses contains a word ending in -*ed*. Identify the word class of that word (adjective or verb) and if you opt for verb, tell us whether the -*ed* is the past-tense morpheme or the past participle, as in the following example:

    a. *The spiders frightened the children.* <u>*Verb, past*</u>
    b. *The child was frightened.*
    c. *Joseph was a professed Christian.*
    d. *She was annoyed by them.*
    e. *She was annoyed with them.*
    f. *The student was satisfied with her assignment.*
    g. *He was worn out by the kids.*
    h. *He was disgusted by the news.*
    i. *The student passed the exam.*
    j. *I was informed by the police.*
    k. *It is accepted that there is no proper evidence.*
    l. *They were surprised by the commandos.*
    m. *They were very surprised.*

Further reading

An overview of clause types is Collins (2006). On tag questions, consult Huddleston and Pullum et al. (2002). On negation and passive voice, see Biber et al. (1999); and Wanner (2009). On the *amn't* gap, see Broadbent (2009). See also Radford (2009) (especially Chapter 4 to 6).

CHAPTER 10

Syntactic *hokey cokey*: more on clause types

In this chapter . . .

We will discuss other type of sentences where the default SVO order (as evidenced in declarative sentences) is departed from. This rearrangement of clausal elements is usually carried out to achieve a specific purpose like asking a question, expressing strong emotion, or focusing on a particular constituent (at the expense of others). We start by looking at two types of sentences we have already introduced in earlier chapters, i.e. relative clauses (Section 8.7.1), and interrogative clauses (Section 9.2), but this time we will zoom in on specific aspects of their behaviour in greater detail. We then introduce other types of special sentences (exclamatives and clefts) which share some structural patterns with relative and interrogative clauses.

10.1 **Relative clauses**

We first came across relative clauses in our discussion of subordinate clauses in Chapter 8. Relative clauses are a special and very frequent type of subordinate clause. They are also fairly easy to recognise because they often contain their own subject, verb and other clausal elements. Relative clauses characteristically (i) occur within NP, (ii) function as post-modifiers to the head of that NP, (iii) are often introduced by a *wh*-word (a relative pronoun) or *that*. They are called *relative* clauses because the *wh*-word introducing them is an anaphor of (i.e. it refers back to) the head of the NP which hosts the relative clause. Thus, the *wh*-word connects (or relates) the head noun to the relative clause. Additionally, the *wh*-word referring to the head of the NP has a function within the relative clause itself; in other words, the *wh*-word is a phrase / constituent of the relative clause. Consider example 1:

1. *The looters who attacked the shop were very polite.*

The relative clause *who attacked the shop* is introduced by the *wh*-pronoun *who*, which refers back to the NP *the looters* in the main clause. Within the relative clause, *who* is replacing *the looters* as we can see in example 2:

2. *The looters [the looters attacked the shop] were very polite.*

Furthermore, we can see why a relative clause is a type of subordinate clause: the simpler clauses are easier to discern:

3. *The looters were very polite. The looters attacked the shop.*
4. *The looters [the looters attacked the shop] were very polite.*
5. *The looters [who attacked the shop] were very polite.*

Relative clauses are introduced by a number of elements: relative pronouns (*which, who/m, whose*), *that* and others. As we have seen, *who* is used to refer back to people, normally the agents that are encoded in the subject NP. In example 6 below, *who* is the subject of the relative clause *who attacked the shop*, and its referent '*the looters*' is the subject of the main clause:

6. NP[*The looters [who attacked the shop]]* were very polite.

However, these functions need not coincide. Below, we can see that whereas *who* is functioning as the subject of the relative clause [*who was not a gentleman*], its referent '*her husband*' is in fact the direct object of the main clause.

7. *Alicia left her husband, [who was not a gentleman].*

Another case of functions not coinciding is where the relative pronoun performs the function of direct object in the relative clause, while its referent is the subject of the main clause. This is illustrated in examples 8 and 9:

8. *Alicia's husband* RC[*Alicia left* DO NP[*Alicia's husband*]] *was not a gentleman.*
9. Subj NP[*Alicia's husband [who/m she left]]* was not a gentleman.

In such cases, grammars used to recommend the use of *whom* over *who*, in order to reinforce the fact that the relative pronoun is not the subject of the relative clause. So *whom* is an object case form (like *her, his*, etc.) which can only be used as object and not as subject, as we said in Chapter 2. *Whom*, like most other case-marked word-forms of English, has fallen out of use in spoken language, and it is likely that it will disappear in its entirety very shortly.

Another relative pronoun used to refer to people (better, to people's possessions) is *whose*. Within the relative clause, *whose* functions as a pre-modifier to the head noun, never as head itself:

10.   *Trish is stumbling across the car park. Trish's shoes are wet.*
11.   *Trish [whose shoes are wet] is stumbling across the car park.*

Whose is another case-marked form (like *his*, *hers*, etc.). We will look into this in Activity 10.1.

Can you see how we have come full circle? Or rather how quite nicely this fits together?

Activity 10.1

But *whose* is clearly not an object, so it won't be an object case-marked form. What does *whose* mark?

It marks possession.

Which other forms mark possession?

Whose marks possession (or genitive case) like the possessive *'s* clitic in *Trish's shoes*.

Which word can you replace *Trish's* with?

We can replace *Trish's* with *her* as in _{NP}[*Trish's shoes*] ~ _{NP}[*her shoes*].

What's the function of *her*?

Her functions as a pre-modifier to the head noun *shoes*, the same function *whose* fulfils in relative clauses such as *whose shoes are very wet?*

For NPs which do not refer to people or other animate beings, *which* is used:

12.   *The flagstones [the flagstones are being replaced] are quite heavy.*
13.   *The flagstones [which are being replaced] are quite heavy.*

The final introductory element we will consider is *that*, which strictly is not a pronoun but is nonetheless serving a 'relative' function. We will refer to this use as *relative 'that'*. This word is a very handy relative element, in that it can be used to replace both *who* and *which*. It has the added peculiarity that it can be omitted when it is not the subject of the relative clause. Consider examples 14 to 20:

14.   *The builder [who fixed the floor] wasn't cheap.* (*who* as subject)
15.   **The builder [fixed the floor] wasn't cheap.*

16. *The builder [that fixed the floor] wasn't cheap.* (*that* as subject)
17. **The builder [fixed the floor] wasn't cheap.*
18. *The builder [who you hired _] wasn't cheap.* (*who* as direct object)
19. *The builder [that you hired _] wasn't cheap.* (*that* as direct object)
20. *The builder [Ø you hired _] wasn't cheap.* (Ø as direct object)

In example 20, 'Ø' indicates the place where the relative element would appear, had the speaker / writer chosen to insert it (rather than omit it).

Can you see how the presence of a *wh*-element (*wh*-pronoun or relative *that*) brings relative clauses in close proximity to *wh*-interrogatives? We illustrate it by highlighting the word-order positions the *wh*-elements occupy in relative clauses (21) and *wh*-interrogatives (22).

21. *The builder [who you hired _] wasn't cheap.*
22. *Who did you hire _ ? I hired a builder.*

Both relative clauses and *wh*-interrogatives have a constituent 'missing', and there is a *wh*-phrase 'sitting in' for it.

Activity 10.2

Combine the pair of sentences below so that one becomes a relative clause.

a. *The cat sat on the mat.*
b. *The cat was insane.*

One possibility is *The cat who sat on the mat was insane* (NB this cat is most definitely not Henry), but we can also have *The cat who was insane sat on the mat*. These examples illustrate that any free-standing sentence can embed or be embedded by another.

Activity 10.3

We said that relative *that* can be omitted without the sentence becoming ungrammatical (except when it's functioning as a/an _____). If you can't remember, you just have to flick back a page or two.

Look at the examples below. Which words in sentences (a) to (c) can be omitted? What function/s are they performing in the sentence?

a. *This is the city [that I was born in].*
b. *This is [why you shouldn't complain].*
c. *December is the month [when assignments are done].*

When the NPs substituted for are adverbials of place, time and reason (*where* / *when* / *why*, respectively) they are sometimes omissible, as in the revisited examples below:

a'. *This is the city [I was born in].*
b'. *This is [the reason you shouldn't complain].*
c'. *December is the month [assignments are done in].*

Relative clauses are classified according to their interpretation within NP structure. This often also has an effect on their grammar. We distinguish between *restrictive* and *non-restrictive* relative clauses.

10.1.1 Restrictive

Restrictive relative clauses (also known as 'defining' or 'integrated' relative clauses) serve to restrict the reference of the noun which they modify. They accurately specify a well-defined set of the elements referred to by the head noun. This type of relative clause cannot really be omitted: if it is left out, the resulting sentence suffers quite a drastic change in meaning.

23.   *The man [Ø/who I killed] was the President.*
24.   *The road [Ø/which/that we should avoid] is waterlogged.*

10.1.2 Non-restrictive

Non-restrictive relative clauses (also known as 'non-defining', 'appositive', 'supplementary') do not specify or limit the referent of the head noun. Rather, they give additional information, which is why they are optional elements which are easily omitted. Unlike restrictive relative clauses, they are typically marked off (separated from the main clause) either by means of intonation or by punctuation, usually by commas or dashes. (You may have wondered why the person marking your essays sometimes puts commas round your relative clauses, and sometimes not. Now you know why, and you can do it yourself next time.)

25.   *My landlord, who believes in UFOs, is in hospital.*

Because the internal structure of restrictive vs. non-restrictive clauses is identical, it may be good to summarise the difference between them. The first or 'restrictive' type lives up to their name because they restrict the set of things being mentioned (by specifying which of the things selected by the head noun are being mentioned). Non-restrictive relative clauses, on the other hand, merely add extra information. This makes a fairly big difference at the semantic / pragmatic level: restrictive clauses only make one statement, but non-restrictive ones make two statements.

Activity 10.4

Which one of the following two examples (a or b) alerts you more if you have foxes in your back garden?

a. *Foxes which have rabies are dangerous.*
b. *Foxes, which have rabies, are dangerous.*

Example (b) should alert you more because it states that foxes (in general) are dangerous, and all have rabies. The speaker of sentence (a) is less afraid of foxes, because he / she only considers rabid foxes to be dangerous.

10.1.3 Sentential

This is a special type of relative clause, introduced only by *which*. These clauses are still 'relative' in that their interpretation (specially that of its relative pronoun) depends on – and is related to – a previous structure; but whereas all other types of relative clauses are related to NPs, sentential relative clauses have wider scope, i.e. they relate to entire clauses.

26. *I forgot my umbrella, <u>which</u> was unfortunate.*
27. *The rain came down hard, <u>which</u> was even more unfortunate.*

The relative pronoun *which* is understood with reference to the whole preceding clause, not to any one noun phrase. These clauses are very useful for passing comments on whole propositions which have just been mentioned, *which is nice.*

Activity 10.5

What kind of relative clause is *which is nice* above? What's its scope? Is it restrictive, non-restrictive or sentential?

It is a sentential relative clause.

We have seen that under certain conditions (i.e. when it is not functioning as subject in the relative clause), the relative pronoun may be omitted.

28. *The woman I love lives in another country.*

These clauses are called *zero-relative clauses*.

Some relatives are further reduced in that they don't have (i) a tensed auxiliary, and (ii) their lexical verb is also in its *-ed* or *-ing* form.

29. *The man [dismissed from his job] walked straight into a wall.*
30. *The film [playing on TV] is ghastly.*

If you want a name for these clauses, they are called *reduced relative clauses*.

Do their morpho-syntactic characteristics remind you of something? Reduced relative clauses are non-finite subordinate clauses (cf. Section 8.6.2), i.e. clauses which don't have a tensed verb form and which modify either one part of the main clause or the entire main clause. Reduced relative clauses can only be restrictive (as opposed to non-restrictive) in function.

Free relative clauses, on the other hand, are introduced by *what*, *where*, *when* or one of the *-ever* pronouns (e.g. *whatever*, etc.). These clauses (also known as *nominal relative clauses* and *fused relatives*) are not part of an NP, but rather behave more freely as an element of the main clause:

31.   *Whatever he says, he is lying.*

10.2 **Relative clauses and movement**

We have already mentioned a parallel between relative clauses and questions. Consider now example 32:

32.   *The horse [which Mike was riding _] jumped over the fence [which Rob had built _].*

Not only do these *wh*-relative pronouns look a lot like *wh*-interrogative pronouns, but they have also been dislocated from their canonical position after the verb. This type of syntactic operation has been called wh-*movement* (in generative grammar), and it is evidenced in both relative and interrogative clauses. Compare examples 33–36:

33.   *The horse [which Mike was riding _]*
34.   *The fence [which Rob had built _]*
35.   *Which horse was Mike riding _ ?*
36.   *Which fence had Rob built _ ?*

Examples 33 and 34 are of course *wh*-relative clauses, and the last two examples *wh*-interrogatives. Despite their similarities, there is also a clear difference between examples 33 and 34 (and *wh*-relatives and *wh*-interrogatives in general): whereas in relative clauses there is no need for the auxiliary to invert with the subject (what we have called *SAI*) and we get the default SV order; the converse is true in interrogatives. This is illustrated in examples 37 and 39:

37.   *The horse [which Mike was riding _]*
38.   **The horse [which was Mike riding _]*
39.   *Which horse was Mike riding _ ?*
40.   **Which horse Mike was riding _ ?*

Examples 38 illustrates that SAI renders relative clauses ungrammatical; conversely, example 40 illustrates that *wh*-interrogatives become ungrammatical if the auxiliary does **not** invert with the subject.

We can explain different constructions as the interplay between SAI and *wh*-movement:

- *Tom chased Jerry.* (declarative sentence, no SAI, no *wh*-movement)
- *Did Tom chase Jerry?* (Y/N interrogative, SAI <tensed aux>, no *wh*-movement)
- *Who did Tom chase?* (*wh*-interrogative, SAI <tensed aux>, *wh*-movement) *wh*-word as direct object
- *Who chased Jerry?* (*wh*-interrogative, no SAI <no tensed aux>, *wh*-movement) *wh*-word as subject
- *The cat [who chased Jerry] is Tom.* (relative clause: no SAI <no tensed aux>, *wh*-movement) *wh*-word as subject
- *The mouse [who Tom chased] is Jerry.* (relative clause: SAI <no tensed aux>, *wh*-movement) *wh*-word as direct object

To summarise what we've seen so far, relative clauses share some syntactic characteristics with *wh*-interrogatives: (i) both contain *wh*-elements (or *that* for relative clauses only) which can be omitted under certain circumstances; (ii) in both constructions the *wh*-element acts as a place-holder for a 'missing' phrase; (iii) in standard sentences, the missing element is in its canonical default position; (iv) the *wh*-element that sits in for the missing phrase in relative clauses and *wh*-interrogatives has been dislocated to the front of the clause, and the default SVO order (as evidenced in declarative sentences) is departed from. The main difference between relative clauses and *wh*-interrogative clauses is that subject-auxiliary inversion is required in *wh*-interrogatives, whereas it (SAI) renders relative clauses ungrammatical.

10.3 Interrogative clauses and movement

In this section we are highlighting similarities between relative clauses and interrogatives in terms of the two processes SAI and *wh*-movement.

Wh-interrogatives are subject to SAI, as we have seen. This is further illustrated below:

41. *The dog had an operation.*
42. *What did the dog have _ ?*

The interrogative example 42 shows three main characteristics: it begins with a *wh*-word; it shows evidence of SAI; and it has a verb (*have* in example 42) whose direct object (*an operation* in example 41) has been moved out of its default position. In *wh*-interrogatives, the *wh*-word is associated with a gap in the clause, which refers to the information the speaker / writer is seeking. In example 42, *what* refers to 'an operation', and both *an operation* and *what* function as direct objects in their corresponding sentences (41 and 42, respectively). However, while in example 41 the direct object is in its canonical position after the verb (with the sentence showing SVO order), it is in initial position in the *wh*-version (example 42), with the sentence showing OSV order. This is (part of) what we have called SAI.

There is one exception: when the *wh*-word is functioning as the subject of the clause, no SAI is required, and constituent order remains SVO.

43.   *The dog had an operation.*
44.   *Who had an operation?*

Activity 10.6

We have only looked at direct interrogatives. For instance, *what did he buy?* is an interrogative which works well in spoken language. English, however, also gives us the possibility of asking indirect questions.

In written English, we need to identify the speaker of the *wh*-interrogative, which gives us sentences like:

The grandmother asked: 'what did he buy?'

Now turn the direct interrogative *what did he buy?* into an indirect question:

The grandmother asked _____

What's the difference between direct *wh*-questions and indirect questions?

---

*The grandmother asked what did he buy? shows that we cannot just use a *wh*-interrogative and embed it into the indirect structure by adding it to *The grandmother asked*_____. *The grandmother asked what he bought* is the correct answer. While the *wh*-word is OK in indirect questions, no auxiliary or 'dummy' *do* is needed to carry tense. This is easy for native speakers because they have heard these structures so many times when their parents told them stories containing indirect questions; but it's not exactly intuitive for non-native speakers.

Let us now turn to Y/N questions. What is the interrogative version of the following examples?

45.   *Michael is running to work.*
46.   *Gabriel has written many letters.*

47. *Raphael was given singing lessons.*

The procedure is quite straightforward. In all cases, it involves moving the first auxiliary to the left over the subject, which results in:

48. *Is Michael _ running to work?*
49. *Has Gabriel _ written many letters?*
50. *Was Raphael _ given singing lessons?*

Notice that the lexical verbs *running*, *written* and *given* are no longer next to their auxiliaries, but their form is still determined by them (see Chapter 2). We can try this out by changing the forms of these verbs, and illustrate the impossibility of this on *run*:

51. **Is Michael _ run to work?*
52. **Is Michael _ ran to work?*
53. **Is Michael _ to run to work?*

In other words, *is*, *has* and *was* have been moved away from their default positions, but they are still carrying tense, as well as determining the form of their main verbs.

Activity 10.7
Turn *wh*-questions (a) to (c) into declarative sentences, filling the slots created by the *wh*-words with adequate phrases. Describe the procedure you followed in all three examples.

a. *When is Santa _ coming _ ?*
b. *What has Santa _ brought _ ?*
c. *Where will he _ leave the presents _ ?*

You should have noticed that in order to arrive at the declarative versions of the interrogatives, you have to reverse the procedure whereby the auxiliary inverted with the subject, and the *wh*-word also dislocated to the front.

10.4 Exclamative clauses

Recall that we classify different sentence types according to their syntactic behaviour and formal structure. In this respect, exclamative sentences are very easy to identify. They begin with a fronted exclamative phrase (usually introduced by *what* or *how*), followed by the subject, which is in turn followed by the rest of the sentence, as in:

54. *What a mess this is!*
55. *How naive I have been _ !*

> ### Activity 10.8
> In written language, the presence of this type of sentence is further indicated by an exclamation mark. What's the equivalent of the exclamation mark in spoken language?

Exclamations are variably accompanied by raised volume, marked intonation, exaggerated aspiration, breathy voice, etc. That's why in written language, where none of those elements are available, we rely more on sentence structure to identify exclamatives.

What is used to introduce a noun phrase, whereas *how* serves to introduce other kinds of constituents (frequently an adjective or adverb phrase). Notice that while there is rearrangement of constituents in exclamatives (away from the default SVO order), there is no SAI. This is partly because these sentences do not seek information. What exclamatives do is communicate strong feelings and emotions.

> ### Activity 10.9
> Like there are many ways of delivering exclamatives in spoken language (Activity 10.8 above), there are also many ways of conveying exclamatory meaning besides using exclamative clause type.
>
> *How on earth am I supposed to know that!*
> *Look at that gorgeous frock!*
> *Don't be so ridiculously absurd.*
>
> What clause type is used in all these examples? What are the most prominent structural characteristics of this clause type? To check your answer, go back to Section 9.3.

10.5 Clefts and pseudo-clefts

These types of clauses allow the rearrangement of sentence constituents in order to highlight one element by syntactic means. For instance, if you want to emphasise that it was Elvis (and not Lady Gaga) who spent her summers in Ormskirk, the default word order won't do, no matter how much you stress the word *Elvis* in spoken language.

56. *Elvis spent his summers in Ormskirk.*

You will therefore come up with something like:

57.   *It was Elvis who spent his summers in Ormskirk.* (not Lady Gaga)

What did you do with the original sentence? You divided it into two clauses: the first one is a main clause with a semantically empty subject (*it*) and a semantically empty verb (*to be*):

58.   *It was Elvis*

And what's the other clause?

59.   *who spent his summers in Ormskirk*

Structurally it is like a very restrictive *wh*-relative (see Section 10.1.1). The function of clefts is to highlight the communicative import of the sentence. Example 57 highlights the subject of the sentence, i.e. *Elvis*. Clefts, however, can highlight pretty much any part of a sentence, as we can see below. (There is, however, one very useful caveat, which we will turn to in a moment.)

60.   *Elvis spent his summers in Ormskirk.*
61.   *It was his summers that Elvis spent in Ormskirk.*
62.   *It was in Ormskirk that / where Elvis spent his summers.*

The emphasized constituent is called the *focus* of the cleft. And the anticipated caveat is that the string of words in the focus position must be a phrase (or constituent). Since Chapter 6 we have stressed the importance of being able to identify which words belong together and form sub-units of clauses, i.e. phrases. They were first introduced in this book in the section on tool kits to identify phrases, and the clefts in this section have done exactly this, i.e. they have correctly identified NP[*Elvis*], NP[*his summers*] and PP[*in Ormskirk*] as phrasal constituents.

Activity 10.10

Bracket and label the phrases that clefting identifies as constituents in the following sentences.

a.   *It was that trouser suit with a herringbone pattern that I took to the charity shop.*
b.   *It was that suit that I left with my parents.*
c.   *It was that trouser suit with my parents that I left.*
d.   *It was with my parents that I left the suit.*

Which sequence is not a constituent and consequently renders the sentence it is contained in ungrammatical? Mark the sentence with an asterisk and state why it is ungrammatical (although it is identical to a sequence of words in one of the other sentences).

That trouser suit with my parents from example (c) is not a constituent. Thus it cannot occur in the focus position of a cleft sentence. That's why (c) is ungrammatical, although *that trouser suit with my parents* (from sentence (c)) and *that trouser suit with a herringbone pattern* (from sentence (a)) consist of the same sequence of words. The crucial difference is that *with a herringbone pattern* post-modifies the *trouser suit* as shown in $_{NP}$[*that trouser suit* $_{PP}$[*with a herringbone pattern*]], but the $_{PP}$[*with my parents*] can't post-modify the trouser suit.

To summarise clefts so far, clefts have a very distinct structure: they are introduced by *it*, followed by a form of the verb *to be*, followed by the focus; the last element is a relative clause which refers to the focus, so IT + BE + FOCUS + (*who/that* + CL) in short.

Pseudo-cleft sentences serve a similar purpose, i.e. that of giving syntactic prominence to a constituent, but their structure and constituent parts are a bit different.

63.   *He needs a stiff drink.*
64.   *What he needs is a stiff drink.*

Example 64 shows that the structure of pseudo-clefts is not dissimilar to that of clefts. Pseudo-clefts consist of a subordinate clause (whose first element is a *wh*-word), followed by a form of the verb '*to be*', which is followed by the focus. This structure can be summarised as: (*wh*-item + CL) + BE + FOCUS; ('standard' clefts are IT + BE + FOCUS + (*who / that* + CL)). Pseudo-clefts can also be inverted, as in examples 65 and 66.

65.   *What Simon wanted to buy is a Maserati.*
66.   *A Maserati is what Simon wanted to buy.*

As with real clefts, it is only phrases / constituents that can occur in the focus position of a pseudo-cleft.

Activity 10.11

Turn the sentences below into cleft sentences in which the element in bold is the emphasised part.

a.   *Mary had a little **lamb**.*
b.   *She can't book **a study room**.*
c.   ***Peter** fell asleep in the orchard.*

10.6 Chapter summary

This and the previous chapter are linked by a focus on clause types which depart from the default SVO order of English declarative sentences. English likes this SVO structure so much that there is always a specific purpose behind a rearrangement of clausal elements, e.g. speakers want to ask a question, express a strong emotion or focus on a particular clause constituent. We returned to relative clauses (which we first introduced in Chapter 8), with the aim of highlighting what they have in common with *wh*-interrogatives (first introduced in Chapter 9). It turns out they have so much in common that we can describe relative clauses as non-interrogative *wh*-clauses. Relative clauses, however, are always subordinate because they modify other linguistic categories (most frequently the head of a noun phrase but also entire clauses), either in a restrictive or non-restrictive way (see Section 10.1.1 and 10.1.2). We then moved on to other types of special sentences (exclamatives and clefts), which share some structural characteristics with relative and interrogative clauses. Exclamatives are easy to recognise because they begin with a fronted exclamative phrase (usually introduced by *what* or *how*), followed by the subject, which is in turn followed by the rest of the sentence, as in *But Grandmother! What big teeth you have!*

All clefts have the function of highlighting a particular part of a sentence. This can be done in two ways: either with cleft structures like *It is the air conditioning that turns my nose red* (IT + BE + FOCUS + (*who / that* + CL)) or with pseudo-clefts, such as *What she is going to buy now is an inhaler* ((*wh*-item + CL) + BE + FOCUS). The group of words that receives prominence is always a phrasal constituent, which is why clefts form part of our tool kit for identifying phrases.

We promised you we'd step it up a bit in the second half of this book and we most certainly did. If you have enjoyed working with us so far, you have widened your career prospects by adding 'linguist' to your career path options.

Key terms
Exclamatives; clefts; pseudo-clefts.

Exercises

Sometimes it's a bit tricky to distinguish nominal relative clauses and dependent *wh*-interrogative clauses from each other. Here is a set of a few short exercises that will help you identify which clause is which (examples are adapted from Huddleston and Pullum 2005).

Exercise 10.1 Which word class does *what* belong to in sentences (a) and (b)?

a. *I wasted what I had saved.*
b. *I wasted what money I had had.*
In sentence (a) *what* is a _____; in (b) *what* pre-modifies *money* and therefore is a _____; so example (a) is a (delete as appropriate) [nominal relative clause / *wh*-interrogative clause], whereas example (b) is a (delete as appropriate) [nominal relative clause / *wh*-interrogative clause].

Exercise 10.2 Examples (c) and (d) are quite similar in structure, but note that there is a difference between them in terms of agreement marking (between subject and verb, remember?). Identify the subjects first. Then check the finite verbs of the main clauses. What's their number?

c. *What cranberries she has left are in the kitchen cupboard.*
d. *What other dried fruits she has to offer remains to be seen.*

In (c) the verb of the main clause is *are*, which is in its plural form; in sentence (c) the verb of the main clause is *remains*. What number is *remains*? It's singular and agrees in person (third) and number (singular) with the subject *What other dried fruits she has to offer*. The singular is commonly used when clauses are used as subjects. Example (c) therefore is a nominal relative clause and example (d) a dependent *wh*-interrogative clause

---

Exercise 10.3   What kind of deviation from the default SVO structure of canonical English sentences do examples (e) and (f) represent?

    e.   *Is what my husband suggests unreasonable?*

    f.   *?Is that he proposes to go Cyprus alone unreasonable?*

We can see from the question mark that this word-order variation renders sentence (f) unwieldy. We discussed this in detail in the chapter: can you tell what kind of construction (e) is and what construction is represented in (f)? Nominal relative clause? *Wh*-interrogative clause?

Exercise 10.4   What kind of constructions are sentences (g)–(h)?

    g.   *What she suggests is unreasonable.*

    h.   *??It is unreasonable what she suggests.*

    i.   *It is unreasonable that we should have to do it ourselves.*

    j.   *It is unclear what she wrote.*

Example (h) is of dubious grammaticality, for the same reason that example (e) from Exercise 10.3 is grammatical. What's this reason? (For an exercise which uses functional criteria to distinguish nominal relatives from dependent *wh*-interrogatives, see the next Consolidation section.)

Further reading

See Collins (1991) on clefts. See also Radford (2009) (especially Chapter 5); Lambrecht (2001); Calude (2009); and Malá (2005).

Consolidation chapter 2

Task 7.1

Consolidation Chapter 2 builds on everything we have done so far. To illustrate how the components of language work together, we now recycle the examples from Tasks 3.7 and 3.8 and your answers to them, and add the knowledge you acquired by working through Chapter 7. In Task 3.8 you conveyed the meaning of synthetic compounds like *user-friendly* through clauses, as in

you use this book; you are the user of this book	V→ N
we intend the book's content to be approachable/friendly	ADJ which post-modifies N
the book is user-friendly	ADJ which post-modifies N

By doing this, you made the functions of the various components of *user-friendly* transparent.

After working through Chapter 7, you are now in a position to integrate all components of language: structure, form and function. We prepared this in Task 3.8 by not only asking you to embed the compounds in sentences; we also encouraged you to identify the phrasal categories you embedded the left-hand compound elements in, and determine whether these phrases were optional or obligatory. Here we have a few more examples:

a. brick-laying conveys that somebody is laying NP[bricks]	obligatory
b. an eye-catching smile is a smile that catches NP[the eye]	obligatory
c. a daydreamer is a person who dreams PP[during NP[the day]	optional
d. spring-cleaning is the cleaning that is carried out PP[in NP[spring]	optional

(Data drawn from Katamba and Stonham (2006))

The phrasal categories you embedded the left-hand compound elements in are NPs in both tasks, but these NPs are further embedded in PPs in (c) and (d). The NPs in (a) and (b) are obligatory (complements), whereas the PPs in (c) and (d) are optional (adjuncts).

Now that we have completed the structural analysis (Chapters 5 and 6) of the clauses derived from synthetic compounds, we can move on to their functional analysis (Chapter 7). *User-friendly* in *This book is user-friendly* is a **subject complement**.

- What is the function of the NPs derived from the left-hand component of the compounds in (a) and (b)?
- What is the function of the PPs derived from the left-hand component of the compounds in (c) and (d)?

And as you have already done so much good work on these examples, we will link them to another short task; one which addresses core facts about clause structure through the functional analysis of synthetic compounds.

Task 7.2

Why is it possible to make sentences from *brick-laying*, *eye-catching*, *day-dreamer*, *spring-cleaning*, i.e. the words in Task 7.1, in the first place? Can you make sentences from all compounds? Try it out on *brickbat*, *eye infection*, *midday* and *spring flower*.

Clue: examples (a) to (d) in Task 7.1 are all **synthetic compounds**. This means that their head, i.e. the right-hand element according to the English right-hand rule, is morphologically derived from a verb. Verbs, we said, are the fundamental building blocks of clauses; they determine both the minimum number and the type of obligatory sentence elements.

Brickbat, *eye infection*, *midday* and *spring flower*, on the other hand, are **root compounds**, they consist of two _____ .

Task 7.3

In each of the following sentences, identify the appropriate sentence structure from the choices given.
Key: S = Subject; V = Verb; DO = Direct Object; IO = Indirect Object; SC = Subject Complement; OC = Object Complement; A = Adverbial.

a. *Amy retired in June.*
 i. S + V + A
 ii. S + V + SC
 iii. S + V + DO
b. *During the war, his family emigrated to London.*
 i. S + V + A
 ii. A + S + V + A
 iii. A + S + V + IO

c. *I'll make you some supper.*
    i. S + V + IO + DO
    ii. S + V + DO + A
    iii. S + V + A + DO

d. *The climate makes life really difficult.*
    i. S + V + DO
    ii. S + V + IO + DO
    iii. S + V + DO + OC

e. *She caught a cold at the weekend.*
    i. S + V + IO + DO
    ii. S + V + DO + A
    iii. S + V + A + IO

Task 7.4

Conduct a structural and functional analysis on sentences (a)–(e) below. First, identify the phrasal categories and their heads so that you can label the square brackets you introduce to the analysis with the appropriate subscripts, as in:

$_{AdvP}$[*Yesterday*] $_{NP}$[*the venue* $_{PP}$[*in* $_{NP}$[*Camden*]] $_{VP}$[*was* $_{AdjP}$[*full*]].

Second, identify the functions of each sentence element by writing the appropriate abbreviations in the round brackets after it, as in

$_{AdvP}$[*Yesterday*] (A) $_{NP}$[*the venue* $_{PP}$[*in* $_{NP}$[*Camden*]] (S) $_{VP}$[*was* (V) $_{AdjP}$[*full*]] (SC).

Key for **structural analysis**: NP = Noun Phrase; PP = Prepositional Phrase; AdjP = Adjective Phrase; AdvP = Adverb Phrase; VP = Verb Phrase.
Key for **functional analysis**: S = Subject; V = Verb; DO = Direct Object; IO = Indirect Object; SC = Subject Complement; OC = Object Complement; A = Adverbial.

a. *Perhaps (_) a lunatic (_) was (_) simply (_) a minority of one (_).*
b. *No news (_) is (_) good news (_), apparently (_).*
c. *The woman (_) donated (_) a kidney (_) to a complete stranger (_).*
d. *His heart (_) leaped (_) in his chest (_).*
e. *The cold (_) turned (_) the woman (_) blue (_).*
f. *The youths (_) looked (_) menacingly (_) at the stranger (_).*
g. *They (_) brought (_) him (_) his food (_) at lunchtime (_).*

Task 7.5

Underline the adverbials in the examples below. Recall that adverbials are recursive / 'stackable', i.e. there may be more than one per sentence.

a. *The festival was opened a few days after our arrival.*
b. *Attendance at the opening ceremony was obviously compulsory.*
c. *The ceremony was prepared with military precision.*
d. *We arrived in the stadium two hours earlier.*
e. *The fireworks were undoubtedly wonderful because of their scale.*
f. *The citizens felt fulfilled afterwards.*
g. *The whole ceremony up till then had been very impressive.*
h. *I am not brave by nature.*

Apart from adverbials, can any other syntactic function feature more than once in a clause? Delete as appropriate: **S** (subject); **SC** (subject complement); **V** (verb); **OC** (object complement); **O** (object).

Task 7.6

In examples (a) to (c) below, identify the sentence elements that are either semantically empty (i.e. they have no meaning) or repeat information that is already known.

a. *Leg it / Beat it.*
b. *There is no point in going for a walk when it rains.*
c. *Mary smiled a toothy smile.*

Given that these sentence elements have no meaning or repeat information we already know, what is their purpose in the sentence?

   A good starting point for this task is to carry out the deletion test. Once you have decided that you can't leave these phrasal categories out, determine their function within the sentence.

All semantically empty sentence elements in (a) are _____ (function).
All semantically empty sentence elements in (b) are _____ (function).
In (c), the sentence elements that cover the same meaning twice are the
   _____ and the head of an _____ (function) _____
   phrase respectively.

Sentence (c) of this task therefore also illustrates that not all noun phrases are complements, just like not all prepositional phrases are adjuncts.

Task 7.7

In each of the following sentences, indicate whether the highlighted (in bold) string is a direct object (DO) or an indirect object (IO).

a. *The neighbour's drunken assaults caused **a great deal of resentment** in the block.*
b. *Give **her** your coat, it is cold out there.*
c. *And I'll call her **a cab**.*
d. *The footballer owes the fans **an apology**.*

Task 8.1

Identify all the conjunctions in the extract below, and specify whether they are subordinating or coordinating.

The user interface rests on a specialised database management system ... Although this is optimised for a read-only distribution, a simple switch enables the editing and revision of the corpus. A sophisticated tree editor is thereby enabled, and the software permits numbers of linguists to edit the corpus simultaneously ... Cross-sectional correction ... is not unfamiliar to corpus linguists, and has been exploited in tag correction, etc. However, in parsing, this presents new problems but also creates new benefits.

Task 8.2

Or tends to be classified as a coordinating conjunction that links elements describing alternative possibilities, as in (a) and (b):

a. *My way or the highway.*
b. *Either I'm wrong or you are.*

Is this also the case in (c)?

c. *Hallowe'en or 'All Hallows' Eve' is round the corner.*

Task 8.3

In Chapter 8 we simply noted that:

- coordination looks simple (but it isn't);
- the analysis and representation of coordinated structures is controversial for almost every linguistic theory.

233

Let's first look at examples which illustrate some of the issues coordination raises.

Describe the coordinates and the relation between them (i) in plain English and (ii) with fully labelled bracketing and / or trees.

You will notice that the structural analysis will help you 'see' things you may have missed in the prose description; *and* it will make you appreciate the difficulties involved in representing coordination (we talk you through this on the companion web-site).

a. *The pen is green and the car is fast.*
b. *She started the car and he drove off.*
c. *Helen left right after the conference had finished and arrived just before it started.*
d. *She started the car and drove off.*
e. *The green and the red pen ran out at the same time.*
f. *She has but he hasn't understood the question.*
g. *The student works evenings and during the holidays.*
h. *Sharon had tea and Dawn coffee.*

Now for the possible representations of coordinate structures. First match trees (a), (b), (c) and (d) with the corresponding brackets (A), (B), (C) and (D):

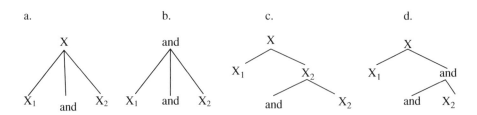

A)   B)   C)   D)
$_{and}$[[X$_1$] and [X$_2$]]   X[X1 $_{x2}$[and X$_2$]]   X[X$_1$ $_{and}$[and [X2]]   X[[X$_1$] and [X$_2$]]

What is the difference between them? There are two fundamental differences (and we have spared you another possible distinction by not representing it with trees and brackets). One has to do with hierarchy / levels, the other one with what is assumed to be the head of coordinate structures.

This makes different notations more suitable for different types of coordination. Which tree / bracketing system 'fits' each sentence in (a) to (h) above better?

And finally, which tree and bracketing system corresponds to the representation of coordination illustrated by two examples Word Grammar?

a.

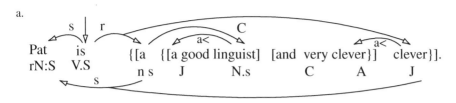

b.

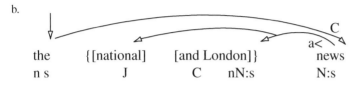

(www.phon.ucl.ac.uk/home/dick/enc2010/frames/frameset.htm)

Task 8.4

Underline the subordinate clauses in the following extract:

When these results are broken down according to their occurrence in a written or spoken medium, additional curiosities surface. Written language results are particularly solid. We can still see the tendency noted in previous totals, whereby first elements are informationally new. In the prepositional phrase, given material occurs as often as new. Surprisingly, these predictions are inverted in the case of spoken language, where it is prediction 1 that is confirmed, and 2 that is disconfirmed.

Task 8.5

Indicate whether the underlined non-finite subordinate clauses are *-ing* clauses, *-ed* clauses, infinitive clauses, or verbless clauses.

a. *England's initial target was to scrape together 22 runs from their last two wickets.*
b. *The Finnish boat capsized after losing its keel 120 miles off the Argentine coast.*
c. *If the Rugby Football Union had wanted to engineer the triumph of the western region it could not have done better than keep Bath and Gloucester apart in the Cup semi-final draw.*
d. *It was from a cross by Ryan Giggs that Ronaldo had his first shot, although pulled wide.*

e. *Blackpool, <u>lying second from bottom</u>, must now concentrate on avoiding relegation.*

f. *<u>3–0 down at half-time</u>, West Ham never really looked like scoring.*

g. *The season begins in earnest on Sunday with the Worth tournament, <u>won by Sevenoaks last year</u>.*

h. *<u>With two minutes left in the game</u>, Michael Owen beat three defenders to place a perfect ball in the Arsenal net.*

i. *There may be as many as 400 players in the game of street football, <u>with the goals being separated by up to three or four miles of open countryside</u>.*

j. *The two weightlifters <u>stripped of their medals following positive drug tests at the Commonwealth Games</u> will learn of their punishment today.*

Task 8.6

We said in Chapter 8 that in comparison with main clauses, subordinate clauses can lack sentence elements and / or morpho-syntactic features. Some subordinate clauses, for example, don't have an overt subject, and some of them (like the ones in Task 8.5) don't have tense. If they are also not introduced by a subordinating conjunction, they can be rather difficult to recognise.

To get used to what can be missing, first identify the subordinate clause(s) within the following sentences; then build them up by giving them whatever they lack. This is what we have in mind:

(1) Identify the subordinate clause in the sentence

The subordinate clause in the sentence *I have nothing to wear* is . . . *I have nothing* [*to wear*].

(2) Identify what is missing in comparison with a fully fledged subordinate clause.

Well, a lot: a subordinating conjunction, a subject, tense/a tensed verb. So we'll give it:

(i) an explicit (not understood) subject, e.g. *I*, as in *I have nothing* [*I to wear*],

(ii) and a subordinating conjunction, e.g. *that*, as in *I have nothing* [*that I to wear*].

(3) We give it tense or a tensed verb, e.g. the modal *can* to render *I have nothing* [*that I can wear*].

Not all intermediate steps are grammatical, but the start and the end points are. When you embark on this exercise now, bear in mind that not all subordinate clauses below lack all the sentence elements and / or morpho-syntactic characteristics that were missing in the example we illustrated.

a. *The neglected allotment waiting to be tended still looks nice.*
b. *The dog which belongs to the old neighbour wants to be stroked.*
c. *He left him crying his eyes out.*
d. *Has the trade-union member already decided who to vote for?*
e. *For Lauren to attempt the London marathon would be very brave indeed.*
f. *We set off, up-lifted by expectation.*
g. *The tutor, approaching the automatic gate, realised she had forgotten her swipe card.*
h. *Andy hoped to hire a room in a hall of residence.*
i. *Simon is reluctant to try Ali's vegetarian sausage.*
j. *This was the unfortunate result of him having drunk too much alcohol.*

So far so good? Yes? Then we can move on to the functions the subordinate clauses have in these sentences. They can be:

S = Subject; DO = Direct Object; IO = Indirect Object; A = Adverbial.

They can also be relative clauses or (when non-finite) post-modifiers in a noun phrase; complements of adjectives (within an AdjP); or complements of prepositions (within a PP). What is the function of the subordinate clauses you identified in (a) to (j)?

Task 9.1

Consider the following extract from a student essay (taken from the British version of the International Corpus of English). Underline all passive verbs and highlight the forms of BE verbs in their *-ed* participle forms that help you identify the passive constructions.

'Behaviour' has now been incorporated into modern evolutionary theory. It is recognised that natural selection acts on phenotypes and not on genotypes, and it is acknowledged that behaviour constitutes a significant part of phenotype expression. It follows that 'intelligence' may be considered as an adaptationary set of behaviours which have evolved … [Many] definitions emphasise what has been called 'the Evolutionary Analogy' … Some writers have hardened the analogy to assert that cognitive development and evolution are the product of identical processes … It is an approach to evolution that has been fostered by biologists with a particular interest in cognition, intelligence and culture.

[ICE-GB:W1A-009]

237

What effect do you think the writer/student is trying to create by using passive constructions?

Task 9.2

What kind of clause type are the following sentences?

a. *Long live the Queen.* [*Don't long live the Queen*]
b. *God bless America.* [*Don't God bless America*]
c. *Bless you!* [*Don't bless you!*]
d. *Damn you!* [*Don't damn you!*]

Did you go for 'imperative'? After all, the verbs are in the base forms, and the sentences appear to be expressing wishes. However, looking at their negative versions (in brackets) shows that they are not imperative sentences. Check again using the three structural characteristics of imperatives discussed and exemplified in Section 9.3. (You may also want to check Section 4.3.3.)

Task 9.3

Ditransitive sentences have two objects. Given what you know about objects and passive constructions, does this suggest that ditransitive sentences may have two passive versions?
  Create two different passive sentences from examples (a) to (d).

a. *Mary gave Paul a black eye.*
b. *Kathryn showed the students a video.*
c. *She sent Paul a new vase.*
d. *Tara made Jeremy a sandwich.*

Which one of the two passive constructions you generated from sentences (a) to (d) do you think is more 'natural'? Why do you think this is the case? You may want to look into:

● which object (i.e. the direct or the indirect one) yields 'better' passives; and
● the semantic properties of the referents of the object / subject noun phrases.

Task 9.4

Negation is one of the few English sentence structures where we still find a considerable amount of regional and social variation. Turn the following two sentences into the negative and interrogative forms (avoid using the word *got*).

a. *My brother has a girlfriend.*
b. *He has many friends.*

Compare your negative constructions with those of other speakers of English from different regions.

Task 9.5

There are two different types of double negation. One of them is intentional and generally regarded as acceptable (although George Orwell railed against it in his 1946 essay 'Politics and the English Language', because he thought it provided an additional degree of obfuscation); the other one is considered as ungrammatical in Standard English (but not in other varieties of English).

Which one is the acceptable one, A or B?

A.

    a. *It is not unusual to be loved by anyone.*
    b. *The editor of the newspaper claimed that phone tapping was not unethical.*

B.

    c. *I didn't do nothing.*
    d. *I can't never do nothing about it neither.*

What's the difference between the examples under A and B in terms of how double negation is achieved? Which sentence elements are involved in each case of double negation?

Here is a hint: as a cure against the use of the acceptable yet obfuscating construction, George Orwell suggested memorising the following sentence: 'A not unblack dog was chasing a not unsmall rabbit across a not ungreen field.'

Task 9.6

In the following sentences, identify non-standard double negatives and state what renders them ungrammatical.

a. *We couldn't see nothing at all.*
b. *The suspect is not unknown to the police.*

c. *They haven't done nothing.*
d. *I can't say I haven't been in the biscuit tin.*
e. *They've never hardly done it.*

Task 9.7

Add tag questions to the following sentences:

a. *Don't tell Joanna, _____ ?*
b. *Make yourself at home, _____ ?*
c. *Switch the i-Pad off before you go out, _____ ?*
d. *Don't use the very heavy weights, _____ ?*

Compare your answers to (a) to (d) with those of colleagues. What do you notice about the tag questions you (and most other people) construct? There is a strange conformity among native speakers of English in terms of which auxiliary they use for the tags.

For the remaining sub-tasks of 9.7 you will need to put your syntactician hat on. Here are a few hints again:

- What clause type do all the examples in this task belong to?
- What does this clause type share with non-finite subordinate clauses?
- What do you therefore have to do to add a tag to these clauses?

Why most people choose *will / won't*, nobody seems to know. (You may want to remember this when you are looking for a dissertation topic.)

Task 9.8

Here are another two utterances featuring tags. What is unusual about them? Compare them with the tags you have just created for Task 9.7, paying particular attention to the use of anaphoric versus cataphoric pronominal reference in the main clause and the tag question.

a. *He is a true supporter, is Simon.*
b. *She has been busy, has Hermione.*

Do you think that anaphoric or cataphoric reference is easier to process for listeners / readers?

Why do writers use cataphoric reference at all then? Link your answer to the concepts of marked versus unmarked language use we discussed in Chapter 9.

Task 9.9

Indicate whether the sentences below are *Y/N* questions, *wh*-questions, declarative questions or alternative questions.

a. *When will working conditions be improved?*
b. *Will there be a large increase in car ownership in this country by the end of the decade?*
c. *How many people do you think will attend our meeting, twenty or thirty?*
d. *How often should I take the medicine?*
e. *You say that she took your car without your permission?*
f. *Hasn't the book been published yet?*
g. *Do bears suffer from toothache?*
h. *Do you want me to buy tickets for your sisters as well or just for us?*

Task 10.1

What's the grammatical function of the bracketed clauses in (a) and (b)?

a. *The pickets give [whoever supports them] a thumbs up.*
b. *The linguistics course she successfully completed made her [what she is].*

The string *whoever supports them* is a _____.
The string *what she is* is a _____.
Key for functional analysis: S = Subject; V = Verb; DO = Direct Object; IO = Indirect Object; SC = Subject Complement; OC = Object Complement; A = Adverbial.

To further consolidate your ability to use (not just recognise) specific linguistic structures, construct sentences in which *wh*-interrogative clauses fulfil the function of direct object and subject complement respectively.

Before we move away from examples (a) and (b), extract the *wh*-relatives and dislocate them to the front of the sentence. What happens? Why?

Task 10.2

Remember clefts? We first came across them in Chapter 6 when we built our tool kit for recognising words which hold / belong together as a group or phrase, and then again in Chapter 10. To remind yourself what cleft constructions are and of how many clauses they consist of, take a look at:

a. *It was this computer that Kim bought with his first French salary.*
b. *It was with his first French salary that Kim bought this computer.*

Do (c) and (d) also consist of two clauses?

c. *Why can't we go the park?*
   It is because I say so.
d. *Why on earth did he buy this huge car?*
   It's just that he is a fool.

Why is it possible to leave out the *that*-clause in the clefts in (a) and (b) above?

Task 10.3

Leave the restrictive clauses below unpunctuated. Punctuate the non-restrictive clauses with commas. If you think that a clause can be both restrictive or non-restrictive, insert the commas in the appropriate positions and discuss the two interpretations.

a. *I hate attending meetings which last longer than an hour.*
b. *She gives the impression of an umpire judging a game in which the players have no idea of the rules.*
c. *Look out for grey or brown fungi which may or may not be edible.*
d. *Sporting bodies can punish those who break their rules by fines, suspensions, or permanent bans withdrawing the right to participate in the sport altogether.*
e. *The 'cab-rank' rule requires advocates to represent any client in an area of law in which they practise.*
f. *Some 2000 fans who began queuing at six that morning barely slept the night before.*
g. *They seem gloomy about the prospects for the domestic film industry which has experienced all the problems British filmmakers have agonised over for twenty years.*
h. *The concert is the first in the twelfth annual music festival which is devoted to electro-acoustic music.*
i. *Teenagers who drive carelessly should be banned from driving until they are twenty-one.*

Task 10.4

Rewrite each sentence below, turning it into an exclamative, the construction type the surprised Little Red Riding Hood used a lot when looking at the wolf in her grandmother's bed. Use *what* or *how* in combination with the underlined words.

a. *Those paintings look peculiar.*
b. *He's been behaving foolishly today.*
c. *It's been a long time since I've enjoyed myself so much.*
d. *She seems young.*
e. *That was a party.*
f. *He has a very loud voice.*
g. *It's cold today.*
g. *You did well in your exams.*

Task 10.5

In a conversation, you didn't catch the name of the woman in (a), the person the burglar confessed to in (b) and the translation of what he insisted on in (c). You have to ask the speakers of (a), (b) and (c) for clarification. How do you do this?

a. *He is engaged to Heidi.*
b. *The burglar confessed to the night warden.*
c. *He insisted on a translation of the marriage certificate. It is ready.*

In English (and a few other languages) you've got two options: you either sound quite stilted and old-fashioned or you upset prescriptive grammarians. If you only had one version of the questions so far, see if you can come up with an equally grammatical question with a slightly different word order for (a) to (c).

Both versions / construction types have quite good names. One is called **pied-piping**, because the preposition is not left stranded, but pied-piped along with the *wh*-pronoun (the name comes from the story of the Pied Piper of Hamelin who lured all the rats (and children) of Hamelin to a watery death by getting them to follow him). Now that you know what pied-piping is, which of the two version of (c) below represents pied-piping, (i) or (ii)? *The translation of the marriage certificate ...*

(i) *[which he insisted on ___] is ready.*
(ii) *[on which he insisted ___] is ready.*

The one that upsets prescriptivists is called **preposition stranding**, because the preposition is left behind / stranded when the *wh*-pronoun that stands in for the sentence element you are questioning is moved to the front of the clause. Winston Churchill is said to have made fun of a particularly stilted

avoidance of preposition stranding with the following joke: 'This is something up with which I will not put.' Some people assume that Churchill's joke
is intentionally and playfully ungrammatical. Why? Note that two words
which look like a preposition have been pied-piped to the front, but only one
of these words is really a preposition. What is the other one? Hint: you may
want to look back at Chapter 3 and Task 2.7 (the latter one is in
Consolidation chapter 1).

Glossary

Adjectives Lexemes that can typically modify nouns and in turn be modified by the adverb *very*. Adjectives can either be **predicative** or **attributive**.

Adjuncts Typically optional elements which do not require licence from the verb to occur in the predicate (e.g. *My sister bought a great house last week*).

Adverbs Lexemes that are frequently derived from adjectives by addition of the suffix *-ly* (*clever =>cleverly*). They usually modify verbs, but also adjectives and other adverbs.

Affix A bound morpheme which only occurs when attached to a root / free morpheme (e.g. *predetermine, painter*).

Agreement A type of syntactic relation in which the inflectional form of a word (or phrase) is determined by the properties of another word or phrase, which is almost always a noun (e.g. *Two men are crossing the road*, cf. **Two men is crossing the road*).

Apposition A relation between two units (usually noun phrases), whereby they share the same referent and can have the same function. The relation between *Henry* and *the white cat with a stripy tail* is one of apposition: they are both NPs and both can function as subject of the sentence *Henry, the white cat with a stripy tail, pounced clumsily on those sparrows*.

Aspect Aspect refers to how the speaker views the situation described in a clause with respect to its temporal structure or properties, not with respect to its location in time. English has two aspects, *progressive* (e.g. *Mary is selling all her paintings*) and *perfective* (e.g. *Mary has sold all her paintings*).

Attributive When an adjective precedes the noun it modifies, it is said to function attributively (e.g. *My old car is in need of repair*).

Base Any unit to which affixes can be attached (e.g. *predetermine*, but also *predetermination*).

Case A distinction in nouns and pronouns related to their grammatical functions. For example, the first-person-singular pronoun has two forms depending on the function it is performing in a clause (e.g. *I shot the sheriff* vs. *The sheriff shot me*).

Clause A clause is a sentence that contains one lexical verb, as well as any other sentence elements required by the verb.

Cleft A type of clause where sentence constituents have been rearranged in order to highlight one element by syntactic means. Clefts are introduced by *it*, followed by a form of the verb *to be*, followed by the focused element (e.g. *It was in Cleveland that they got lost*). Pseudo-clefts are similar to clefts, only they consist of a subordinate clause (whose first element is a *wh*-word), followed by a form of the verb *to be*, which is followed by the focused element (e.g. *What Nigel wanted to be was a shoe salesman*).

Clitic In English, reduced forms of auxiliaries and negatives (*'m, -ve, -n't*) which attach to the preceding word.

Comparative The form of a gradable adjective / adverb indicating a comparison of two things on some scale. These forms typically end in the inflectional suffix *-er*, or for those words longer than a syllable, the adverb *more* is employed (e.g. *colder, more beautiful*).

Complement Elements required by the verb, a term which in this book includes direct objects, indirect objects, subject complements and object complements.

Complementiser An alternative term for a subordinating conjunction or subordinator.

Compounds Words formed by adjoining two (or more) lexemes (e.g. *arm chair, head phone*).

Conjunction Conjunctions link together, or conjoin, linguistics units. They form a closed class, or rather two: **coordinators** (such as *and, or, but*) and **subordinators** (e.g. *because, if, when, although*, etc.).

Coordination The joining of two or more sentences (or phrases), without any one element being dependent on the other (e.g. *egg and mayonnaise; we cried but they laughed*).

Dependent An element that combines with a **head**.

Derivation A morphological process which creates new lexemes (e.g. *beauty* => *beautiful*), can change the word class (or grammatical sub-class) of the base (e.g. *home* (N) => *homeless* (Adj)) and / or can change the meaning of the base (e.g. *plane* => *de-plane*).

Determiner Determiners introduce noun phrases. Their name derives from the fact that they determine or specify how (the reference of) a noun phrase is to be understood. They are classified into several types: definite (*the*), indefinite (*a, an*), possessive (*his, their*), relative (*which*), etc.

Do-*support* The use of the verb *do* as an auxiliary to form negative or interrogative sentences.

Ellipsis Omission of words from a sentence where the omitted forms are retrievable. Ellipsis does not result in ungrammaticality (e.g. *They wanted to go to the party, but they decided not to <go to the party>*).

Exclamatives Exclamative sentences begin with a fronted exclamative phrase (usually *what* or *how*), followed by the subject, followed by the rest of the sentence (e.g. *How extraordinarily agile that ballet dancer is!*).

Finiteness Finite verbs carry tense. Non-finite verbs do not. Most verb forms are finite, with the exception of participles (present and past) and infinitives. In turn, finite clauses are those headed by a finite verb.

Gerund Nouns derived from verbs, such as *washing* in *I enjoy not washing clothes*. Gerunds combine the characteristics of both nouns and verbs.

Gradable Most adjectives denote properties of people or things. Because properties can be possessed in varying degrees, adjectives (as well as adverbs) tend to be gradable, and have **comparative** and **superlative** forms.

Grammar   A general term for morphology and syntax. It describes how morphemes group together to make words, and how words group together to make phrases, clauses and sentences.

Head   The head of a phrase bears the most important semantic information and incorporates the most essential grammatical characteristics of the whole group of words (e.g. *all those fantastic little grammar books on the table*).

Imperative   A type of sentence structure used largely for directives, orders or commands. In English, a verb in imperative form is indistinguishable from its infinitive form (e.g. *Stop using your phone*).

Inflection   The inflection of a lexeme is the variation of its form determined by syntactic properties (like number in nouns, or tense in verbs). Inflection also refers to obligatory morphological operations.

Lexeme   Lexemes are vocabulary items listed in a dictionary.

Mood   The grammatical category that indicates the attitude of the speaker to what is said. Mood is mostly marked in English by means of modal verbs.

Morph   The concrete physical shape of a morpheme.

Morpheme   Morphemes are abstract entities expressing a single concept within a word. They are the smallest indivisible units of language which carry meaning or grammatical function. Words are formed out of morphemes. *Bound* morphemes cannot stand on their own (e.g. *-ity* in *continuity*), whereas free morphemes are roots which can stand on their own (e.g. *aware* in *unawareness*).

Negation   The operation of changing a clause into its negative form, for example by means of the word *not* (e.g. *I have not agreed to these terms*).

Noun   Nouns are a certain type of lexemes which denote physical as well as inanimate objects (e.g. *ball*, *rights*). A typical characteristic of nouns is that they inflect for number (e.g. *cat / cats*; *child / children*).

Number   A grammatical category contrasting singular and plural, mainly seen in nouns (*cat* vs. *cats*) and pronouns (*he* vs. *they*) but also verbs via agreement (*she dances* vs. *they dance*).

Object   A complement of the verb, which can become the subject of a passive voice sentence (e.g. *The islanders speak a local dialect*).

Phrase   A group of semantically and grammatically related words with an internal structure. Phrases can consist of one word and can frequently be replaced by one word, i.e. the **head**. A phrase is often seen as a grammatical unit intermediate between the word and the clause (e.g. *The old woman must sit down and talk*).

Postmodifier   A modifier occurring to the right of its **head**.

Predicate   Everything but the **subject** of the sentence. Predicates tend to convey the majority of the information contained in a clause (e.g. *Commander Bond could not see the light at the end of the tunnel*).

Predicative   When adjectives are placed to the right of the noun they express a property of, they are said to function predicatively (e.g. *Her eyes were green*).

Prefix   An affix attached to the left of a word (e.g. *undisclosed*).

Pre-modifier   A modifier occurring to the left of its **head** (e.g. *the cold, thick, torrential rain*).

Preposition   A closed word-class denoting relations of space and / or time (*in*, *under*, *on*, *over*, etc.), and normally appearing in front of a noun phrase.

Pronoun A type of lexeme which can perform the same functions as nouns and can occur in the same range of positions. This word-class includes personal pronouns (*you*, *me*), demonstrative pronouns (*that*, *these*) and others.

Relative clause A (subordinate) clause functioning as post-modifier to the **head** of a noun phrase (e.g. *The man who was stuck at airport security was called Derek*).

Root The irreducible core of a word (e.g. *antiorganisational*).

SAI Subject-auxiliary inversion. A syntactic operation which reverses the order of the auxiliary and the subject. SAI occurs largely in questions, e.g. *Can you drive?*

Sentence Sentences are strings of words held together by syntactic relations.

Stem A **root** or **base** without inflectional affixes (e.g. *cold* and *reorganise*, but not *colder* and *reorganised*).

Subject A function in clause structure normally associated with the agent / doer of the action in active clauses (e.g. *The audience booed the band*). Subjects tend to appear before the verb, and are obligatory in English (with the exception of imperative sentences).

Subject/Object Complement Complements in VP structure which are not objects. *Subject complements* occur with copulative verbs and refer to the subject (e.g. *David was very calm*), whereas *object complements* co-occur with (and modify) direct objects (e.g. *Critics called the new album a disaster*).

Subordination Subordination involves the use of a clause as a constituent part of a larger clause (e.g. *Because of the interference, Nigel left the band*).

Suffix An affix attached to the right of a word (e.g. *reproduction*).

Superlative The form of a gradable adjective / adverb indicating the highest or lowest position on some scale. These forms typically end in the inflectional suffix *-est*, or for those words longer than a syllable, the adverbs *most* or *least* are employed (e.g. *coldest*, *most beautiful*, *least intelligent*).

Syntax Syntax refers to how words group together to make phrases and sentences.

Tense A morpho-syntactic way of referring to the time when some action, event or state takes place (e.g. in the past, present or future) in relation to the moment of speaking. Tense is marked inflectionally on verbs (e.g. *he thinks*; *they danced*).

Transitivity The type and number of complements a verb needs.

Verb Verbs are a type of lexeme which normally inflects for tense. *Lexical verbs* are also known as main verbs. *Auxiliary verbs* are a type of verb which can appear before the main verb in a sentence, and tend to mark **tense, aspect, mood** and voice. *Modal verbs* are a type of auxiliary verbs used to indicate mood (possibility, necessity, obligation, permission, etc.).

Voice The grammatical category contrasting active and passive clauses. *Active voice* clauses express the action of the verb, linking it directly to the person or thing carrying out the action, which has the thematic role of agent (e.g. *The tutor marked the exam*). *Passive voice* changes the focus of the sentence by reordering the elements / units (NPs) that express its constituent roles (e.g. *The exam was marked by the tutor*).

Wh-interrogatives A type of interrogative beginning with an interrogative word, which (except for *how*) begin with *wh-*, e.g. *when, where, what, which*, etc. (e.g. *Which album cover was chosen?*).

Word   The basic unit of syntax (and of language itself). Words can have different forms; can occur in both written and spoken language; can form larger units such as phrases, clauses and sentences; and can often be segmented into smaller meaningful units.

Y/N Interrogatives   An interrogative which expects *yes* or *no* as answer (e.g. *Have they chosen a new manager yet?*).

References

Aarts, Bas (2008) *English syntax and argumentation*. 3rd edition. Basingstoke: Palgrave Macmillan.

(2011) *Oxford modern English grammar*. Oxford: Oxford University Press.

Aarts, Bas and Liliane Haegeman (2006) English word classes and phrases. In: Bas Aarts, and April McMahon (eds.) *The handbook of English linguistics*. Malden, MA: Blackwell Publishers. 117–45.

Aarts, Flor and Jan Aarts (1982) *English syntactic structures*. Oxford: Pergamon Press.

Adams, Valerie (2001) *Complex words in English*. Harlow: Pearson Education.

Aronoff, Mark and Kirsten Fudeman (2005) *What is morphology?* Oxford: Blackwell.

Bauer, Laurie (1983) *English word-formation*. Cambridge University Press.

(2003) *Introducing linguistic morphology*. 2nd edition. Edinburgh University Press.

(2004) *A glossary of morphology*. Edinburgh University Press.

Biber, Douglas, Stig Johansson, Geoffrey Leech, Susan Conrad and Edward Finegan (1999) *Longman grammar of spoken and written English*. London and New York: Longman.

Blevins, James P. (2006) English inflection and derivation. In: Bas Aarts and April McMahon (eds.) *The handbook of English linguistics*. Malden MA: Blackwell Publishers. 507–36.

Borjars, Kerstie and Burridge, Kate (2006) *Introducing English grammar*. London: Arnold.

Brinton, Laurel (2000) *The structure of modern English*. Amsterdam/Philadelphia: John Benjamins.

Broadbent, Judith (2009) The *amn't gap: the view from West Yorkshire. *Journal of Linguistics* 45: 251–84.

Burton-Roberts, Noel (2011) *Analysing sentences: an introduction to English syntax*. 2nd edition. Harlow: Pearson Longman.

Calude, Andrea S. (2009) *Cleft constructions in spoken English*. Berlin: VDM-Verlag.

Carnie, Andrew (2002) *Syntax: a generative introduction*. Oxford: Blackwell.

Carstairs-McCarthy, Andrew (2002) *An introduction to English morphology*. Edinburgh University Press.

Cash Cash, Philipp (2004) Nez Perce verb morphology. www.u.arizona.edu/~cashcash/Nez%20Perce%20Verb%20Morphology.pdf (accessed 15 February 2012).

Coates, Jennifer (1983) *The semantics of the modal auxiliaries*. London: Croom Helm.

Collins, Peter (1991) *Cleft and pseudo-cleft constructions in English*. London: Routledge.

(2006) Clause types. In: Bas Aarts and April McMahon (eds.) *The handbook of English linguistics*. Malden, MA: Blackwell Publishers. 180–97.

(2009) *Modals and quasi-modals in English*. Language and Computers: Studies in Practical Linguistics 67. Amsterdam: Rodopi.

Collins, Peter and Hollo, Carmella (2000) *English grammar: an introduction*. London: Macmillan.

Comrie, Bernard (1976) *Aspect*. Cambridge University Press.

(1985) *Tense*. Cambridge University Press.

Corbett, Greville G. (2007) Canonical typology, suppletion, and possible words. *Language* 83: 24.

Crystal, David (2003) *The Cambridge encyclopedia of the English language*. 2nd edition. Cambridge University Press.

(2006) *The fight for English: how language pundits ate, shot, and left*. Oxford University Press.

Depraetere, Ilse and Susan Reed (2006) Mood and modality in English. In: Bas Aarts, and April McMahon (eds.) *The handbook of English linguistics*. Malden MA: Blackwell Publishers. 269–90.

Fabb, Nigel (2005) *Sentence structure*. London: Routledge.

Facchinetti, Roberta, Manfred G. Krug and Frank Palmer (2003) (eds.) *Modality in contemporary English*. Berlin: Mouton de Gruyter.

Gelderen, Elly van (2002) *An introduction to the grammar of English*. Amsterdam/ Philadelphia: John Benjamins.

Greenbaum, Sidney and Gerald Nelson (2009) *An introduction to English grammar*. 3rd edition. Harlow: Pearson.

Haspelmath, Martin (2002) *Understanding morphology*. London: Arnold.

Haspelmath, Martin and Andrea D. Sims (2010) *Understanding morphology*. London: Hodder Arnold.

Heiman, John and Sandra A. Thompson (1998) *Clause combining in grammar and discourse*. Amsterdam/Philadelphia: John Benjamins.

Hornstein, Norbert and Maria Polinsky (2010) *Movement theory of control*. Amsterdam/Philadelphia: John Benjamins.

Huddleston, Rodney and Geoffrey K. Pullum (2005) *A student's introduction to English grammar*. Cambridge University Press.

Huddleston, Rodney and Geoffrey K. Pullum et al. (2002) *The Cambridge grammar of the English grammar*. Cambridge University Press.

Hudson, Richard A. (2004). Are determiners heads? *Functions of language* 11: 7–43.

(2010) *An introduction to Word Grammar*. Cambridge University Press.

Hudson, Richard A. and Jasper Holmes (1995) Children's use of spoken standard English. *School Curriculum and Assessment Authority*. Discussion Paper No. 1.

Katamba, Francis (2004) *English words*. 2nd edition. London: Routledge.

Katamba, Francis and John T. Stonham (2006) *Morphology*. 2nd edition. Basingstoke: Palgrave Macmillan.

Keizer, M. Evelien (2007) *The English noun phrase: the nature of linguistic categorization*. Cambridge University Press.

Lambrecht, Knud (2001) *Information structure and sentence form.* Cambridge University Press.

Leech, Geoffrey N. (2004) *Meaning and the English verb.* 3rd edition. Harlow: Pearson Longman.

Leech, Geoffrey N., Margaret Deuchar and Robert Hoogenraad (1982) *English grammar for today.* London: Macmillan.

Lieber, Rochelle (1992) *Deconstructing morphology.* Chicago: University of Chicago Press.

Mahlberg, Michaela (2005) *English general nouns: a corpus theoretical approach.* Amsterdam/Philadelphia: John Benjamins.

Malá, Marcela (2005) Syntactic and semantic differences between nominal relative clauses and dependent wh-interrogative clauses. *Theory and practice in English studies* 3: 85–9.

Matthews, Peter H. (1991) *Morphology.* 2nd edition. Cambridge University Press.

Max Planck Institute for Evolutionary Anthropology; Department of Linguistics (2008) Conventions for interlinear morpheme-by-morpheme glosses. www.eva.mpg.de/lingua/resources/glossing-rules.php (accessed 15 February 2012).

McCully, Chris (2009) *The sound structure of English: an introduction.* Cambridge University Press.

Minkova, Donka and Robert Stockwell (2009) *English words: history and structure.* 2nd edition. Cambridge University Press.

Nelson, Gerald (2010) *English: an essential grammar.* 2nd edition. London: Routledge.

Nelson, Gerald, Sean Wallis and Bas Aarts (2002) *Exploring natural language: the British component of the International Corpus of English.* Varieties of English around the World series. Amsterdam: John Benjamins.

O'Grady, William D. and John Archibald (2008) (eds.) *Contemporary linguistic analysis.* Toronto: Pearson Education Canada.

Owens, Robert E. (2008) *Language development: an introduction.* 8th edition. Boston: Pearson.

Ozón, Gabriel (2006) The Given Before New principle, and textual retrievability: a corpus-based study. In: Antoinette Renouf, and Andrew Kehoe (eds.) *The changing face of corpus linguistics.* Rodopi: Amsterdam. 243–62.

(2009) *Alternating ditransitives in English: a corpus based study.* PhD thesis, English Department, University College London.

Palmer, Frank (1987) *The English verb.* 2nd edition. London: Longman.

(1990) *Modality and the English modals.* 2nd edition. London: Longman.

(2001) *Mood and modality.* 2nd edition. Cambridge University Press.

Plag, Ingo (2003) *Word-formation in English.* Cambridge University Press.

Pullum, Geoffrey K. (2007) Ungrammaticality, rarity, and corpus use. *Corpus linguistics and linguistic theory* 3: 33–47.

Quirk, Randolph, Sidney Greenbaum, Geoffrey N. Leech and Jan Svartvik (1985) *A comprehensive grammar of the English language.* Longman: London.

Radford, Andrew (2004) *Minimalist syntax: exploring the structure of English.* Cambridge University Press.

(2009) *Analysing English sentences.* Cambridge University Press.

Saaed, J. (1997) *Semantics.* Oxford: Blackwell.

Spencer, Andrew (1991) *Morphological theory*. Oxford: Blackwell.

Spencer, Andrew and Arnold M. Zwicky (1998) (eds.) *The handbook of morphology*. Oxford: Blackwell.

Spinillo, Mariangela (2004) *Reconceptualising the English determiner class*. PhD thesis, English Department, University College London.

Tallerman Maggie (2005) *Understanding syntax*. 2nd edition. London: Arnold.

Tesnière, Lucien (1959) *Éléments de syntaxe structurale*. Paris: Klincksieck.

Thomas, Linda (1993) *Beginning syntax*. Oxford: Blackwell.

Thompson, Sandra A. (1988) A discourse approach to the cross-linguistic category 'adjective'. In: John A. Hawkins (ed.) *Explaining language universals*. Oxford/ New York: Blackwell. 167–85.

Trask, R. L. (1994) *Language change*. London/New York: Routledge.

Wales, Katie (1996) *Personal pronouns in present-day English*. Cambridge University Press.

Warner, Anja (2009) *Deconstructing the passive*. Berlin: de Gruyter.

Warner, Anthony (1993) *English auxiliaries: structure and history*. Cambridge University Press.

Williams, E. (1981) On the notions 'lexically related' and 'head of a word'. *Linguistic inquiry* 12: 245–74.

Index

12499504R00148

Printed in Great Britain
by Amazon.co.uk, Ltd.,
Marston Gate.